AT SPEED WITH THE WORLD'S GREATEST MOTORSPORT

FORMULA 1
75
YEARS

Stuart Codling, James Roberts, and James Mann

motorbooks

Quarto.com

© 2025 Quarto Publishing Group USA Inc.
Text © 2025 Stuart Codling, James Roberts, James Mann
Images © 2025 Motorsport Images, except where noted

First Published in 2025 by Motorbooks, an imprint of The Quarto Group,
100 Cummings Center, Suite 265-D, Beverly, MA 01915, USA.
T (978) 282-9590 F (978) 283-2742

Motorbooks titles are also available at discount for retail, wholesale, promotional, and bulk
purchase. For details, contact the Special Sales Manager by email at specialsales@quarto.com
or by mail at The Quarto Group, Attn: Special Sales Manager, 100 Cummings Center, Suite
265-D, Beverly, MA 01915, USA.

29 28 27 26 25   1 2 3 4 5

ISBN: 978-0-7603-9443-4

Digital edition published in 2025
eISBN: 978-0-7603-9444-1

Library of Congress Cataloging-in-Publication Data

Names: Codling, Stuart, 1972- author. | Roberts, James (Motorsports
   journalist), author. | Mann, James, 1963- author.
Title: Formula 1 75 years : at speed with the world's greatest motorsport /
   Stuart Codling, James Roberts, James Mann.
Other titles: Formula One seventy-five years
Description: Beverly, MA : Motorbooks, 2025. | Includes index. | Summary:
   "Formula 1 75 Years celebrates the sport's full history with a
   stunningly illustrated ride through its greatest teams, drivers, and
   events"-- Provided by publisher.
Identifiers: LCCN 2024049918 | ISBN 9780760394434 | ISBN 9780760394441
   (ebook)
Subjects: LCSH: Grand Prix racing--History. | Formula One
   automobiles--History. | Automobile racing drivers--History.
Classification: LCC GV1029.15 .C638 2025 | DDC 796.7209--dc23/eng/20241203
LC record available at https://lccn.loc.gov/2024049918

Design: Cindy Samargia Laun
Cover images and endpapers: Motorsports Images
Photography: MotorTrend

Printed in China

DEDICATION

In loving memory of Jasper Codling 2006–2024.

CONTENTS

INTRODUCTION: FORMULA 1'S ORIGINS

Tick-tock of the clock. The driver who completes the distance in the shortest possible time wins the race. Many other facets of motor racing have changed since Hungarian-born Ferenc Szisz won the first Grand Prix in 1906, but the passage of time–implacable, inscrutable time–remains a racing driver's greatest foe.

Motor racing as a pursuit began within a decade of Carl Benz unveiling his Patent Motorwagen on July 3, 1886, publicly demonstrating it on the streets of Mannheim, Germany, at the heady maximum speed of 10 mph (16 kmh). The earliest races to feature this new-fangled contraption, still known to many as the "auto-car," had little in common with competitions for the horse-and-cart it would quickly supplant as humanity's prime mode of transport. Historic records are muddy and incomplete, but popular consensus enshrines the Paris to Rouen Horseless Carriages contest, a 78-mile (126 km) point-to-point time trial on public roads on July 22, 1894, as the first organized competitive motoring event. Wheel-to-wheel battles around purpose-built courses lay decades in the future.

By the turn of the century, the pace of technological development was pushing top speeds towards the 100 mph (160 kmh) mark. Tire, suspension, and braking technology were yet to catch up. Racing on public roads–not the sealed bitumen surfaces of today, but crude and dusty at best, littered with rocks and sharp stones as well as other traffic–was truly perilous. Did that dust cloud up ahead contain another competitor, a child, or a domestic animal, or some other vehicle coming the other way?

National automobile clubs took on the responsibility of organizing and promoting races. Naturally power struggles erupted. What's now known as the Fédération Internationale de l'Automobile (FIA), the governing body of world motorsport, evolved from the various national auto clubs grudgingly and gradually setting their petty differences aside to form the Association Internationale des Automobile Clubs Reconnus (AIACR) in 1904.

That wasn't the end of the power plays, though.

American newspaper magnate James Gordon Bennett Jr. organized a handful of point-to-point races on European soil just after the turn of the 20th century. The Gordon Bennett Cup limited each national club to just three entrants to encourage an inter-nation element, but this didn't sit well with the rapidly growing French motor industry. Having won the 1905 Cup, the Automobile Club de France had earned the honor of hosting for a sixth time in 1906, but instead it decided to create its own event, with unlimited national entrants and a substantial 45,000 francs in cash for the winner. Grand Prix ("great prize"), already a familiar monicker in horse racing circles, entered motoring parlance as the Grand Prix de l'ACF. French honor and preeminence was upheld as, of the 34 cars entered, 26 were French-built. And in an echo of other battles to come, the motoring industry ousted the upstart media man.

In photographs, Ferenc Szisz looks dapper and slight of build, but make no mistake, these races required muscle and willpower in equal measure. Based on a 65-mile (105 km) lap east of the French city of Le Mans, later home of the annual 24-hour race, the Grand Prix de l'ACF was a grueling two-day event in which only 11 entrants finished. The race consisted of six laps a day, timed with the competitors setting off at intervals to thunder off into the countryside, wrestling with cumbersome steering, agricultural gearboxes, and cable-operated brakes working on the rear axle only. Yet the pace was anything but slow; early leader Paul Baras, in a 12-liter Brasier, averaged 73.3 mph (118 kmh), setting the fastest lap.

While the ACF got its wish of a French car winning (Szisz was driving a Renault), manufacturers from Germany and Italy would dominate the following decades as the philosophy of Grand Prix racing spread internationally. For racing to cross borders and for it to not become ruinously expensive for the manufacturers, commonly agreed

rules and technical benchmarks would be required. This was an early driver toward the founding of the Commission Sportive Internationale (CSI) in 1922 with a mandate to set a technical formula and, in the same decade, to take the first steps toward establishing a world championship.

This was probably too much too soon for an automobile industry still in flux after World War I. Despite the economic boom of the 1920s, many small European manufacturers went out of business or were driven to merge with others. Cars remained expensive and slow to build until the Europeans followed Henry Ford's lead. Motor racing was a rich man's sport in which manufacturer backing was vital—and in many cases that commitment was fragile. The AIACR inaugurated its world championship for constructors in 1925, got spooked by increasing car performance, and introduced a new and needlessly complicated set of rules for the following season—and then wondered why there were so few takers. But the preconditions for failure had already been set out. The world championship calendar included the Indianapolis 500, where just one privately entered Fiat faced the might of a U.S. motor industry, relatively untouched by the European war. At the European Grand Prix, the first to be held at Spa-Francorchamps in Belgium, Alfa Romeo's P2 cars proved so dominant that the crowd began to boo and jeer. The team set out a picnic in the pits and called its drivers in to enjoy it while the few other remaining competitors could catch up a little.

Despite competitive inequalities, speed fever was catching on in Europe. New purpose-built speedbowls in Montlhéry, France, and the Milanese suburb of Monza followed the lead of Brooklands and the Indianapolis Motor Speedway in producing fast, spectator-, and competitor-friendly environments. Grand Prix racing completed its transition from a time-trial format to mass-start wheel-to-wheel combat. Poor choice of materials meant none of the European venues enjoyed the longevity of Indy's brick-paved oval: their concrete banking sections distorted with changing weather conditions and became dangerously bumpy.

Drivers as well as cars became an integral part of racing's box-office appeal, as promoters rewarded the biggest names with appearance fees (known euphemistically as "starting money") as well as cash prizes. Former motorcycle racer Tazio Nuvolari became the bellwether of the 1930s. Against a tapestry of rapidly evolving technology, he was among the first drivers to race for Scuderia Ferrari, in Alfa Romeo machinery designed by pioneering engineer Vittorio Jano, the technical genius of his time. Nuvolari drove Alfa's Tipo B, the seminal single-seater of the early 1930s, alongside Germany's Rudolf Caracciola in what was arguably the first "superteam." Nuvolari was at the center of the 1934 Tripoli GP race-fixing scandal (though it's now known that there was no such thing, merely an agreement to share prize money); and his move to Auto Union in 1938 represented a definitive capitulation to the dominance of the Nazi-backed German teams.

During the 1920s, Nuvolari had raced against fellow Italian Enzo Ferrari. Having quit driving, the entrepreneurial Ferrari went into business for himself during one of Alfa Romeo's periodic withdrawals from racing. What he offered, in essence, was an arrive-and-race experience for wealthy individuals. Backed by two such customers and with support from Alfa Romeo, Scuderia Ferrari prepared and ran cars with such efficiency that the team became Alfa's de facto works entry when the company returned to Grand Prix racing—an arrangement that endured even after Benito Mussolini's government took Alfa into state ownership.

Maximum speeds went from around 130 mph (209 kmh) to nearly 200 mph (322 kmh) during the 1930s, as the fascist governments in Germany and Italy turned Grand Prix racing into national propaganda exercises. Not only did the Germans generally beat off the Italians, but they were pushing the limits of what was technically achievable given certain well-established limitations. For all the advances in aerodynamic shapes, lightweight materials, chassis trickery (such as locating the engine behind the driver rather than in front), and horsepower-liberating fuel additives, suspension and braking technologies remained primitive, as did the skinny cotton-carcass tires of the era.

Ferrari's solution to being outgunned on track was to shift the parameters of competition. In 1937 he directed Jano's protégé Gioacchino Colombo to design a new car and 1.5-liter supercharged engine for the "Voiturette" sub-class, a step down from the Grand Prix cars. The upper strata of management and their political masters were unimpressed by this attempted sleight of hand, and, the following year, Alfa Romeo bought Enzo out and brought his operation in-house, to be supervised by engineers recruited from outside. Ferrari disliked life as an employee and left to form his own company, and the outbreak of World War II rendered the four-year non-compete clause in his severance agreement moot.

Bizarre as such an exercise may seem given the devastation wrought by the six-year conflict, Paris hosted the first peacetime motor race on September 9, 1945, just a week after Japan's formal surrender. The Coupes de Paris was contested by a ragtag assortment of whatever machinery remained available, driven by an eclectic cast including prewar heroes such as winner Jean-Pierre Wimille and ex-servicemen who needed a replacement source of adrenaline.

Since many racing cars had been looted or melted down for munitions, events organized in the immediate postwar years tended to be held to "Formula Libre" rules: anything goes. As national automobile clubs felt their way back towards a properly structured "world" championship, it became clear that a better-defined rulebook would be required—but prudence would dictate the first steps.

THE ① 1950s

One of the factors that had stymied Grand Prix racing's growth in the prewar era was the too-frequent tinkering with the technical formula. While (usually) well-intentioned, aiming to level the playing field or stimulate different technical solutions, its effect was to allow the best-resourced organizations to dominate. This kind of regime was never going to work in the postwar environment.

1959 Dutch GP
After Hawthorn's demise and Fangio's retirement, the field was without a world champion. At the Dutch GP, Swedish driver Jo Bonnier sealed his first pole and took BRM's inaugural win after nine years, ahead of Jack Brabham (No. 7) in the Cooper-Climax.

The first iteration of we what we now know as Formula 1, then known as Formula A (sources differ as to when this transition took place), was ratified by the AIACR at the 1947 Paris Salon and dictated by pragmatism. In allowing space for 1.5-liter super-charged and 4.5-liter naturally aspirated engines, it acknowledged that, in the short term at least, most competitors would be "making do" with prewar cars. At some point there would have to be a new technical formula, but when?

Ensuring full and competitive grids became a key challenge for race promoters and the governing body, even after the inauguration of a world championship to provide focus. Alfa Romeo's fleet of prewar 158 voiturettes–the ones created at Enzo Ferrari's behest–had dominated the most significant Grands Prix of 1948 before lack of funds and the deaths of all three star drivers (Jean-Pierre Wimille and Achille Varzi suffered

1950 British GP
Winner of the first Formula 1 race, Giuseppe Farina leads Luigi Fagioli, both in Alfa Romeo 158s, around the perimeter track of the ex-WWII airfield at Silverstone.

1950 Italian GP
After qualifying on pole, Fangio's Alfa Romeo retired with engine failure on lap 23. Fangio took over Piero Taruffi's Alfa, but this car also retired, leaving Giuseppe Farina to take the win and the championship.

(ABOVE)

1950 French GP

Alfa Romeos piloted by Juan Manuel Fangio (No. 6), Giuseppe Farina (No. 2), and Luigi Fagioli lead the field down the Reims main straight. Farina led initially but dropped to third after a lengthy pit stop to cure a fuel problem. Fangio took the checkered flag, with Fagioli second and almost three laps ahead of British driver Peter Whitehead in the Ferrari 125.

(RIGHT)

1951 Swiss GP

Fangio leads Farina in the supercharged Alfa Romeos around the slippery Bremgarten circuit at the first round in Switzerland. At the flag, Fangio was in first place, with Taruffi in a Ferrari 375 splitting the Alfas on the podium.

(OPPOSITE BOTTOM)

1950 Monaco GP

The Mediterranean principality hosted round two of the F1 championship, which was marred by an opening lap pileup at a wet Tabac corner. Farina's Alfa almost blocked the track, but teammate Juan Manuel Fangio squeezed past to win.

(ABOVE)

1951 Italian GP

Following Alfa Romeo's dominance, the 1951 drivers' championship remained popular. Fangio retired from pole with engine failure at half distance. Milanese hero Alberto Ascari won the Italian Grand Prix at the Monza Autodrome in his Ferrari.

(LEFT)

1951 British GP

Ferrari won its inaugural Formula 1 at the British Grand Prix. There, Argentine driver Jose Froilán González took the 4.5-liter V12 375 to the top step, beating the thirsty supercharged Alfas for the first time. Fellow Argentine Fangio, who finished second, congratulates him.

(ABOVE LEFT)

1952 Belgian GP

Alberto Ascari had his first season outing in the simple but effective Ferrari 500 at Spa-Francorchamps in round three. He had missed the first rounds competing in the Indianapolis 500. Here, he leads teammate Giuseppe Farina and Jean Behra's Gordini into Eau Rouge on lap two.

(ABOVE RIGHT)

1952 French GP

Qualifying in Rouen, Ferrari was locked out of the front row, with Ascari on pole next to Farina and Piero Taruffi. Despite the Gordini team's valiant battle for third, Taruffi took the place on lap four, allowing a clean sweep for Ferrari with Ascari the winner. Ascari leads Farina with Gordini behind.

(RIGHT)

1951 Spanish GP

Ascari's Ferrari (No. 2) took the pole in the first Spanish Grand Prix at the Pedralbes street circuit in Barcelona. He shared the front row with teammate González alongside Fangio (winner) and Farina in their Alfa Romeos.

fatal accidents, while Count Trossi died of cancer) prompted the company to pull out of racing once again. In 1949, facing little serious competition, Ferrari's new, supercharged 125s led the way, even though chassis were so flimsy that the cars achieved frightening yaw angles traveling in a straight line. One early customer, British prewar ace Raymond Mays, returned his 125 to Modena after just one race.

If the hope was that the inauguration of the world championship in 1950 would foster greater international competition and technical development, it was only partly successful in the short term. Alfa Romeo returned to the fray, lured by bigger prize purses. The inclusion of the Indianapolis 500 as a hands-across-the-ocean exercise failed because the cars were too different and the distance too great in this epoch before jet aviation. Scant few competitors crossed the great divide. There was great aural diversity among the entrants, with the thudding straight-8 of the Alfettas ranged against the screaming V12 and V16 of Ferrari and BRM, and the more luxuriant roar of the 4.5-liter straight-6 Talbot-Lago. However, there was little variation in terms of the winning team—Alfa Romeo—and its three Fs: Giuseppe Farina, Juan Manuel Fangio, and Luigi Fagioli. None of them was young; Fagioli remains both the oldest man to win a world championship race (in 1951, aged 53), and the only Grand Prix winner to have been born in the 19th century.

Was it too soon to begin a world championship? Perhaps. The first venue was Silverstone, a redundant wartime bomber airfield in rural England whose racing potential had been "discovered" by ex-servicemen breaking in to exercise their cars at speed on the abandoned runways and perimeter roads. Gasoline was still rationed in the UK when Farina led an Alfa 1-2-3 in that first world championship Grand Prix on May 13, 1950. The fourth-place finisher was two laps down, BRM (the British national prestige project backed by Mays after his Ferrari disappointment) was a no-show because its car wasn't ready, and Ferrari was absent because Enzo thought the prize fund insufficient to warrant the trouble of crossing the English Channel. Unlike the modern era, with its centralized prize pot, there was no requirement to enter every event and competitors negotiated appearance fees with the individual race promoters.

(ABOVE)
1952 British GP
In another dominant race for the Ferraris, Farina took pole next to Ascari, but dropped down the field after returning to the pits with engine trouble. Recovering from a bad start, Piero Taruffi (left) finished in second place behind Ascari (center). Both received silverware.

(TOP LEFT)
1953 Argentinian GP
World champion Ascari's Ferrari 500 leads Fangio in a Maserati A6GCM at the start of the first Formula 1 race held in South America, in Buenos Aires, Argentina. Ascari won, but the race was marred by accidents involving spectators spilling onto the circuit.

(TOP RIGHT)
1953 Dutch GP
Ascari's Ferrari leads Fangio's Maserati among the sand dunes in the Dutch Grand Prix at Zandvoort. The Ferrari had superior handling on the slippery, freshly resurfaced track. Ascari won again after Fangio retired with a broken axle.

(RIGHT)
1953 French GP
Mike Hawthorn signed to Ferrari at the end of 1952 and started seventh on the grid at Reims. After an epic battle slip-streaming Fangio in his Maserati on the long straights, Hawthorn won his first Grand Prix.

(NEXT PAGE)
1952 Italian GP
The final round in Monza saw a great start for the Argentinian Maserati driver Froilán González taking the lead, only to lose it to a slow pit stop. Ascari took the win on the cobbles and the driver's title, but González split the Ferraris finishing second. André Simon is lapped by Farina (fourth) and Luigi Villoresi (third).

Change was in the air even though Farina swept to the championship in 1950 and teammate Fangio did likewise the following season. Ferrari's swap to natural aspiration with a new V12 designed by Aurelio Lampredi, though it took until mid-'51 to register a Grand Prix victory, would hasten Alfa Romeo's withdrawal at the end of that year as funds ran short again and efforts to squeeze more power from the engine made it uncompetitively thirsty. A new technical formula based on 750cc supercharged and 2.5-liter naturally aspirated engines was in the offing, but not until 1954. In theory this gave sufficient notice for aspiring entrants to gear up, but it also acted as a disincentive to build new cars for the outgoing regulations. Fearing thin grids and Ferrari whitewashes—a mood exacerbated by further BRM no-shows in early 1952—race promoters lobbied to have Formula 1 shelved in favor of Formula 2 as the class for world championship events.

As it happened, Ferrari dominated anyway since its Formula 2 car was the fastest and most robust in the class. Alberto Ascari won six out of eight championship races in 1952, a victory ratio that wouldn't be matched for another 71 years, and then became the first double world champion in 1953.

BEHIND THE SCENES

THE EARLY SIGNS OF PROFESSIONALISM

The 48-page program for the first-ever World Championship race at Silverstone, offers a remarkable glimpse into a bygone age. One of the paragraphs inside that 1950 publication is head-lined "Smoking Permitted." It adds: "Grand Prix drivers do not normally have to undergo strict physical training. Moderation in eating, drinking and smoking is sufficient, for motor racing is a test of brain rather than brawn."

A second passage on the protocols of the sport is almost unrecognizable in today's world. It starts with "Pass Friend" and continues: "The French were the pioneers of motor racing and ever since it has been a tradition to use their rule-of-the-road. Therefore, overtaking drivers should pull over to the left-hand side of the road."

While the 1950s were predominantly an era for wealthy amateurs, one man was starting to take a more professional approach to the sport. Stirling Moss was the first to seize on commercial opportunities—even if it meant smoking six cigarettes a day. His first sponsorship deal was with Craven A tobacco. He also employed a manager, Ken Gregory, who helped him establish Stirling Moss Limited.

When Mercedes-Benz returned to motor racing, it soon hired Moss who mirrored its own professional high standards. However, Gregory revealed that the flight to Argentina for its first race together, in January 1955, was particularly fraught.

"I was horrified to learn from a Pan-American official there was a panic at Stuttgart as Mercedes-Benz had omitted to tell me that Stirling needed an Argentine visa," said Gregory. With the airliner crossing the South Atlantic, Moss's manager was engaged in a series of frantic calls with the Foreign Office in London and the British Consul in Buenos Aires to resolve the vexatious customs issue. Meanwhile, at 30,000 feet, Stirling encountered his own calamity.

"Neubauer [Mercedes's competition director], of course, is a huge man, weighing around 20 or 21 stone [280–294 lbs] with a vast frame and massive shoulders," continued Gregory. "About an hour after take-off he lumbered to the back of the plane and found he could not get through the [toilet] door. In the end Stirling and teammate Hans Herrmann were enlisted to help, and they turned him sideways to force him through the door. They had to get him out again by grabbing his arm and pulling like fury until he popped out like a cork from a champagne bottle."

Neubauer was a brilliant organizer, and with Rudolf Uhlenhaut as the team's technical chief, the German cars were engineered to suit each individual driver's needs with an almost obsessive attention to detail. In addition to its slick operations, Mercedes-Benz was one of the first to recognize the importance of public relations and the team's press attaché would ensure a team photographer flew to every race, accompanied by an expensive Leica camera carefully clipped into a beautifully lined case. The age of friendly amateurs passing each other on the left was coming to an end.

"The Motor" Copyright

The Royal Automobile Club

Grand Prix d'Europe

Incorporating

THE BRITISH
GRAND PRIX

Silverstone
Saturday,
13th May, 1950

OFFICIAL PROGRAMME

ONE SHILLING

(ABOVE)
1953 German GP
Farina qualified third at the Nürburgring GP in Germany. When Ascari's front wheel came off, Farina passed Fangio to win. It would be Farina's final Grand Prix win, and he clinched the driver's title for Ascari.

After this faltering start, the world championship rapidly gained status with the first proper postwar Formula 1 in 1954. While there were no takers for the 750cc supercharged engine concept, the 2.5-liter naturally aspirated format attracted enlarged version of existing six- and four-cylinder designs from Maserati, Gordini, and Ferrari, plus a new fuel-injected straight-8 from Mercedes, a V8 from Lancia, and an unusual hybrid of motorcycle and automobile-derived elements in the form of Vanwall's straight-4. Energetic competition involving both recognized automobile industry names and engineering specialists would drive developments in aerodynamics, braking, and chassis dynamics, as well as engine performance in the years to come.

The year 1954 also provided another "first" as Hollywood made a maiden appearance on the grid, albeit in a far more low-key way than the 2025 Brad Pitt—starring *F1* movie filmed in and around the championship 70 years later. At the Belgian Grand Prix, 14 cars entered and qualified, but, in an unbilled 15th, Emmanuel "Toulo" de Graffenried doubled for Kirk Douglas to collect opening-lap film footage for *The Racers,* a melodrama based loosely on the life of prewar ace Rudolf Caracciola.

While posterity—and rapturous encomiums from some of the greatest drivers of the era—enshrines Maserati's sweet-handling 250F as one of the all-time great race cars, the remarkable Mercedes W196 did most of the winning from its first appearance (in "streamliner" form) at Reims in 1954 until the team withdrew from racing at the end of the '55 season. Fuel injection and desmodromic valves made the engine a technological showcase while the sheer efficiency of Mercedes's works team set new operational standards. By contrast, Maserati struggled to cope with customer demand for 250Fs, lacking the quality materials and manpower to achieve quality as well as quantity. Fangio won the first two championship GPs in a factory-entered 250F, then ruthlessly jumped ship to Mercedes when the silver arrows returned to racing in France. The following season, partnered by the young Briton Stirling Moss, Fangio romped to a third world title driving solely for Mercedes.

1954 French GP

Mercedes returned to Formula 1 for round four in France. Fangio won for Maserati in Argentina and Belgium, switching to Mercedes and winning first time out at the French GP in Reims with the new "Silver Arrow," the streamlined W196. Here Fangio leads Kling.

1954 German Grand Prix

At the fearsome Nürburgring, Fangio in Mercedes (No. 18) qualified on pole with Hawthorn (No. 3) in the Ferrari second and young privateer Stirling Moss (No. 16) in a Maserati third. After González (No. 1) retired his Ferrari, Hawthorn took over the car, but couldn't catch Fangio, who won after three hours and 45 minutes.

One-team dominance highlighted the fact that competitive inequalities remained. The Italian teams suffered for lack of material resources and organization: Maserati could scrap for race wins, but Ferrari's effort, in effect an enlarged F2 car, proved so hopeless that Ascari bailed out before the end of 1954, lured by the late but more promising Lancia D50 overseen by the great Vittorio Jano.

While the D50's prolonged gestation meant it didn't compete until the end of the 1954 season, it arrived freighted with innovative thinking. Chassis engineering was moving on from the rugged simplicity favored by (and holding back) Ferrari, where the bodyshell was attached to a basic ladder-frame structure with twin horizontal beams. Maserati and Mercedes had a more sophisticated "spaceframe" consisting of thin, interconnected metal tubes; the 250F was over-engineered compared with the W196, in which every section had been rigorously stress-tested so as to use minimal materials, saving weight. The D50, as well as holding fuel and oil in pannier tanks between the front and rear wheels to facilitate a shorter, nimbler wheelbase and (theoretically) better balance, positioned the engine off-center within the spaceframe so the

(ABOVE)

1955 Monaco GP
World champion Fangio and Stirling Moss, new to the Mercedes team, led the Monaco GP before both retired with mechanical problems. Ascari led, overshot the chicane, and crashed into the harbor in his Lancia. This allowed outsider Maurice Trintignant (No. 44) through to win in his Ferrari 625. Ascari was killed four days later in an accident while testing.

(OPPOSITE TOP LEFT)
1954 Italian GP
Stirling Moss in a Maserati 250F in third place leads Mike Hawthorn in the Ferrari 625 at Monza. The dynamic race saw the lead change many times, challenging the dominance of Mercedes. After Moss lost oil pressure, Fangio in the W196 Streamliner took the win.

(OPPOSITE TOP RIGHT)
1954 Spain GP
World champion Ascari signed for new F1 team Lancia, but their innovative D50 wasn't ready until the final round in Spain. Although Ascari was quick, putting the car on pole, he, and Luigi Villoresi in the other D50, failed to finish the race due to clutch and brake failure.

(BELOW)
1955 British GP
At the new circuit at Aintree, the open-wheel Mercedes showed their dominance, taking the first four out of five places in qualifying and top four at the flag. On home turf, Stirling Moss achieved his first win, but Fangio pushed all the way, finishing just two-tenths behind.

driveshaft could pass beside rather than under the driver, who could then sit lower. Not only that, the top end of each side of the V8 was rigidly bolted to the chassis so the block absorbed some chassis loadings.

Tragedy confined the D50's achievements under Lancia's ownership to a handful of pole positions and wins in non-championship races. Just days after crashing his D50 into the Monaco harbor Ascari was testing a Ferrari sportscar at Monza when he crashed, with fatal consequences, at the corner which still bears his name. Out of money and the will to compete, Lancia withdrew from racing, and ultimately the D50s fell into Ferrari's hands, where Enzo's people somehow contrived to reverse some of the more innovative developments and make the cars slower—though not before Fangio had secured a fourth world title in 1956.

A gentleman on and off the track, Fangio was ruthless in targeting the most competitive drives. His season with Ferrari in 1956 was an outlier, for his hand had been forced by Mercedes's withdrawal. He quickly despaired of Ferrari's abilities to prepare cars to the same standard and, by mid-season, was threatening to quit, and only mollified by the permanent assignment of a respected mechanic to his car. Even then, he owed his world championship to another quirk of the era, which modern readers will find peculiar: when Fangio retired from the season-closing Italian Grand Prix with a broken steering arm, teammate Peter Collins pulled into the pits and handed over his car, sacrificing his own (albeit remote) title chances in doing so. The points, though shared with Collins, were enough for Fangio to beat Moss, the Italian GP winner for Maserati, 30–27.

His former teammate's performance at Monza was enough to embolden Fangio to quit Ferrari and enjoy the final flurries of development applied by Maserati to the 250F in 1957, when the company returned as a works team. With a lighter chassis, a V12 engine in development, and a healthy stockpile of Pirelli tires (the company had quit racing at the end of 1956), Maserati became the team to beat in 1957 and Fangio secured his final world championship.

CASABLANCA 1958

There was a considerable amount of press attention ahead of the 1958 title showdown. The location for the season's climax was the fearsome Ain Diab road course on the outskirts of Casablanca. It's the only time Morocco has held a World Championship Grand Prix.

Already a national hero, Stirling Moss was spearheading the attack for Vanwall. To beat Mike Hawthorn to the title, Moss had to win and set fastest lap.

Despite the tension, this was still an age of fair play. At the Portuguese round in August, Moss had given evidence in support of Hawthorn, to prevent the Ferrari man from disqualification—despite the points swing, it would have given Stirling.

Usually laid-back, Hawthorn felt uneasy throughout the season. When he arrived in Casablanca, he was spooked to have been given number two on the entry list, the number that his Ferrari teammates Luigi Musso and close friend Peter Collins had run when they had been killed earlier in the year.

In the race, Moss was imperious and brilliantly triumphed on the high-speed North African course. But Hawthorn's teammate Phil Hill dutifully gave up second place, which ensured the title went to Mike by one point.

"I didn't drink anyway, and I restrained my running around a bit," said Moss, who lost the championship with four wins to Hawthorn's one. "I wasn't going out with girls quite as much as I had been, and I really had taken it seriously. Then I go and lose it to Mike, who was really having a ball. I thought it was very unfair. There was no justice at all, and I do remember being a bit teed-off."

Moss would never win the championship in his career, but he'd done enough to give Tony Vandervell's smart green Vanwalls the honor of winning for Britain the first-ever championship for Constructors'—but celebrations were muted.

In the race, Oliver Gendebien upended his Ferrari, injuring his chest and ribs. François Picard crashed his Formula 2 Cooper and sustained a fractured skull. But devastatingly, Moss's Vanwall teammate, Stuart Lewis-Evans, had an accident that left him with terrible burns. Still alive, he flew back to Britain and was admitted to the famous McIndoe unit at East Grinstead hospital. Sadly, he succumbed to his dreadful injuries over a week later.

His death took its toll on the friend who had flown home with Lewis-Evans, and who had been helping him negotiate contracts and starting money. Ultimately, he would go on to manage the day-to-day operations of the whole of Formula 1—a man called Bernie Ecclestone.

1958 Moroccan GP
Four drivers were killed during a tragic season. Musso in France, Collins in Germany, Pat O' Connor in Indianapolis, and Stuart Lewis-Evans in the newly added Moroccan Grand Prix in Casablanca. Moss leads the pack with the ill-fated Lewis-Evans behind in car No. 12.

(ABOVE)

1955 Italian GP
Mercedes bowed out of all motor racing after the terrible Le Mans accident in which 84 spectators died after a Mercedes disintegrated into the crowd. It would be 57 years before Nico Rosberg would win again for the Silver Arrows at the 2012 Chinese Grand Prix.

More significant change was blowing through Grand Prix racing, initiated by two simple-sounding measures that would have a profound impact. For 1958, race distances were cut from 500km to 300km, and methanol-based fuels were banned in favor of Avgas. The competitive advantage swung towards small British manufacturers with experience of building lightweight cars around smaller fuel tanks for the junior categories—not that this was recognized at first.

The leading British constructor at this point was Vanwall, founded by the industrialist Tony Vandervell with the explicit intention of beating "those bloody red cars"—by which, in these days of national racing colors, he meant the Italians. Initially part of the BRM consortium, Vandervell had tired of the lack of progress at the beginning of the decade and acquired a handful of Ferrari cars (requiring a substantial battle

(TOP LEFT)

1955 Italian GP
On the new steeply banked circuit of Monza, Mercedes put out both types of W196 with open-wheel cars for Kling and Taruffi and streamliners for Moss and Fangio. This was the last time closed-wheeled cars would be used in Formula 1, but they were effective as Fangio won his third driver's title.

(TOP RIGHT)

1956 British GP
Ferrari was back in control after Mercedes had withdrawn from motor racing the previous season. Fangio now led the team, winning the opener in Argentina. He would not win again until round six in Britain with teammate Collins and Maserati's new hot shoe Moss taking two wins each. Fangio drifts his Ferrari to win at Silverstone.

(ABOVE)

1956 French GP

British driver Peter Collins joined an already strong Ferrari team for 1956. Qualifying third for the French Grand Prix behind teammates Eugenio Castellotti and Fangio, Collins takes the lead past the long Reims pit straight. He would go on to take his second win in a row after victory in Belgium in round four.

(RIGHT)

1956 Monaco GP

Fangio qualified on pole in Monaco, but had a bad race, hitting the barrier twice and damaging a rear wheel. Moss, consummate in his Maserati 250F, led from the first lap to win, despite nearly losing his bonnet late in the race after contact with teammate Cesare Perdisa.

(LEFT)
1957 British GP
Brooks and Moss embrace after their shared victory in the Vanwall at Aintree, the first British car to win any Grand Prix since the 1920s. Moss started well but retired. Still suffering from leg pain after an accident at Le Mans a month earlier, Brooks surrendered his car to Moss, who seized the win.

(BELOW)
1957 German GP
Fangio disliked the political side of Ferrari and moved to Maserati for 1957. He won his fifth title for four different teams at the age of 46. Here he is seen (No. 1) leading the field away from the start of the German Grand Prix, which he won.

with the British Board of Trade over import duties) to showcase his patented Thinwall bearing technology. He then bankrolled development of a four-cylinder engine based on a Rolls-Royce crankcase allied to the top end of a Norton motorcycle design, but Vanwall's efforts in 2.5-liter F1 with a Cooper chassis were largely fruitless, until Vandervell engaged the aerodynamicist Frank Costin and the promising young engineer Colin Chapman to create an in-house design. Developments of this raced competitively in 1957, and, the following year, Vanwall became the first team to win the new constructor's championship. Stirling Moss, who raced most of the '58 season with Vanwall, might have taken the drivers' title had he not declined to protest an illegal push-start for Ferrari's Mike Hawthorn in the final Grand Prix of the year.

(RIGHT)
1957 Italian GP

With the Belgian and Dutch GP cancelled, Pescara in Italy was added to the calendar. The 16-mile road course was the longest F1 circuit. Fangio took pole, but Musso, in the Ferrari, led at the end of lap one, followed closely by Moss. After an epic drive in hot and rough conditions, Moss took the checkered flag.

(BELOW)
1957 French GP

After dominance in '56, Ferrari couldn't win a race in '57. Their aging modified Lancia Ferrari D50/801 wasn't competitive against the Vanwalls and Maseratis. Musso and Hawthorn still finished fourth and fifth in the championships, respectively, having finished on the podium in three races. D50/801 pit lineup, French GP.

MASERATI 250F

At a time when grids were dwindling, a new 2.5-liter formula for normally aspirated and 750cc supercharged engines began in 1954—and Maserati took full advantage.

With the aid of legendary designer Gioacchino Colombo, the Italian manufacturer produced a new low-cost car for private customers. The elegant, front-engined 250F epitomized the era, appearing on grids across the seven years of the formula.

As a development of Maserati's F2 car, the 250F featured a tube-frame chassis with aluminum panels, independent front and de Dion rear suspension, and drum brakes all round. The driver positioned his legs on either side of the clutch housing with the brake pedal positioned on the right and the accelerator and clutch on the left.

With the oil tank mounted under the carburetor, the former would often overheat and leak, which resulted in an early redesign. While the 250F only won eight World Championship races, it has been long revered, not only because it exemplified a beautifully proportioned racing car, but also because it was a joy to drive.

The positioning of the driveline to lower the center of gravity gave the 250F exquisite handling, especially in the hands of great talents such as Fangio and Moss.

Fangio drove the 250F to victory on its championship debut at his home track in Argentina, 1954, while Moss, in a privately run entry, gave the car its first European victory in a Formula Libre race at Aintree.

"The 250F steered beautifully and inclined towards stable oversteer," said the British driver. "Which one could exploit by balancing it against power and steering in long, sustained drifts."

One of the most famous motor racing photographs of the 1950s pictured Fangio at the wheel of the 250F, in a perfectly balanced slide through the high-speed sweeps of Rouen-les-Essarts in 1957. That year's 250F T2 was a lighter and stiffer model, featuring another 30bhp extracted from the six-cylinder engine. Seven years after making its debut, a privateer 250F in the hands of Bob Drake entered the final race of the 2.5-liter formula at the end of 1960, marking the last dance for front-engined machinery in Grand Prix racing.

James Mann

(OPPOSITE)

1958 French GP

Under new FIA rules, races were now limited to two hours. World champion Fangio competes in only two races—his home GP in Argentina and in France as a privateer. Hawthorn clinches his only win in Reims, and Fangio retires after finishing fourth. Fangio in Maserati 250F leads Moss in Vanwall.

(TOP)

1958 Portuguese GP

Despite winning only one race, Hawthorn took the driver's title from Moss by a single point in his Ferrari after consistently being on the podium. Hawthorn was killed in a road accident a few months later. Here at the Portuguese GP, he was second to Moss.

(RIGHT)

1958 Monaco GP

Front engine cars would last be competitive in the 1958 season. French driver Maurice Trintignant won the Monaco Grand Prix in his Cooper Climax T45 ahead of Musso and Collins's Ferraris.

It was Moss who acted as the canary in the coal mine for the next generation of cars in the opening Grand Prix of 1958, which Vanwall sat out while its engines were modified to accommodate the new fuel. Instead Moss raced a Cooper privately entered by his friend, the whisky heir Rob Walker, who in his passport listed his occupation as "gentleman." The Cooper's four-cylinder Climax engine was half a liter short of the maximum allowed and mounted behind the driver—a practice drawn from 500cc Formula 3, where the use of motorcycle engines made retaining the donor vehicle's gearbox and chain drive prudent. Moss's guile in preserving his tires offset his engine's relative lack of power, as heavier rival cars lost track position while pitting for fresh rubber.

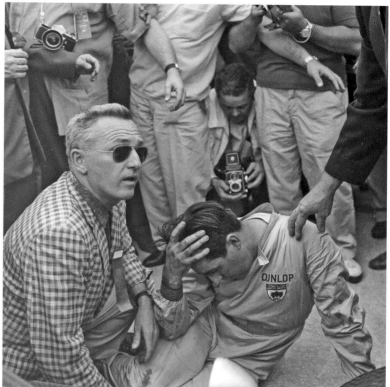

Initially the result was believed to be an outlier owing to the thin entry of ten cars, along with Maserati proving to be a spent force since the parent company was on the verge of bankruptcy. This perspective lasted until the next Grand Prix, Monaco, which Maurice Trintignant won in a newer Cooper chassis with a 2.1-liter engine. And while front-engined cars were victorious in the remainder of the championship races, in 1959 they won just three Grands Prix—four if you count the anomalous Indianapolis 500.

Vanwall's 1958 constructors' championship win proved to be the British team's high water mark. In that tumultuous final round in Morocco, the team's promising young driver, Stuart Lewis-Evans, who had qualified third behind Hawthorn and Moss, was holding fifth place when his engine seized mid-corner and spun him into a rocky bank. His Vanwall caught fire in the impact and a sheared oil pipe sprayed him with hot oil as he tried to escape. Vandervell paid for Lewis-Evans to be flown home immediately, but he succumbed to his injuries six days later. Advised by his own doctors to step back from running the team for the sake of his health, a distraught Vandervell announced he would be leaving Vanwall to its own devices. The team contested just two more world championship Grands Prix as Cooper and Colin Chapman's new Lotus company effectively picked up the baton for British constructors. Lewis-Evans's manager Bernie Ecclestone, a former motorcycle dealer, vanished from the scene—but he would be back . . .

The 1950s ended with New Zealander Bruce McLaren becoming the youngest Grand Prix winner of all time, at 22 years 104 days, at Sebring, Florida, while teammate Jack Brabham pushed his Cooper over the finishing line to claim fourth place and three points, which enabled him to see off Ferrari's Tony Brooks for the drivers' title. Enzo Ferrari hated it, but soon enough he would have to join the rear-engined revolution.

(ABOVE LEFT)
1959 Italian GP
At the Italian GP in Monza, Moss in his Cooper-Climax drove a carefully controlled race after qualifying on pole. He saved both fuel and tires, slipstreaming the Ferraris and winning without a pit stop. Moss leads, with Hill's Ferrari second.

(ABOVE RIGHT)
1959 United States GP
For the final round at Sebring, Florida, Moss, Brabham, or Brooks could win the driver's title. Although the Cooper-Climaxes were dominant, Jack Brabham on the last lap ran out of fuel and pushed his car a mile over the line to finish fourth. It was enough for him to win his first of three championships.

(OPPOSITE)
1959 German GP
The German GP relocated to the steeply banked AVUS circuit in West Berlin. Brooks took his second win of the season in his Ferrari 246. Teammates Dan Gurney and Phil Hill were also on the podium. Brooks (No. 4) leads Gurney (No. 6) and Brabham (No. 1).

THE WORLD CHAMPIONS

**GIUSEPPE FARINA
(1950)**

**JUAN MANUEL FANGIO
(1951, 1954, 1955, 1956, 1957)**

"Nino" was a tough and uncompromising competitor. Born into a Turin coach-building dynasty, Farina made an inauspicious debut in motorsport, breaking his shoulder and suffering facial lacerations in a hillclimb event in 1925.

When the World Championship was inaugurated in 1950, the 44-year-old veteran—known for his arms-stretched style—took pole and victory in a supercharged Alfa 158 in the first round at Silverstone 1950.

While marginally behind on points heading into Monza, he was crowned champion when teammate Juan Manuel Fangio retired with a broken gearbox. Farina quit racing in 1957, but his impetuosity led to a fatal road crash while driving to the 1966 French Grand Prix.

From humble origins, Fangio is regarded as one the greatest drivers of all time. In the course of his life, the Argentine always retained a quiet, undemonstrative demeanor. The Maestro had few accidents, but his worst came in Peru in 1948. Due to fatigue, he tumbled down a mountainside, and the shunt killed his co-driver Daniel Urrutia—his best friend from his home town of Balcarce.

Fangio traveled to postwar Europe in 1949. Noted for his physical strength and stamina—not to mention outright speed—the short and stocky 38-year-old was immediately winning races. When he finally returned home, part-way through 1958, he'd claimed five World Championships with an incredible 47 percent win ratio—24 Grand Prix victories from 51 starts.

Car reliability issues saw him miss out in 1950, but "El Chueco" won the title with his Alfetta the following year, before switching to Maserati for 1952. He sat out most of the season after breaking his neck at Monza. When Mercedes-Benz returned to racing, it hired the peerless Fangio, and during 1954–55 he was untouchable. He moved to Ferrari to claim another title, but disliked the politics in the Italian camp.

For 1957, he rejoined Maserati and his prodigious talent shone through at the wheel of the sublime 250F. His greatest and final win came at the notorious Nürburgring, where a tardy pit stop left him a minute behind the race leader. He broke the lap record ten times en route to a remarkable triumph.

"The Nürburgring was my favourite circuit," said the soft-spoken Fangio. "I think that day I conquered it. On another day it might have conquered me."

After he hung up his helmet, Fangio ran a successful Mercedes-Benz dealership in Buenos Aires. He passed away in 1995 at the age of 84. He is still considered one of the most talented drivers to grace the sport.

ALBERTO ASCARI
(1952, 1953)

Alberto was just seven years old when his famous racing driver father Antonio was killed in the 1925 French Grand Prix. Growing up, the Milanese youngster began racing motorcycles, then cars, before hostilities intervened. When Ascari returned to racing after World War II, it was with Enzo Ferrari, his father's former teammate and friend.

Intensely superstitious (his light blue crash helmet was his lucky charm), Ascari raced with a precise, though relaxed driving style. When the World Championship was run to Formula 2 regulations, he was unrivaled. He won at Spa in the summer of 1952 and did so again one year later. Nobody else won a Grand Prix in the intervening 12 months. His nine consecutive wins was a record that stood for 70 years.

After his two world titles, he signed for Lancia to drive its new D50. At Monaco in early '55, fading brakes pitched him into the harbor. He survived with just a broken nose. Four days later the Italian paid a surprise visit to Monza. After lunch with his protégé Eugenio Castellotti, he asked whether he could drive a few laps of his Ferrari.

Ascari slipped his jacket off, donned Castellotti's white helmet, and with his tie billowing in the breeze, accelerated out of the pits. He never finished his third lap. When the mechanics found him, he had been thrown clear from the car.

Italy went into shock and Alberto was laid to rest alongside his father.

MIKE HAWTHORN
(1958)

Hawthorn enjoyed a meteoric rise to eclipse Stirling Moss to become Britain's first World Champion in 1958. Often sporting a bow tie behind the wheel, the debonaire racer's most successful years were with the Prancing Horse. His hopes rested on the new V6-powered Ferrari Dino 246 for 1958, his title year, when he was partnered by his close friend Peter Collins.

Hawthorn fended off the threat from the Vanwalls of Moss and Tony Brooks, but he was heavily impacted by witnessing the crash that killed Collins at the Nürburgring. When Luigi Musso also lost his life that year, Hawthorn swore he would retire at the year's end to focus on his garage business.

After clinching the title, he lost his life tragically on a cold January morning just a few months later when his Jaguar left the road and hit a tree on the Guildford bypass.

JACK BRABHAM
(1959)

A dirt-track competitor who won titles with midgets and hillclimbs in his native Australia, "Black Jack" came to England in 1955 and formed a close relationship with John Cooper's pioneering car company. Brabham helped to develop the rear-engined concept, which would transform the face of Grand Prix racing forever.

In 1959 Brabham won at Monaco and Aintree to propel Cooper towards its first World Championship. At Sebring, the final race of the year, Brabham ran out of fuel within sight of the checkered flag and pushed his car across the line to secure fourth place and the points he needed for the crown.

THE
② 1960s

Fittingly, the underlying theme of Formula 1 in the 1960s began to percolate in the two-month hinterland between Jack Brabham winning the drivers' title at Sebring in December '59 and the first round of the following decade getting underway on a hot February Sunday in Buenos Aires. The world championship had begun in 1950 with a make-do-and-mend ethos, survived two seasons with no F1 cars at all, then settled into a rhythm where technical development yielded results, and yet there was no great rush to design all-new cars every year. Drivers and many team bosses tended to be individuals of established means rather than professionals or businessmen.

1967 Dutch GP
In 1965 Ford announced a partnership with Lotus to build a race engine. The DFV V8 arrived in round three at Zandvoort mounted in the superb Lotus 49. Graham Hill, who had moved to Lotus from BRM, retired from pole, but Clark took the new car to a historic win on its debut.

While some competitors took longer than others to recognize that the ground rules had–almost imperceptibly–begun to change over the winter, events in Argentina that February provided a clear warning flag for the new world champion.

The catalyst was a new car from Lotus, a tiny organization operating from a garage in a North London suburb. Lotus had scored just a handful of points with its front-engined F1 car over the preceding two seasons despite gaining access to the 2.5-liter Climax engine. But now it unveiled the 18, rear-engined like Brabham's championship-winning Cooper if rather ugly and boxy. Jack thought it resembled a biscuit tin on wheels.

Were you to do business with Lotus founder Colin Chapman, it would be advisable to check your wrist, after shaking hands on a deal, to make sure your watch was still attached. Nevertheless, he was a clever and instinctive self-taught engineer who believed in the mantra of "added lightness." In the coming years, his company would acquire a reputation for making light, innovative, and agile cars that had a tendency to fall apart–hopefully after passing the finishing line.

(OPPOSITE TOP LEFT)
1960 Portuguese GP
Australian Brabham won his second drivers' title at the Portuguese GP with two rounds still remaining. Despite the bumpy street circuit, John Surtees won his first pole in the Lotus-Climax ahead of Dan Gurney's BRM. After an epic battle, including Hill's Ferrari and a recovering Moss in another Lotus, "Black Jack" prevailed.

(OPPOSITE TOP RIGHT)
1960 French GP
At the French GP, the lead switched between Jack Brabham in his Cooper-T53 (rear car), Phil Hill (No. 4) and Wolfgang Von Trips (Ferrari 246) in third before the Ferraris fell back with gearbox problems. At the flag, Brabham won with the next three places also Cooper-Climaxes.

(OPPOSITE BOTTOM LEFT)
1960 Italian GP
With the championship already decided in favor of Brabham, the British teams boycotted the Italian GP citing safety concerns for the new, lightweight rear-engined cars on Monza's banking. Monza would mark Phil Hill's first Formula 1 win in the Ferrari 246.

(OPPOSITE BOTTOM RIGHT)
1960 Monaco GP
Stirling Moss, driving for Rob Walker's private team, dominated the Monaco race in a Lotus 18, scoring the builder's first Formula 1 win. He was later injured in practice at Spa in Belgium, breaking both legs and missing much of the season. Moss returned in the final round winning at California's Riverside Raceway.

(RIGHT)
1961 Monaco GP
F1's rule change to a 1.5-liter engine caught many of the British teams unprepared, benefitting Ferrari and its new mid-engined "Sharknose" 156. Only Moss in the outdated Lotus 18 Climax was competitive, winning two races starting with the opener in Monaco.

While Brabham could only qualify tenth for the season opener in Buenos Aires, Stirling Moss claimed pole in his Rob Walker-entered Cooper. Come the race, though, it was the performance of second-place qualifier Innes Ireland in the new Lotus 18 that drew the eye, even though a broken gear linkage caused him to spin out of contention. Brabham's teammate, Bruce McLaren, took his second consecutive victory, while Jack himself exited at half-distance with gearbox failure.

In terms of hard results, then, it was business as usual. Brabham knew better, his mind made up after watching Ireland's speed in a subsequent non-championship race in Cordoba, where neither factory Cooper made it past the opening lap. On the plane back to the UK, Brabham started sketching ideas with John Cooper.

"I told John 'we've really got to do something or we'll be left for dead this year,'" he wrote in his autobiography, "and we began planning a new car right there on the airliner."

Team patriarch Charles Cooper thought changing a winning car was madness. He had failed to grasp that F1 was now a business in which competitors had to be constantly moving forwards or they would soon–relatively speaking–be heading backwards. Despite the elder Cooper's staunch opposition, Brabham and chief designer Owen Maddock completed the new "Lowline" T53 in two months. A second chassis was

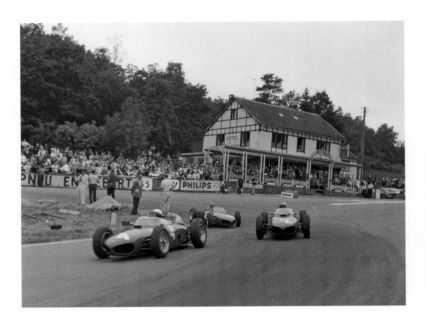

hidden away from the boss, ditto paperwork detailing the expense of a new five-speed gearbox design. Nevertheless, in the interim, Ireland claimed the Lotus 18's first victory in a non-championship race at Goodwood, leaving Moss in his wake. Moss returned to the pits and informed his friend Walker that they needed to get their hands on a Lotus as soon as humanly possible.

While the Cooper T53's curved-tube chassis design was unusual, and a point of contention between Maddock and Brabham, other elements of the car established a theme others would have to follow. More compact than its predecessor, with an elongated nose allowing the radiator and pedals to be brought forward and the driver taking a more reclined position, it cleaved a smoother path through the air. Coil springs marked a definitive break from the leaf springs still espoused by some competitors (including Old Man Cooper).

Moss claimed Lotus's first world championship race victory in Monaco, though Brabham passed him early on before spinning into the wall. Thereafter Jack's title defense began to click with victory at Zandvoort, then Moss ceased to be a factor when he suffered a serious injury after a wheel fell off in Belgium–that Lotus fragility

(ABOVE)

1962 Dutch GP
For the 1962 season, the British teams had developed a new range of 1.5-liter V8 engines to compete with Ferrari, as was demonstrated by Graham Hill (No. 17) winning for BRM at the season opener at Zandvoort. He would go on to win his first drivers' title.

(OPPOSITE TOP LEFT)
1961 Belgian GP
In a tightly fought Belgian GP, the Ferraris dominated with teammates Phil Hill (No. 4), Von Trips (No. 2), Richie Ginther (No. 6), and Olivier Gendebien (No. 8) swapping the lead through the steep curves and long straights at Spa-Francorchamps. At the flag, it was a Ferrari 1-2-3-4 sweep with Hill taking top honors.

(OPPOSITE TOP RIGHT)
1961 United States GP
New York's Watkins Glen circuit hosted the final round of the 1961 season. Ferrari was still reeling from the accident at Monza, and since the title was already decided, the team did not attend. Brabham made pole, but it was Innes Ireland who won his and team Lotus's first grand prix.

(RIGHT)
1961 Italian GP
Ferrari drivers Von Trips (No. 4) and Hill (No. 2) were both vying for the title at Monza, but after a collision with Clark's Lotus, Von Trips was thrown from his car and died instantly, the car rolling into the crowd killing 14 spectators. The race continued with Hill winning to clinch the championship.

(BELOW)
1962 Monaco GP
After an early laps crash at Monaco in round two took out Gurney, Maurice Trintignant, and Richie Ginther, New Zealander Bruce McLaren in his Cooper-Climax (No. 14) led the race. Graham Hill in the BRM then took the lead on lap seven before retiring and handing the win to McLaren.

THE POWER STRUGGLE

For 1966, the sport's governing body, the CSI, decided to change the Formula 1 engine regulations by doubling the capacity to more powerful 3-liter units. It led to a design that was to have a profound effect on the sport.

The Ford-Cosworth DFV triumphed on its debut at the 1967 Dutch Grand Prix and went on to take another 155 wins over the following 18 seasons. It was cheap, reliable, competitive and enabled teams to enter F1 with an off-the-shelf solution for as little as £7,500.

The DFV (double four valve) was designed by the brilliant Keith Duckworth thanks to a £100,000 fund from the Ford Motor Company. As a former transmission engineer, he'd established his own business with Mike Costin, producing Ford-based engines for racing purposes.

The partnership between Ford and Cosworth was initiated by former Fleet Street journalist Walter Hayes. Appointed director of public affairs for Ford, he saw the potential in creating a Grand Prix engine to fill the breach left by Coventry-Climax, as it had withdrawn from F1 at the end of 1965.

Duckworth understood that while the engine might not be powerful enough in its own right, it could offer more potential if it was fully integrated with the chassis. Bankrolled by Ford, Lotus's Colin Chapman began working on the 49, which would utilize the DFV as a fully stressed member of the car.

When the Lotus broke cover at Zandvoort in 1967, it effectively rendered the opposition obsolete. The light and compact 90-degree, 85.7 × 64.8 mm, 2,993cc V8 developed 400bhp at 9,000rpm car powered Jim Clark to victory on its debut. Initially the DFV was exclusive to Lotus, but Chapman generously agreed to allow the sale of the engine to his rivals for the wider interest of the sport.

Bruce McLaren was soon writing a check for one, and in time, more teams were making the transition to the pioneering V8s, including Brabham who ditched his title-winning Repco. As a mark of the engine's success, in 1973, every round of the World Championship was won by this era-defining power unit.

New for 1967, the all-conquering 3.0-liter Ford Cosworth DFV V8 engine, here in Graham Hill's Lotus 49.

manifesting itself. A front-engined car would win just one more race, and then only because the Italian GP promoters used Monza's dangerous banked layout in the hope it would favor the outmoded Ferraris. Relative performance became a moot point when the British teams boycotted the event on safety grounds—not that it mattered since Brabham had the championship in the bag by then.

Shortly before Moss's accident at Spa, Brabham had sliced 7s from the lap record. Within moments of Moss's car coming to rest, a steering column weld failed on the privately entered Lotus 18 of Mike Taylor, pitching him off the track and into the trees. So severe were his injuries that he raced again only once, and he pursued Chapman for damages through the courts. Two more drivers—Alan Stacey and Chris Bristow—would die during a race weekend which would have profound consequences for Grand Prix racing.

(LEFT)
1962 French GP
After qualifying sixth at the French GP, Gurney probably didn't hold out much hope of victory in his flat-eight, air-cooled Porsche. But as Brabham retired, McLaren spun off, and Clark's suspension failed, Gurney found himself in the lead. It was his first, and Porsche's only, Formula 1 win.

(BOTTOM)
1962 British GP
Jim Clark's new monocoque Lotus 25 (No. 20) was the shape of the future. He won at Spa in Belgium and he also took pole at Aintree for the British GP. The 25's superiority was obvious during the race, with Clark leading from start to finish.

(OPPOSITE BOTTOM)
1963 Italian GP
Originally planned to run on Monza's rough concrete banking, the race was switched to use the road course after a petition from the newly formed Grand Prix Drivers' Association. Surtees achieved pole in front of Ferrari's home crowd, but his engine failed and Clark (No. 8) went on to win.

(TOP LEFT)

1963 Monaco GP

The 1962 world champion Graham Hill won the first race of the calendar in Monaco in his BRM, despite trailing Clark's Lotus from pole. After an epic battle with Surtees's Ferrari, Clark retired with a gearbox problem and Surtees slowed, allowing Hill and Ginther to take a 1-2 for BRM.

(TOP RIGHT)

1963 German GP

Seven-times world motorcycle champion John Surtees had signed for Ferrari at the start of the 1963 season. He qualified second for the German GP behind Clark's Lotus. Surtees hung in there while many of his competitors crashed or broke down, resulting in his first Grand Prix victory.

In a bid to cut speeds, the governing body announced a 1.5-liter naturally aspirated engine formula for 1961 and beyond. It was a rather footling measure since lap times were also falling because of improved aerodynamics and handling, plus tire development, and few among the British racing establishment believed it would actually be enshrined in the regulations. However, they were fooled because it came to pass, and Enzo Ferrari had a perfectly good 1.5-liter V6 ready to go. In 1961 Ferrari belatedly embraced rear-engined design (having told John Cooper in '59 that it was never going to happen) and cleaned the clocks of opposition teams limping around with inadequate power. Moss's remarkable victory in Monaco in '61 was a rare outlier.

Drivers hated the 1.5-liter formula because the lack of power reduced differentiation between the elite level of racing and the lower formulae. But it drove technical and tire development at an ever-faster pace as engineers sought to overcome the power deficit. The seminal cars of this era came from the Lotus workshops. Popular myth has it that Chapman first sketched the concept of the 25 on a napkin while dining out with Frank Costin. Developed alongside the 24, a conventional spaceframe design, the 25 located the driver in an ultra-reclined position between two horizontal box-sections that also housed fuel tanks. These pontoons were then held rigidly together not by a frame but by the bodywork itself. It was the first true monocoque chassis in which the bodyshell functioned as a stress-bearing element of the chassis. Those who had bought a 24 on the assurance that it would be "mechanically identical" were not amused.

Driven by new superstar Jim Clark, the 25 was a racing force stoppable only by its fragility, which cost Clark titles in 1962 and '64. Its more refined replacement, the 33, furnished his second drivers' championship in 1965. The farmer from the village of Duns in the Scottish borders was shy out of the cockpit, a born winner in it. If his car could last the distance–by no means a given in this era–the peerless Clark would usually cross the line first. He finished second just once in his world championship career.

More manufacturers were declaring an interest in motor racing, a trend which both drove technical development and accelerated the trend towards professionalism. Honda arrived in Formula 1 in 1964, partnered by Goodyear tires. Soon Firestone would join the threat to Dunlop's virtual monopoly position. In sportscar racing, Ford was throwing resources at combatting Ferrari on track after Enzo rebuffed the Blue Oval's

(TOP LEFT)
1963 Dutch GP
Clark won seven of ten races to secure the driver's title with three rounds still to run. He won two of those remaining, ending the season with 73 points, more than double second-place finisher Graham Hill. Clark and Lotus principal Colin Chapman celebrate on the Dutch GP podium.

(TOP RIGHT)
1964 British GP
World champion Clark put his Lotus 25 on pole at hilly Brands Hatch in Kent ahead of main rival Graham Hill in his BRM and Gurney in a Brabham. After a hard-fought race, Clark won by less than three seconds from Hill.

(OPPOSITE BOTTOM LEFT)
1964 Monaco GP
In a season of mixed results, no team dominated. Graham Hill in his improved BRM P261 won in Monaco ahead of teammate Ginther after retirements by Clark, Surtees, Brabham, and Gurney.

(OPPOSITE BOTTOM RIGHT)
1964 Mexican GP
Gurney took his second win of the year in the Brabham BT7. Clark would have won the Mexican GP, but his Lotus's engine blew on the last lap. Surtees won the 1964 driver's title for Ferrari, becoming the only man ever to claim both motorcycle grand prix and F1 championships.

(TOP)
1964 Italian GP
Surtees's (No. 2) second win of the season would be from pole at Ferrari's home GP in Monza following on from Bandini's success in Austria. Jumped at the start by McLaren's Cooper, Surtees recaptured the lead at the end of lap one and never looked back.

attempt to buy his company. As sportscar engine displacements grew to 7 liters, F1's supposed position as the premier motorsport formula became untenable. By 1966 the governing body was ready to capitulate and proudly announce "the return to power" with 3-liter engines.

As with the downsizing of 1961, there were those who were unprepared for and disadvantaged by the change. Ferrari, distracted by the tin-top war with Ford, tried to make do with an existing V12 concept designed for sportscars. BRM, as was the company's habit, became embroiled in engineering overshoot and tried to spin its 1.5-liter V8 into a 3-liter H16 by flattening out the vee and mating two cylinder banks to a single crankcase. Climax abandoned plans for a 3-liter engine entirely. Maserati's V12 was based on designs from a decade earlier.

Enter Jack Brabham again. Having tired of Cooper's conservatism and inability to move with the times, he'd gone into partnership with fellow Australian Ron Tauranac

THE 1966 BELGIAN GP

The majestic Spa-Francorchamps is considered one of the greatest circuits in the world, but today's layout is a much shorter version than the original. In the 1920s, a 14km (8.7 mile) course was first mapped out using public roads that linked the villages of Francorchamps, Malmedy, and Stavelot. It was fearsomely quick. Long-radius curves such as Burnenville were taken at 170 mph (274 kmh), while the left-right Masta Kink required huge levels of bravery and immense skill.

The original layout featured on the F1 calendar from 1950 until 1970. But it was discontinued for safety reasons. The lack of roadside protection meant it was extremely dangerous if a driver left the track, and the high-speed venue suffered a number of fatalities. The risk of an accident was also increased by the capricious nature of the weather.

The Belgian High Fens have a micro-climate that can bring torrential rain one moment, sunshine the next. At the start of the 1966 race, the field streamed towards a wall of water. Cars flew in all directions as they aquaplaned on the flooded course.

Jackie Stewart was heading to the Masta Kink at 170 mph (274 kmh) when he hit a river of water. His BRM went instantly out of control, hitting a telegraph pole as it careered off the circuit and down an eight-foot drop. Stewart was trapped in his car and two fellow drivers, Graham Hill and Bob Bondurant (who had also shunted), came to his aid.

With the fuel tank leaking corrosive liquid into the cockpit, Bondurant managed to find a spanner from the car trunk of some local spectators to help clear Jackie from the wreckage.

"They carried me to a barn beside a farmhouse, but by now I could feel my skin being burned by the high octane fuel," wrote Stewart in his autobiography *Winning Is Not Enough*. While sliding in and out of consciousness, he pleaded to have his overalls removed. Thirty minutes passed after his accident and there was no sign of any medical intervention—although Jackie does recall a surprise visit by a couple of nuns—who were alarmed at their discovery.

Eventually the Scot was taken to the track's so-called medical center and lay on a canvas stretcher on a filthy floor strewn with cigarette ends. The police escort for the ambulance he rode to Liege hospital then got lost en route.

The ordeal was too much for Stewart to allow such a farce to continue. In the course of 11 years, Jackie lost 57 of his fellow drivers. "Why were so many of my friends being killed? Why did our community have to cope with so much carnage? Why were people so regularly walking down the pit lane saying: 'Oh no, not again' and shaking their heads? I decided my response should be to do everything within my control to minimize the risk I faced as a racing driver," he wrote.

During Stewart's crusade in transforming safety measures for drivers, its cars, and the circuits, he faced bitter resistance, but ultimately—while still dangerous—Formula 1's impressive safety record is a testament to Jackie's determination to end the tragedies.

Heavy rains challenged drivers,
film crews, and fans alike.

and set up as a constructor himself. In the Australia/New Zealand-based Tasman Series, Brabham had enjoyed success with a 2.5-liter V8 based on an Oldsmobile alloy block and modified with bespoke cylinder heads and a flat-plane crank by the Repco company. It was small and light enough to fit in an F1 car even when expanded to 3-liter form in 1966. What it lacked in all-out power, it compensated for in torque and durability; after winning four of the nine rounds, Brabham became, at the age of 40, the first world champion to win in a car bearing his name.

(LEFT)

1965 Monaco GP

No Lotuses in Monaco as the Automobile Club only allowed one car per team entry, so Chapman withdrew both cars in protest. Hill (No. 3) led from pole before being forced by a backmarker into the escape lane and having to push his BRM back onto the circuit. He still won ahead of Bandini's Ferrari (No. 17) and new BRM teammate Jackie Stewart (No. 4).

(BOTTOM)

1965 German GP

Clark dominated the season, winning his sixth race in Germany and the championship. He further proved his mastery by winning the Indy 500 for Lotus that year. Clark might have won the remaining rounds had it not been for mechanical failures in each race.

1965 Italian GP
At Monza, Clark (No. 24) was on pole, with Surtees's Ferrari (No. 8) second and Stewart's BRM (No. 32) third. Both Clark and Surtees retired, leaving Stewart to take his first GP win for BRM ahead of teammate Graham Hill. Gurney's Brabham came third.

1965 Mexican GP
The last race of the 1.5-liter era was in Mexico and won by American Richie Ginther in his Honda RA272. Ginther had qualified third before taking his sole F1 win and Honda's first.

1966 Monaco GP
For the 1966 season, engine capacity was doubled to 3.0 liters. Stewart managed a great start and win at the season opener on Monaco's twisty street circuit despite only 2.0-liter displacement in his BRM P261.

(ABOVE)

1966 United States GP

1966 was a disappointing season for world champion Jim Clark. He took his only win at Watkins Glen in the typically unreliable Lotus 43 with its highly complex and heavy H16 engine.

(OPPOSITE TOP)

1966 Belgian GP

Surtees (No. 6) won the Belgian GP then left Ferrari following a disagreement with team principal Enzo, he moved to the Cooper team, finishing second in the championship behind Brabham.

(OPPOSITE BOTTOM LEFT)

1966 German GP

Jack Brabham won his fourth consecutive race of the season and third title at Germany's Nürburgring. It was the first time a driver had won the F1 championship in a car bearing his own name.

(OPPOSITE BOTTOM RIGHT)

1967 Belgian GP

At Belgium's Spa, Clark put the new Lotus 49 on pole with Gurney (pictured) in the stunning All American Racing Eagle Weslake V12 sitting second. After mechanical failures for the Lotus and Stewart's BRM, Gurney went on to win at an average speed of 143 mph (230 kmh), a circuit record at the time.

Another development in 1966 would have profound significance for F1 and motor racing in general. In this era, the Spa-Francorchamps circuit covered nearly 9 miles (14 km) of the Ardennes countryside where, then as now, the fickle climate can leave one portion of the track almost under water while other areas remain dry. On the first lap of the Belgian GP, a sudden storm triggered chaos–some of which can be seen in the movie *Grand Prix* owing to the presence of 1961 world champion Phil Hill on the grid in a camera car.

In one of several accidents, the up-and-coming talent Jackie Stewart's BRM spun into a telegraph pole and bounced off a house before coming to rest in the basement of a farmyard building with Stewart trapped inside, soaked in leaking fuel. There were no marshals and he was only freed by other drivers who stopped and came to his aid. The circuit doctor was a gynecologist by trade, volunteering for the weekend. The ambulance driver taking Stewart to the hospital in Liège got lost.

From this point on, Stewart began a tireless campaign to demand better safety facilities, for which he was vilified by those who thought such concerns were an affront to masculinity. When Lorenzo Bandini crashed at the chicane, with fatal consequences, during the 1967 Monaco Grand Prix, Stewart was the only driver on the grid wearing seat belts.

The return to power brought a surfeit of grunt over grip, even more so after the arrival of the Ford-bankrolled Cosworth DFV at the Dutch GP in June 1967. Exclusive to Lotus in its first year, the DFV was designed to be strong enough to accept chassis loadings and was bolted direct to the new 49's monocoque as an integral element of the structure–the consummation of an idea first explored by Lancia the previous decade. Clark won first time out but the Lotus's unreliability enabled Denny Hulme to claim a final title for Brabham-Repco before the Cosworth V8 became de rigueur.

LOTUS 49B

Throughout the 1960s, Colin Chapman's Team Lotus was often a step ahead of the opposition when it came to technical innovation. In 1962, he'd developed a pioneering monocoque design for the Lotus 25 whereby the body panels formed a structured part of the chassis.

With the development of the Ford-Cosworth DFV, Chapman—in conjunction with designer Maurice Philippe—set to work on a new model. The revolutionary engineering featured a monocoque that was bolted onto the engine at one end, while the rear suspension and gearbox were mounted on the other side of the DFV.

The result was the beautiful, streamlined, and compact Lotus 49. After sensationally winning on its debut, the car took ten consecutive pole positions in the hands of Jimmy Clark and Graham Hill, but lost the title through poor reliability.

For 1968 two developments took place that would change the face of Grand Prix racing forever. First, Lotus had ditched its traditional yellow and green livery in favor of a sponsorship deal with Gold Leaf tobacco. This was the first step towards F1's big-money era, and the major backing was estimated to bring in £60,000 a season. Second, the adoption of aerofoils was to radically alter the look of a Formula 1 car. Enzo Ferrari had trialed the use of spoilers on his sports cars. Exploiting airflow to create "negative lift" aerodynamic design has since dominated racing car form to this day.

When the 49B appeared at Monaco in 1968, it did so with fins on either side of the nose and an uplifted tail section. With the oil tank repositioned to the rear and with improved suspension geometry, Graham Hill triumphed on the streets of the Principality.

As more teams started to experiment with aerofoils, Chapman went one step further, adding a high, stilt-mounted wing fixed to the rear suspension. It looked rudimentary and the stilts often bucked under the high forces they sustained.

British racer Jackie Oliver suffered a crash in the fast sweeps of Rouen that year. In qualifying, the back of the car stepped out suddenly. It was suggested the wing fell backwards, lifting the rear of the car off the road. Further incidents took place at Montjuic Park in Barcelona, the second round of the 1969 season. Both Hill and new teammate Jochen Rindt suffered failures at the same point of the lap, with Rindt lucky to survive with just a broken nose.

Rindt did though, score a memorable final win for the celebrated 49B. At Monaco in 1970 leader Jack Brabham went off at the last corner, to enable Rindt to nip through and give the 49B one last moment of glory.

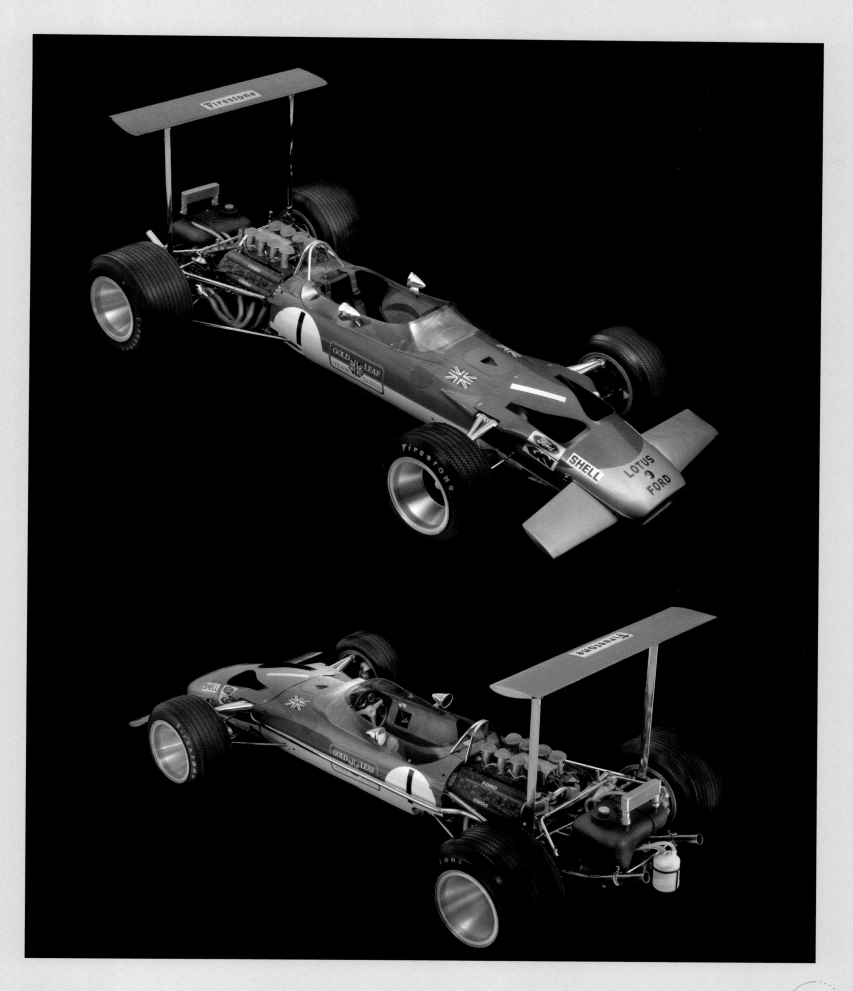

1967 Italian GP
Monza proved an epic battle as Surtees fought his way from 14th to win. Clark started from pole, then Brabham led, then Gurney, then Hulme, then Clark again until he ran out of fuel. Surtees pipped Brabham by just 0.2 seconds at the finish line to secure Honda's second grand prix win.

Further events of great significance played out over the winter of 1967 and spring of '68. Several team sponsors, notably Esso, had withdrawn from racing because they felt the level of exposure they received didn't warrant the expense. In response, racing's governing body dropped regulations that demanded competitors race in "national" colors and keep sponsor logos to a minimum. When Clark won the South African Grand Prix on New Year's Day, it was easy to overlook the presence of local privateers John Love and Sam Tingle in cars bearing the colors of the Gunston cigarette brand. Less so three weeks later at a Tasman Series race, when Team Lotus disgorged its cars from the transporter in the red and gold of Imperial Tobacco's Gold Leaf brand. Arguments followed, but overt commercial sponsorship was here to stay.

Clark's death in a still-unexplained accident during an F2 race at Hockenheim that April shook the motor racing world to its core, for here was a driver who seemed untouchable even as tragedies regularly befell others. And yet still the movement towards better safety proved grudging. Progress was slow in relation to car performance, which continued to increase at an almost alarming rate: teams added small wings and dive planes to encourage downward aerodynamic pressure for better cornering performance. These continued to grow in size and height until a succession of structural failures prompted the governing body to ban high-mounted wings in the spring of 1969. But, as with the burgeoning presence of sponsor logos, there would be no halting the aerodynamic revolution.

Before his passing, Clark had moved to Bermuda to circumvent the UK's punitive tax regime. In 1969 his friend Stewart claimed his first of three world championships and relocated his young family to Switzerland. As well as more power and performance, greater professionalism had come to F1, and with it the financial rewards. This did not go unnoticed by the man who had recently reappeared on the racing scene looking after the business affairs of another of Stewart's racing buddies, Jochen Rindt: Bernard Charles Ecclestone.

(TOP LEFT)
1968 South African GP
Tragedy struck Colin Chapman's dream team of Graham Hill and Jim Clark when Clark was killed in an F2 race at Hockenheim at the start of the season. He had won round one in South Africa. Jackie Oliver was drafted in to fill his spot.

(BOTTOM LEFT)
1968 Belgian GP
Ferrari driver Chris Amon set pole in Belgium with Stewart in the Matra second. Hill, Brabham, Surtees, and Amon all retired with mechanical problems, leaving Stewart in the lead until he ran out of fuel. Voila! Bruce McLaren inherited the win, the first for team McLaren.

(TOP RIGHT)
1968 Monaco GP
Graham Hill won round two in Spain and again in Monaco after Ferrari didn't race citing safety concerns. For the first time, front and rear aerofoil wings were added to the Lotus 49B. The advantages were clear, and Ferrari and Matra would soon follow suit.

(BOTTOM RIGHT)
1968 United States GP
High wings were in for the final rounds, and every team ran them. In America, local hero Mario Andretti took pole as Lotus's third driver but dropped out after he lost his front wing. Stewart took advantage in his Matra, now with Ford DFV power, for the win.

(LEFT)
1969 Spanish GP
The Belgian GP had been boycotted over safety issues, but round two in Spain fared no better, marred by a nasty accident when pole sitter Jochen Rindt's Lotus's rear wing collapsed, catapulting him into catch fencing, destroying the car and breaking his jaw. Stewart in the Matra took the win.

(BELOW)
1969 Monaco GP
There was much FIA deliberation in Monaco regarding aerodynamics, and adjustable rear wings were banned for future races. Although Stewart was on pole again, he retired on lap 22 and Hill took his final F1 win, his fifth at Monaco.

(OPPOSITE TOP)
1969 United States GP
The Williams F1 team moved from F2 to F1 for the 1969 season. Despite some unreliability issues with the car, Piers Courage (No. 18) reached the podium twice, in Monaco and America at Watkins Glen. He finished eighth in the season standings.

(OPPOSITE BOTTOM)
1969 Italian GP
Stewart wrapped the 1969 championship at Monza having won seven out of 11 rounds that season. Matra's F1 team was now run by Ken Tyrrell, while the factory team focused on sports car racing. Every race in 1969 was won by a car using Ford's all-conquering DFV V8 engine. Here, Stewart leads Hulme's McLaren.

THE WORLD CHAMPIONS

JACK BRABHAM
(1960, 1966)

PHIL HILL
(1961)

GRAHAM HILL
(1962, 1968)

At the start of the decade, Australian Jack Brabham took his second consecutive title at the wheel of a rear-engined Cooper-Climax. Despite retiring at the season opener in Buenos Aires (and disqualification at Monaco for outside assistance), Brabham scored five victories in a row. He wrapped up the championship in Portugal with two rounds to spare.

After leaving Cooper to establish his own team with Ron Tauranac as designer, Brabham failed to win again until the 3-liter formula came into effect in 1966. The new engine regulations led Brabham to acquire a V8 from Australian company Repco. It wasn't the most powerful, but it was lightweight and reliable. He won four races in '66, thereby becoming the first and only driver to win a world title in a car bearing his own name.

Originally hailing from Miami, Florida, Phil Hill resided on America's West Coast where he started racing sports cars. His turn of speed led to a partnership with Ferrari, and he was eager to try his hand at Grand Prix racing in Europe. He made the breakthrough in 1958, but it was the beginning of a period of decline for the Scuderia.

For 1961, Ferrari produced its first rear-engined car for the 1.5-liter formula. In addition to victory at two endurance classics, Sebring and Le Mans, Hill also won two Grands Prix at the wheel of the fabled 156 "shark nose" at Spa and Monza.

Sadly, his Italian Grand Prix triumph was overshadowed by tragedy. Hill's championship rival and Ferrari teammate, Wolfgang von Trips, crashed on the opening lap of the race. The German star was killed along with 12 spectators. Hill never won another Grand Prix but did continue to enjoy success in endurance racing, winning Le Mans for a third time in 1962.

As one of the sport's most-loved characters, Graham Hill was blessed with a great wit and bags of charm. He also possessed a single-minded determination and work ethic that brought him success in a motor racing career that spanned nearly two decades. He remains the only driver to have won the fabled trinity: the Formula 1 World Championship, the Indianapolis 500, and the Le Mans 24 Hours.

Initially working as a mechanic, he was handed a drive with Lotus at the end of the 1950s. For 1960 he joined BRM and by '63 the team was armed with a new V8. Graham won the season opener at Zandvoort but failed to finish at Monaco and France, races he was leading.

Hill was victorious in Germany, Italy, and the season finale in South Africa to edge out Jim Clark to the crown. In '67 he partnered Clark at the wheel of the Lotus 49. It was a formidable combination tragically shattered by Clark's death at Hockenheim a year later. Hill soldiered on, winning in Spain and Monaco and at the final race of the year in Mexico, to claim his second title in 1968.

Graham continued to compete in F1, latterly with his own team. When flying back from a test session on a foggy November evening in 1975, he crashed his aircraft on a golf course, approaching Elstree airfield outside London. Hill was killed along with promising young racer Tony Brise and four other members of his team.

JIM CLARK
(1963, 1965)

JOHN SURTEES
(1964)

DENNY HULME
(1967)

JACKIE STEWART
(1969)

Jim Clark died at the age of 32 when his Formula 2 Lotus crashed in the wet at Hockenheim on April 7, 1968. His accident rocked the world. Clark is still regarded as one of the greatest racing drivers of all time. His parents would have preferred he'd stayed on the family farm in the Scottish borders, but his prodigious talent took him to the pinnacle of the sport.

His speed was recognized by Colin Chapman, and the soft-spoken Scotsman spent his professional career racing for Lotus. Founded on mutual trust, the legendary Chapman-Clark partnership dominated Formula 1 in the early 1960s.

Clark's first victory came at Spa in 1962, a year he just missed out on the title. He won the following season and again in 1965, losing the '64 championship after his engine seized on the final lap of the Mexican finale.

Clark embodied a golden age of motor racing. Shy and retiring, he unanimously was respected by his peers for his genius behind the wheel. Fellow Scot Jackie Stewart likened the shock of his death to the impact the atomic bomb had on the world.

The Englishman made an immediate and successful transition from two wheels to four, and remains the only Formula 1 World Champion to have also won motorcycle championships. Between 1956 and 1960, he won seven world titles in the 350cc and 500cc classes.

In 1962 Surtees finished a remarkable second in only his second Grand Prix, and he accepted Ferrari's advances to join the Scuderia for the following year. Thanks to his technical prowess, he helped develop its monocoque chassis, and with a new V8 was able to mount a championship challenge for '64.

After a series of early-season setbacks, a commanding win at the Nürburgring put his title aspirations back on course. A memorable victory in front of the feverish *tifosi* at Monza kept him in contention heading towards the final round. Behind the scenes, a disgruntled Enzo Ferrari entered the final races of the year in the blue and white colors of the North American Racing Team (NART) following a disagreement with Italian motorsport bosses.

The unusual livery provided a lucky charm in Mexico City as title rivals Graham Hill and Jim Clark suffered misfortune in the closing stages. Ferrari teammate Lorenzo Bandini gave up second on the final lap to hand Surtees the title.

After winning a "New Zealand Driver to Europe" scheme, Denny Hulme joined forces with fellow Antipodean Jack Brabham, first working as a mechanic, then racing for his fledging outfit from 1965. He accrued four podiums the following season. Hulme imbued a humble, undemonstrative nature, and his drives were characterized by measured, shrewd performances.

"The Bear" scored his first Grand Prix win at the second round of 1967, in Monte Carlo, and he notched up another at the Nürburgring. His German GP drive characterized his style; running second he chose to drop back and nurse his engine, inheriting the win when leader Dan Gurney retired with a broken driveshaft. He pipped Brabham to the crown and soon partnered with fellow Kiwi Bruce McLaren, where he raced in F1 for the next seven seasons. Hulme was still driving sports cars in October 1992, when he suffered a heart attack, aged 56, in the Bathurst 1000km race.

Often regarded as the first truly professional Formula 1 driver, Jackie Stewart understood the commercial and marketing benefits of the sport, as well as having the talent to perform at the highest level. Fifty-five years after winning his first of three World Championships, JYS is still regularly seen at races today, ushering guests through pit garages and around the paddock.

Stewart was also instrumental in transforming motorsport, highlighting the dangers inherent in the cars and circuits to bring about meaningful change in safety.

After suffering at school with undiagnosed dyslexia, Stewart became an ace shot in clay pigeon shooting, just missing out on the 1960 Olympics.

He followed his brother Jimmy into racing and was given an F3 seat by Ken Tyrrell. After making his F1 debut with BRM, he was reunited with the Tyrrell team for 1968. A broken wrist meant two missed races, and he lost out in the points battle. But at the wheel of the beautifully balanced Matra MS80, he swept all aside, winning six times in '69 to take his first drivers' title.

THE ③ 1970s

The great American racer Mark Donohue won in practically every discipline he contested, with the rare exception of the Formula 1 world championship. Nevertheless in titling his autobiographical book *The Unfair Advantage*, he aptly summed up F1's direction of travel in the 1970s and the following decades. Since becoming non-exclusive in 1968, Ford-Cosworth's DFV engine had not only democratized power, it triggered parallel arms races as DFV-powered competitors sought to get ahead of each other by alternative means.

1972 German GP
Ickx (No. 4) won from pole on the Nordschleife in Germany. Stewart (No. 1) took the final two rounds in Canada and the U.S. Meanwhile, Fittipaldi had already won enough points to secure the championship in Italy, making him the youngest to do so at just 25.

Barring the occasional bad batch of components, Cosworth's V8 offered reliability as well as competitive power thanks to greater consistency of manufacture. By 1970 alternative choices were scarce. Brabham had abandoned the Repco V8, not a unit hugely endowed with horsepower anyway, when adding quad-cam heads scuppered its reliability. Ferrari, courtesy of financial security afforded by Fiat buying the company in June 1969, had finally cured the teething troubles that had delayed the introduction of Mauro Forghieri's new flat-12–but this, of course, wouldn't be available to anyone else.

BRM's V12 never made as much power as team boss Louis Stanley claimed for it and, as the team ran short of money, consistency and reliability suffered as damaged units were patched up and pressed back into service. French aerospace manufacturer Matra also made a V12, but this so disappointed 1969 world champion Jackie Stewart when he tested it that it provoked a schism. For years Ken Tyrrell's eponymous team had run Stewart and Matra chassis to great effect; now they went their separate ways, leaving Tyrrell just about managing to secure a Cosworth engine supply but without a car in which to run it.

So the 1970s opened with the champion in the inconvenient position of having no car to race–or so it appeared. In fact, Tyrrell had secretly contracted the engineer Derek Gardner, who had worked on an experimental four-wheel-drive transmission for Matra in the late 1960s, to design a new chassis. Gardner's studio was the bedroom of his house. In the interim, very much in the spirit of this age where if you could get your hands on a Cosworth DFV, you could go racing, Tyrrell bought a chassis from a new manufacturer, March Engineering.

March was nothing if not ambitious, led by former lawyer and amateur racer Max Mosley, who had discovered to his delight that almost nobody in the motor racing world realized he was the son of disgraced British Union of Fascists leader Sir Oswald Mosley. But the company's first F1 chassis, designed and built to tight deadlines, was pendulous and difficult to drive–even though Stewart, who won the second round of the season in one, made it look better than it was. Undoubtedly the best car of this era was the Lotus 72, which channeled IndyCar aerodynamic practice in its radical wedge profile.

1970 Dutch GP
In the sand dunes of Zandvoort in Holland, Piers Courage, driving for Williams, was killed when the car burst into flames. The race continued, and Rindt won again in the upgraded Lotus 72 (No. 25), 30 seconds ahead of Jackie Stewart's March.

1970 Monaco GP
The 1970 season turned out to be tragic—Bruce McLaren was killed testing a Can-Am car at Goodwood. Lotus debuted its new 72 in Spain, but it wasn't sorted. Jochen Rindt reverted to the 49C for a win at Monaco—his first of five.

(ABOVE LEFT)
1970 Italian GP

To increase top speed on the long straights of Monza, Lotus removed the wings, making the cars unstable. Emerson Fittipaldi escaped injury after a qualifying crash at Parabolica. Rindt was not so lucky when his car suddenly veered off into the barrier at the same turn and he was killed. He was awarded the championship posthumously. Nina Rindt is seen here at the fateful race.

(ABOVE RIGHT)
1970 Austrian GP

Belgian Jacky Ickx (No. 12) led a Ferrari 1-2 finish with teammate Clay Regazzoni for round nine in Austria at the Östereichring. Rindt made a poor start from pole and retired with mechanical failure. The Ferraris were a lap ahead of everyone, except third place Rolf Stommelen.

(RIGHT)
1971 South African GP

Tyrrell produced two versions of its Cosworth DFV-engined car after it was proven in Canada the previous season when Stewart took pole. A long chassis for the tall Francois Cevert and a short chassis for the diminutive Scot. At Kyalami in South Africa, Stewart was on pole again, but Andretti in the Ferrari (No. 6) won, his first F1 victory.

1971 French GP
At the new Paul Ricard circuit near Marseilles, it was two races all for Ferrari and Tyrrell. Stewart won pole and took off with Regazzoni close on his tail. Ickx retired with engine trouble as did Petersen's Alfa Romeo, dropping oil that Regazzoni spun on. At the flag, it was a Tyrrell 1-2 win with Cevert second.

1971 Austrian GP
Despite retiring in the race, Stewart (No. 11) won the driver's title in round eight in Austria. Ickx (No. 4) and Petersen (No. 17) failed to score points and Siffert's BRM (No. 14) won.

While the 72 wasn't quick out of the box, requiring some of the more out-there design elements (such as the anti-dive and anti-squat suspension geometry) to be removed, it became the most competitive car in the field and would still be winning Grands Prix four years later. But the weekend where it finally came good, at Zandvoort, was another bleak one for motor racing as Piers Courage crashed with fatal consequences. As was typical of the time, the race was not stopped; for lap after lap the acrid scent of Courage's burning De Tomaso 505/38 assailed the nostrils of the remaining drivers, including Jochen Rindt, one of his best friends. Rindt's victory, the first for the 72, was a joyless one.

(ABOVE)
1972 South African GP
In South Africa, Stewart's Tyrrell won pole by less than half a second from Regazzoni's Ferrari and Fittipaldi's Lotus. During the race, the Tyrrell retired with gearbox problems and Hulme's McLaren (No. 12) fought past the Lotus (No. 8) and Hailwood's Surtees (No. 17) to win.

(RIGHT)
1972 Argentinian GP
World champion Stewart (No. 21) won the opening round in Argentina. Local hero Carlos Reutemann made his debut and took pole. At the start, Stewart went into the lead, and Fittipaldi's Lotus battled Hulme's McLaren. The New Zealander prevailed to finish second with Ickx's Ferrari third.

BEHIND THE SCENES

F1 GOES GLOBAL

On occasion, Formula 1 practice wouldn't start if everyone wasn't ready. Teams conducted their own negotiations with circuits. Ferrari would skip a race if it felt like it. Fans could even wander into the paddock. Bernie Ecclestone saw an opportunity to transform Formula 1 into a professional sport and in the process create untold wealth for himself and the teams.

Ecclestone had been on the fringes of Grand Prix racing for a number of years. In the late 1950s, he'd been British driver Stuart Lewis-Evans's right-hand man, helping with contracts and sponsorship deals. By 1970 he was performing a similar managerial role for Austrian superstar Jochen Rindt.

Despite his size, Bernie was—and remains—a larger-than-life character, who had an eye for a dollar as well as a quick wit. His one liners are legendary too. A few years later when he was asked how many people worked for the Brabham team he owned, he replied: "About half of them."

As a team owner, Bernie would emerge as a major force in the newly established Formula 1 Constructors' Association (FOCA). He became president of the organization and handled negotiations with race promoters. By establishing a unified front, he pushed the sport towards a more professional—and ultimately, more lucrative—era. But he couldn't do it alone, he needed an ally.

Based in Bicester, March Engineering was an ambitious new company that started building cars for F1 at the start of the decade. One of the constructor's directors was Max Mosley.

The son of the British fascist leader, Sir Oswald Mosley, Max was a keen amateur racer who served as a barrister. He became the legal advisor for FOCA and his alliance with Ecclestone made the pair a formidable duo. Over the next 20 years, they took on the motor racing establishment to build Formula 1 into a global success story.

Together they unionized the teams and acted as a single voice against the circuits around the world. They held the keys to the cars, and without their star drivers, the promoters had nothing to sell. As a result their bargaining position blossomed. By the end of the decade, Bernie had established the TV rights to broadcast the sport, and Formula 1 was now being beamed into people's homes every fortnight.

Brabham team owner Bernie Ecclestone (left) with Max Mosley, March Team Owner in 1977. The two would work together as FOCA Chief Executive and FOCA Legal Advisor respectively beginning January 1978.

This being an era where drivers and their families socialized with each other far more than today, not only were Rindt and Courage friends–so too were their wives. Courage's death came 19 days after Bruce McLaren perished in a testing accident at Goodwood. Rindt had long struggled to reconcile the desirability of Lotus cars' speed with their fragility. In the summer of 1970, he was a man burdened by doubts–indeed, at Monaco he had lost his temper with an overly zealous police officer and kicked him in the face. Riding in a car to the airport from Zandvoort with his manager, Bernie Ecclestone, Rindt floated–and ultimately rejected–the idea of quitting the sport straight away. In time they would agree to go into business together as team owners.

(LEFT)
1972 Belgian GP
Fittipaldi took the distinctive black and gold liveried Lotus 72 to the top step in Spain and again in round five in Belgium after Stewart missed it due to an ulcer. Regazzoni and Ickx's Ferraris both retired, so Emerson won with Cevert in the Tyrrell runner up.

(BELOW)
1973 Brazilian GP
The calendar expanded to 15 rounds in 1973 with races added in Brazil and Sweden. World champion Emerson Fittipaldi got off to a good start winning in Argentina, at Interlagos in Brazil, and in Spain in his Lotus 72D. However, he couldn't reach the top step for the rest of the season.

(RIGHT)

1973 British GP

American Peter Revson (No. 8) won two races in Britain and in Canada for McLaren. At Silverstone, a nine-car pileup on lap one earned a red flag. At the restart, Stewart and Lauda in the BRM got away well, but the Scot spun. When Lauda pitted, Revson took the lead to win.

(BELOW)

1973 French GP

At the French GP, a collision between Scheckter and Fittipaldi took out both drivers. Swede Ronnie Peterson (No. 2), whom Lotus signed from March, won his first F1 from fifth on the grid at Paul Ricard.

(LEFT)
1973 German GP
Stewart wrapped up the championship, winning five races. When teammate Cevert was killed in practice at Watkins Glen, Tyrrell withdrew and Lotus won the constructors' title by 10 points. Stewart celebrated his final victory in Germany, then announced his retirement at the end of the season.

(BELOW LEFT)
1974 Spanish GP
Austrian Niki Lauda (No. 12) won his first F1 race for Ferrari in Spain after signing at the start of the season. Peterson's Lotus overtook Lauda at the wet start, but as the track dried, Niki pitted, exiting in the lead to take the checkered flag.

(OPPOSITE TOP)
1974 Swedish GP
In Sweden the Tyrrells were fast with Patrick Depailler (No. 4) taking pole ahead of Scheckter (No. 3), the Ferraris on row two. At the start, Jody got in front with Peterson's Lotus second. Both Ferrari gearboxes failed, giving the South African Scheckter his first win and a Tyrrell 1-2. Hunt's Hesketh was third.

(OPPOSITE BELOW LEFT)
1974 Belgian GP
After a complaint about restrictive practices was upheld, there were 41 cars on the grid in Belgium as the smaller teams jostled to qualify. Pole-sitter Regazzoni's Ferrari took to the grass avoiding Carlos Pace. Fittipaldi won from fourth in his McLaren (No. 5). Lauda was second.

(OPPOSITE BELOW RIGHT)
1974 American GP
After a hotly contested season, Fittipaldi won the drivers' championship and McLaren their first constructors title. Fittipaldi only scored three victories and finished eighth in the final round, but it was enough to beat Regazzoni's Ferrari. Reutemann's Brabham BT44 (shown) won.

Rindt would never achieve this dream, for he too lost his life in an accident before the season was out. To reduce unsprung weight, the Lotus 72 had inboard-mounted front brakes; as Rindt hit the middle pedal at Monza's Parabolica corner during practice for the Italian Grand Prix, the shaft connecting the front-right brake to the wheel sheared and Rindt's car speared left into a barrier that broke on impact, tearing the car apart. By this point, he had built a championship lead that proved insurmountable in the remaining three rounds. He remains, thankfully, the only driver to have become champion posthumously.

Safety improvements came piecemeal and grudgingly, since modifying tracks was expensive and most teams led a hand-to-mouth existence. All this would change in time, but for now Stewart shouldered the burden of pushing for change and being pilloried for it by those who viewed safety in motor racing as an unmasculine contradiction in terms. It was a case of small wins: six-point harnesses, fire-resistant suits, and full-face helmets became mandatory, as did safety foam in fuel tanks, crushable safety structures, and on-board fire extinguishers. Tracks faced more regulations on gradient

changes, the width of grass verges, and the distance of spectators from the action. Monza grew chicanes while Spa-Francorchamps and the Nürburgring briefly vanished from the calendar while long-overdue improvements were completed.

Those who painted Stewart as a coward were, of course, ridiculous, for this was a driver who had won the 1968 German Grand Prix at the Nürburgring by over four minutes in truly dreadful weather conditions. He would win the world championship twice more in the 1970s once Tyrrell became a constructor–helped in 1971, it must be said, by the arrival of the slick racing tires whose extra grip exposed the flimsy nature of the Lotus 72's chassis and suspension. Following Rindt's death, rising Brazilian star Emerson Fittipaldi had joined Lotus and became Stewart's principal rival. Tyrrell's star gradually began to wane after Stewart's retirement in 1973; Jackie's extraordinary ratio

1978 ITALIAN GRAND PRIX

Due to its high speeds, Monza is revered and feared in equal measure. The Italian *autodromo* is not a place for the faint-hearted. In the half century before 1978, it had claimed 50 lives. And there was further tragedy that year. Within seconds of the start of the '78 Italian Grand Prix, a terrifying crash occurred as the pack funneled into the tight, first-corner chicane. In the ensuing chaos, carabinieri and police cordoned off the accident site.

Ronnie Peterson's Lotus came off worse and James Hunt had helped pull the unfortunate Swede from his burning wreck. Attending this race was eminent neurosurgeon Professor Sid Watkins, who was making his first visit to Monza in a professional capacity.

When a conscious Peterson was brought to the medical center, with badly smashed legs, there was chaos, with crowds littering the paddock and even entering the building where Ronnie was being treated.

"We took him on the stretcher across the walkway to a waiting helicopter," wrote Watkins in his autobiography *Life at the Limit*. "There was a great murmur from the crowd and a struggle when the 'tifosi' tried to touch the injured Peterson, as if he were some holy relic."

When "The Prof" was able to reach a nearby hospital, despite more trouble exiting the circuit thanks to the overwhelming number of spectators, he looked at the X-rays and counted 27 fractures in poor Ronnie's feet and legs. That night, surgery was going well and Prof. Watkins managed to extricate himself from the clogged entrance to the hospital and return to his hotel.

At 4 a.m. he was woken by a call that reported things had taken a turn for the worse. After some breathing difficulties, the unconscious Peterson was now on a ventilator and a chest X-ray revealed he'd developed in his lungs multimodal emboli (blood clots and fat globules). A neurological examination showed he had signs of severe brain damage. An autopsy confirmed fat embolism was the cause of death.

"It seemed to me that the start and the response of the rescue team to the accident had been a shambles," wrote Watkins. "Various estimates of the delay getting Ronnie out of the car and the arrival of the ambulance range from 11 to 18 minutes. Bernie [Ecclestone] came to the conclusion that my authority had to be extended to supervising the rescue arrangements on the circuit. There was now a very obvious need for a following car with medical support on the first lap, but there were howls of protest and sabotage of our efforts to achieve this."

Ultimately, with Bernie's help, Watkins transformed the medical rescue and facilities at all Grand Prix tracks to minimize the time a driver has between accident and medical care. An FIA Medical Car continues to circulate at the back on the opening lap to this day. In the wake of Ronnie's fatal accident, many more drivers lives have been saved due to the timely intervention of Professor Sid Watkins and his team.

Tragedy marred the Italian GP. After a botched start at
Monza, a seven-car accident propelled Swede Petersen's
Lotus into the barriers where it caught fire. The race
restarted and Lauda won, but Petersen died the next day.

(ABOVE)
1975 Brazilian GP
World champion Fittipaldi opened 1975
with a first round win in Argentina. In
Brazil, Jean-Pierre Jarier's Shadow (No. 17)
was on pole alongside Fittipaldi's McLaren
(No. 1). Reutemann in the Brabham (No. 7)
took the lead, but Jarier got ahead before
retiring, allowing local Carlos Pace through
to win.

(LEFT)
1975 Monaco GP
Ferrari's new 312T debuted at Kyalami, and
Laudi put it on pole in Spain, but the car's
first win came in round five in Monaco. On
a drying track, Lauda led from pole, and
after tire changes was ahead by 15 seconds
to secure Ferrari's first win in 20 years.

of 27 wins in 99 Grand Prix starts is a testament not only to his skill, but also to what a small niche the world championship calendar occupied in the wider motor racing world. Formula 1 drivers didn't just race in F1, which remained a European championship for the most part with only brief journeys overseas.

Fittipaldi was just one of a new generation of drivers who entered the stage in the 1970s and who elevated the concept of star power to new heights. Niki Lauda was considered a rich kid of only middling talent, though actually his parents disapproved of his racing activities and he had leveraged himself to the hilt via a life insurance policy to buy his way into racing. Combined with a resurgent Ferrari in 1974, he rapidly proved his detractors wrong. Teammate Clay Regazzoni was a similarly colorful character with a penchant for overly forceful racing, as demonstrated when he put Fittipaldi on the grass in the '74 championship finale at Watkins Glen. When Fittipaldi, who had taken Texaco and Marlboro sponsorship to McLaren after leaving Lotus, inexplicably decided to join his brother Wilson's embryonic team in '76, McLaren turned to James Hunt, a high-living womanizer whose career was littered with so many crashes he had once been nicknamed "Hunt the Shunt."

1975 Dutch GP
Poor reliability plagued James Hunt's Hesketh (No. 24) after his second place in Argentina. At the Dutch GP, Hunt was third on the grid behind the Ferraris. The start was wet, but the track dried fast in the breeze at Zandvoort. Lauda (No. 12) led, but Hunt switched to slick tires first and took his and Hesketh's only win.

1975 French GP
Lauda won three consecutive rounds mid-season. The new Ferrari proved dominant, taking pole no less than nine times. In France at Paul Ricard, Lauda was on pole, battling Hunt, Mass, and teammate Regazzoni until the Swiss' engine gave out. Hunt pressed him all the way to the line but Niki won.

1976 Swedish GP
Introduced for round four in Spain, Tyrrell's innovative six-wheel P34 (No. 3) succeeded for Jody Scheckter in round seven in Sweden. Andretti's Lotus led at the start, but retired with engine failure, allowing a 1-2 win for Tyrrell's new car with Depailler second.

(TOP)
1976 British GP
After a first lap pileup at Brands Hatch, Hunt (No. 11) snuck back to the pits on an access road and switched to the spare McLaren. Lauda led at the restart but suffered gearbox problems. Hunt won, only to be disqualified two months later after appeals from other teams.

(ABOVE)
1976 Japanese GP
The championship decider was in a very wet Japan. Andretti's Lotus (No. 5) was on pole, Hunt (No. 11) second, Lauda third. On lap two, Lauda pulled into the pits and withdrew, as did Fittipaldi and Pace due to safety concerns. Hunt got the three points he needed to beat Lauda to the drivers' title.

(TOP RIGHT)
1977 Argentine GP
World champion James Hunt was on pole for the first three rounds but won none of them. Argentina went to Scheckter who had left Tyrrell for the new Walter Wolf team. Brazil went to new Ferrari signing Reutemann. South Africa went to Lauda. Argentina to Scheckter's Wolf.

(RIGHT)
1977 United States GP
With two races in America, the first was a street circuit in Long Beach, south of Los Angeles. After getting past pole sitter Lauda, Scheckter led at first. Andretti avoided a pileup involving Hunt, Watson, and Reutemann. Scheckter suffered a puncture and Andretti won.

(NEXT PAGE)
1976 German GP
At the notorious Nordschleife, the track was damp but drying with Hunt and Lauda in the front row. After changing to slicks, Lauda was on the charge but crashed and was hit by two following cars that caught the Ferrari alight. Drivers pulled him from the car, but he was badly burned.

All this was crucial in F1's evolution towards doubling the number of races held per year and becoming a multi-million-dollar business with a global footprint. And yet, at the time, TV coverage remained patchy and competitors still had to get by on sponsorship and the archaic payment model of prizes and "start money," whereby teams individually negotiated their appearance fees with the race promoters. Naturally the likes of Tyrrell, Lotus, McLaren, and Ferrari, as frontrunners, could command good fees . . . but it was the new owner of the resurgent Brabham team who would ring in the changes.

At the end of 1970 Jack Brabham had retired to Australia, selling his share of the business to his engineering partner Ron Tauranac. Finding the administration side tiresome and distracting, Tauranac grew open to offers, and at the 1971 Monaco Grand Prix he shook hands with Bernie Ecclestone. Like many who have had dealings with "The Bolt," Tauranac would eventually come to realize that the former motorcycle dealer had come out of the negotiation very much on top. Jochen Rindt's death had prompted a delay and a course correction in Ecclestone's journey towards team ownership, but, once there, he was by no means fulfilled. In the coming years, he would become top-level motor racing's principal dealmaker and even finagle commercial control of F1 itself.

Ecclestone found a willing and gifted ally in the form of Mosley, whose similarly sharp mind was imbued with the rigor of legal training—making him the perfect foil to the impulsive, improvisational Bernie. They scored an early victory at Monaco in

LOTUS 72

In April 1970, a pair of Lotus 72s rolled out to make their Formula 1 debut at the Spanish Grand Prix at Jarama. Five years later, in October 1975, the Lotus 72 made its last competitive outing—with Ronnie Peterson taking a fifth place in the USGP at Watkins Glen. It was a remarkable lifespan for the wedge-shaped machine that was initially troublesome, but would become one of F1's most enduring racing cars.

The striking Gold Leaf-liveried 72 appeared with a sleek, low nose and innovative, side-mounted radiators to improve weight distribution. Cars had predominantly housed their radiators at the front, but this hip arrangement would set a new standard.

Another of the car's radical features were its inboard brakes, which were cooled by two ducts on the front of the monocoque—with air exiting via two small chimneys.

But the 72's early running was hampered by its complex torsion bar suspension, which had the joint effect of minimizing the car squatting to the ground at the rear on acceleration and reducing dive at the front under braking.

An inauspicious debut led to the car being withdrawn so that the teething problems with its geometry could be ironed out. When it later appeared at Brands Hatch, the 72 featured two innovative scoops either side of the driver to force air into the engine to boost power. Rindt won the British GP, along with four other races that season, but he was tragically killed at Monza, taking the title posthumously.

Former BRM designer Tony Rudd helped develop the car, and for 1972 it was decorated in its famous gold and black John Player Special colors. Emerson Fittipaldi swept all aside to take five wins to become, at the time, the sport's youngest-ever World Champion.

With a new mandatory crash structure introduced to increase safety, the 72E for 1973 featured integrated sidepods and larger bodywork—as well as a switch from Firestone to Goodyear tires. Ronnie Peterson's prodigious throttle usage and elegant car control defined the era as the 72 looked spectacular in the Super Swede's hands.

Behind the scenes Lotus was working on a replacement, but that was sidelined ensuring the trusty 72 continued to race into the middle of the decade. Despite coming to the end of car's competitive life, Peterson's fifth place on its swansong at the final race of 1975 emphasized what an impressive machine it had been—taking 20 wins, two Drivers', and three Constructors' Championships.

James Mann

(ABOVE)

1977 United States GP

With feuding at Ferrari, Lauda announced he would race for Brabham in 1978. To clinch the championship at Watkins Glen, he needed a single point and Scheckter not to win. Hunt (No. 1) won from pole, Andretti (No. 5) second, Scheckter (No. 20) third, and Lauda (No. 11) fourth to earn three points and his second title.

(LEFT)

1977 British GP

Hunt's first win came at home at Silverstone. Watson's Brabham led until he retired with a fuel problem. Hunt went through to take the checkered flag, with Lauda runner up.

(OPPOSITE TOP)

1978 Monaco GP

In Monaco it was Reutemann's Ferrari on pole. After a clash with Hunt, the Ferrari pitted, Watson led but spun, allowing French driver Patrick Depailler in the Tyrrell to win.

(OPPOSITE BOTTOM)

1978 Swedish GP

To counter Lotus's ground effect, Brabham introduced its 46B fan car in round eight in Sweden. It worked—Watson was second on the grid and Lauda third behind Andretti's Lotus. At the start, Lauda got past Watson, Andretti retired after leading, and Lauda won but the car never raced again.

1972 when the organizers insisted on limiting the race grid to 18 cars. Ecclestone and Mosley corralled the other competitors together and secured their agreement not to practice until the organizers and the FIA signed off on 25. Despite much huffing and puffing from the blazer-wearing officials of Monaco's auto club, and the arrival of a police battalion, the entrants got their way. This victory for collective bargaining emboldened Ecclestone to win over the teams one by one with his proposal to negotiate starting money on their behalf with race promoters. The formerly supine Formula One Constructors Association became a more powerful animal with Ecclestone and Mosley animating it. By 1975 they had sufficient muscle to have the Canadian Grand Prix struck off the calendar when the promoter didn't agree the requested purse within FOCA's deadline.

Pushback came in the form of increasing friction between FOCA and Jean-Marie Balestre, the autocratic head of the governing body's sporting committee. An ex-journalist with a colorful past including a postwar prison stint for collaboration with the Nazis (he claimed he was spying for the French Resistance), Balestre very much stood for the interests of the national automobile clubs and the stuffed shirts who ran them. And unanimity within the teams was never quite guaranteed since they remained competitors on track—Enzo Ferrari in particular liked to play one side off against another. In this dance, he was often joined by other manufacturer-aligned teams such as Renault, who arrived in 1977 as a solo entry with Formula 1's first turbo-powered car.

It would take turbos several years to push Cosworth off the throne and force Ferrari to embrace forced induction. The first Renault's tendency to expire in clouds of smoke and steam led rivals to deride the car as "the yellow teapot." Trick aerodynamics would be the key focus of difference and endeavor in the second half of the decade as Cosworth clients looked for the "unfair advantage." Tyrrell went as far as designing a six-wheeled car with four small wheels at the front, believing this conferred an aerodynamic benefit. Although it won a race, it was unloved by its drivers.

1979 Brazilian GP
With ground effects well proven, other teams sought to emulate the brilliant Lotus 79s. After Ligier swapped its Matra V12s for the reliable and powerful Ford DFV, Jacques Laffite (No. 26) made a great start to the season, taking both poles and wins in Argentina and Brazil, with teammate Depailler (No. 25) second.

1979 Monaco GP
With seven drivers winning races over the season, Scheckter won the title for Ferrari, including Monaco, with just three victories to Jones' (No. 25) four. It would be the last championship for the Italian team for 20 years.

(OPPOSITE TOP LEFT)
1978 German GP
With the death of teammate Ronnie Petersen, no one could catch Mario Andretti who won the title under bittersweet circumstances. In the final two rounds, he qualified on pole at Watkins Glen, but his engine failed and he managed only tenth place in Canada. In German GP, Andretti leads Petersen.

(OPPOSITE TOP RIGHT)
1979 French GP
The new Renault RE10 turbos succeeded in France, taking Jean-Pierre Jabouille and Rene Arnoux to a 1-2 on the grid and a win for Jabouille. Arnoux started badly and battled with Villeneuve's Ferrari to finish third.

Having struggled to follow up the 72 and spent several seasons playing second fiddle to Ferrari and McLaren, Lotus became resurgent thanks to serendipity. While making some of F1's first experiments in the wind tunnel, Lotus engineer Peter Wright noticed his car model sagging in the middle through material fatigue . . . but also that the airflow was taking an interesting pattern. With the 78 and 79 chassis, Wright and his colleagues would harness the power of negative pressure, concealing venturi within the sidepods to accelerate the flow of air under the car, in effect sucking it towards the ground. Mario Andretti became only the second American to win the world championship, describing the 79 as "painted to the road."

This kicked off an arms race that, thanks to broader TV coverage, played out in front of a wider audience than ever before. The 1976 season had been the first to be widely televised, and the dramatic title battle between McLaren's James Hunt and Ferrari's Niki Lauda–with the stakes raised by Lauda's fiery mid-season crash at the Nürburgring–entranced sports fans. Ecclestone took note of the potential value of TV rights sales. Come 1978, as Andretti and Lotus dominated and Brabham's response–a modified car that used ground skirts and an extractor fan to achieve high cornering speeds–caused uproar, Ecclestone withdrew the car rather than alienate the other members of FOCA. He could see bigger payouts on the horizon.

For much of the 1970s, little had changed in the engine bay. Development yielded higher revs and more power but, fundamentally, the virtually ubiquitous Ford-Cosworth DFV V8 remained as it had been at the start of the decade. Likewise Ferrari in 1979 took the championship double with a car powered by a development of the flat-12 engine introduced in 1970. This cozy situation in which engine development made stately progress was soon to change dramatically.

THE WORLD CHAMPIONS

JOCHEN RINDT
(1970)

JACKIE STEWART
(1971, 1973)

EMERSON FITTIPALDI
(1972, 1974)

After his parents were killed in an air raid, Rindt used his inherited wealth to fund his early motor racing exploits. He memorably burst onto the scene in a Formula 2 race at Crystal Palace and toppled the established stars of the day.

The Austrian dovetailed his F1 outings with further F2 success, and along the way, he scored an unlikely Le Mans victory in 1965. He proved to be an exceptional talent, but the F1 Coopers he drove in the mid-1960s were both underpowered and overweight.

Jochen accepted a big-money offer from Lotus for 1969, although his relationship with team boss Colin Chapman was often uneasy—not helped when his rear wing collapsed at Montjuic Park early in the year.

With the promise of Chapman's latest creation, the Lotus 72, Rindt remained with the team for 1970. Once the car was properly ready, he reeled off four consecutive victories. Haunted by the deaths of his friends Piers Courage and Bruce McLaren, Jochen lost his own life when a mechanical failure pitched his car into the barriers at Monza. Jacky Ickx failed in the remaining races to overhaul his points tally, so Rindt became the sport's, and thankfully to date, only posthumous World Champion.

After winning the title in 1969, Stewart's Tyrrell team ended its association with Matra and resorted to a March chassis for 1970. Meanwhile, in the famous Surrey woodshed, designer Derek Gardner was busy creating the first Tyrrell, and for 1971, JYS triumphed six times, netting him more than double the points of his nearest rival.

Stewart was a man in demand and was regularly crossing the Atlantic to compete. But his health suffered and a stomach ulcer caused him to miss six weeks of competition in 1972.

By the start of the next year, the Scot was back to full fitness and swept to another crown in the Tyrrell. He scored five wins to overhaul Jim Clark's record tally of 27 to become the most successful driver at that time.

This was to be Stewart's last season. At the final race of the year in Watkins Glen, at what would have been his 100th start, his teammate and protégé, François Cevert, was tragically killed in practice. It was a devastating end to a meteoric career.

With a father who was a well-known motorsport journalist and commentator, Emerson followed his brother Wilson into racing. Rapid success in his native Brazil led to Fittipaldi selling his Formula Vee car to finance a trip to Europe for 1969. He won the British F3 title that year and was quickly snapped up by Lotus. Following Rindt's death, "Emmo" won on just his fifth F1 outing.

Fittipaldi was given the number one seat for 1971, but his season stalled when he suffered a road car accident. Aided by Stewart's illness in '72, Fittipaldi rattled off a superb sequence of wins to wrap up the World Championship at Monza. At the age of the 25, he became Formula 1's youngest title winner, a record that stood for 33 years.

Fittipaldi joined McLaren for 1974, and his smooth driving netted him a second crown. But it was a close run thing. At the final race of the year an undramatic drive to fourth place secured enough points to overthrow his nearest rivals.

The Brazilian's Formula 1 career stalled when he joined the Copersucar team established by his brother, and he failed to win another race between 1976 and 1980. But he later found a new life in IndyCars, extending his career into the mid-1990s.

NIKI LAUDA
(1975, 1977)

Lauded as one of the great survivors of Formula 1, thanks to his remarkable comeback following his fiery Nürburgring shunt, Niki Lauda was a forthright, no-nonsense racer. He made an inauspicious start to his F1 career and even took out a bank loan to fund his drive with BRM in a pay-as-you-race deal.

But he'd been targeted by Ferrari, which was led at the time by team manager Luca di Montezemolo. Working with designer Mauro Forghieri, Lauda helped develop the transverse-gearbox 312T for 1975. A hat-trick of wins began in Monaco and was followed in quick succession by triumphs in Belgium and Sweden. A podium at Monza gave the Scuderia its first world title for 11 years.

The dominance looked set to continue into 1976, until that fiery crash in the German Grand Prix that nearly cost Lauda his life. His withdrawal from the final race in Japan meant his rival James Hunt took the title by a single point.

Normal service was resumed for '77 and wins at Kyalami, Hockenheim, and Zandvoort netted him his second championship. But at season's end he turned his back on Ferrari for Brabham—and eventually quit F1 midway through a practice session in 1979. Lauda went on to start an airline business, but the sport had not seen the last of the Austrian.

JAMES HUNT
(1976)

Nicknamed "Hunt the Shunt" due to his erratic driving, he found a soulmate in the eccentric aristocrat Lord Alexander Hesketh. With his long blonde hair, plummy voice, and good looks, Hunt captured the imagination of the British public, and his epic duel with Niki Lauda in 1976 electrified the sport.

Hunt had already shown a turn-of-speed in Hesketh's privately run car at Zandvoort in 1975, beating Lauda's works Ferrari in a straight fight. But the cost of running a Formula 1 operation was too much, even for a Lord, and Hunt lucked into a McLaren drive following Fittipaldi's departure.

Hunt's first F1 win in Spain was contentious. His McLaren was disqualified—then reinstated. There was further furor at Brands Hatch. After contact with Ferrari's Clay Regazzoni at Paddock Hill bend, the race was halted. Hunt won the restarted race but was again disqualified.

Lauda's near-fatal crash enabled James to close the points gap. The dramatic Japanese season finale gripped TV viewers worldwide as Hunt took the title by a point, following Lauda's withdrawal.

Hunt retired midway through 1979. It was television that led to a second career, his witty and pithy comments making him the perfect foil to co-commentator Murray Walker's trousers-on-fire style. His death in 1993, at the age of 45 following a heart attack, remains a terrible shock to this day.

MARIO ANDRETTI
(1978)

There has arguably been no driver before or since who has loved racing as much as Mario Andretti. The length and breadth of his career is a testament to his passion for the sport. Born in Italy, Mario and his twin brother Aldo moved to postwar America as refugees. The pair began racing in dirt-track competitions, but Mario would soon shock the establishment with his pace.

He won the IndyCar national championship in his first full season in 1965, and when he accepted a one-off drive with Lotus in the '68 US GP, he qualified on pole position.

In the early 1970s, Mario was racing a mix of IndyCars, sports cars, and in F1 until Colin Chapman got him to agree to a full Grand Prix season in 1976. The following year, the first ground effect car, the Lotus 78, turned the fortunes of the British team around.

For 1978, the upgraded 79 was the class-of-the-field and Andretti dominated, winning the Argentine, Belgian, Spanish, French, German, and Dutch Grands Prix. His world title celebrations at Monza were muted, however, when his teammate and great friend, Ronnie Peterson, sadly lost his life.

After two more seasons with Lotus, Mario joined Alfa Romeo for 1981—and even made a couple of appearances for Ferrari the following year—but settled back to the U.S. where he helped establish a racing team with his son.

JODY SCHECKTER
(1979)

Scheckter's arrival from South Africa was quite a whirlwind. He gained notoriety at the 1973 British Grand Prix when an "off" at Woodcote created a multiple pileup that eliminated over a dozen cars. But by the time of his World Championship at the end of the decade, Jody had matured into a fine, composed racer.

Despite his wild moments, Ken Tyrrell hired Jody for 1974. He finished third that season after winning two Grands Prix. At the wheel of the extraordinary-looking six-wheeled Tyrrell, the South African was once again third overall in 1976.

After scoring a sensational win for the newly established Wolf team in Argentina the following year, Scheckter's time with Walter Wolf yielded yet another third place in the points standings.

He joined Ferrari for 1979, but was beaten early-on by his ultra-quick teammate Gilles Villeneuve. But consistency throughout the year netted him the championship lead, and Gilles dutifully stayed in his wheel tracks for Jody to win the title at Monza. He called it quits at the end of the following year to first set up a successful arms business in the U.S. and more latterly run an organic farm in the English countryside.

THE ④ 1980s

It took Frank Williams over a decade to become an overnight success. Arriving on the Grand Prix scene in 1969, running his friend, the brewery heir Piers Courage, in a second-hand Brabham, Williams scored a handful of podium finishes before a swap to a new chassis from sportscar manufacturer de Tomaso initiated a sharp decline in results and finances. Knocked down but not out by Courage's tragic death in 1970, Frank clung on to the Grand Prix scene by his fingertips, doing deals on public payphones and living a hand-to-mouth existence until Canadian oil magnate Walter Wolf bought him out in 1976.

1981 Monaco GP
By the Monaco GP Ferrari had fitted a version of pneumatic suspension, an idea developed by Brabham. Piquet led from pole but misjudged his line at Tabac and hit the barrier, allowing Jones (No. 1) through. Towards the end of the race, the Williams suffered a fuel problem and Villeneuve (No. 27) got past to win.

(ABOVE)
1980 Belgian GP
New Ligier signing Didier Pironi was getting noticed after qualifying well in rounds one and two and finishing on the podium in South Africa. At Zolder he won his first F1 race, beating both Williams and lightning-fast turbo Renaults.

(TOP LEFT)
1980 Brazilian GP
Williams had shown its strength in '79, winning five rounds from mid-season but not the title. Its dominance would not go unchallenged in 1980. Although Jones won in Argentina, Arnoux (pictured here) in the turbo Renault took the wins in Brazil and South Africa.

(TOP RIGHT)
1980 Canadian GP
A first lap accident caused Piquet to take a spare car before his engine blew. Williams's Alan Jones (No. 27) then took the driver's title and gave the team its first world championship in Canada. Reutemann in the other Williams was second.

(ABOVE)

1980 Dutch GP
Arnoux (No. 16) and Jabouille (No. 15) in the turbo Renaults locked out the front row of the grid at Zandvoort for the Dutch GP. Brabham's Nelson Piquet (No. 5) battled his way through the field to win his second race of the season, keeping the title battle alive.

Even then "Wanker Williams," as he was derisively nicknamed by many in the paddock, wasn't done; setting up under his own name again, he persuaded young engineer Patrick Head to join him and design a new chassis. After a year running Belgian pay driver Patrick Nève in a secondhand March car, it was time to get serious with the first Head creation in 1978. And, while Lotus pioneered ground-effect aerodynamics in that era, it was Head and his colleagues who realized that downforce had to be balanced against chassis rigidity. As Lotus came apart (often literally), the Williams FW07 claimed its first victories in 1979 before the B-spec car delivered the gritty Australian Alan Jones to the world championship in 1980.

In demanding his designers prioritize downforce, Lotus chief Colin Chapman missed the bigger picture. His cars weren't structurally rigid enough to withstand the higher cornering forces, and adding downforce introduced new problems as the

(ABOVE)

1981 British GP

At Silverstone Arnoux and Prost's Renaults were on the front row, almost a second ahead of Piquet in third. Prost led but a collision on lap five took out Villeneuve, Jones, and de Cesaris. Watson's (No. 7) McLaren squeezed past, and when both Renaults retired, he won his home GP.

(LEFT)

1981 San Marino GP

At a wet Imola for the San Marino GP, Villeneuve's Ferrari started on pole alongside the Williams of Reutemann. The Canadian led with teammate Pironi second but pitted too early for slicks when the rain returned. Piquet's Brabham (shown) moved up the field, overtaking Patrese and Pironi on the 47th lap to take the win.

(ABOVE)

1982 Brazilian GP
In an highly competitive 16-round season, 11 drivers from seven different teams won a GP. French driver Prost got off to a good start in his Renault turbo, winning in South Africa despite a puncture and again in Brazil.

aerodynamic center of pressure migrated under braking and acceleration, compromising the handling. And like teams across the grid, Lotus encountered and then failed to understand a phenomenon that would return when F1 re-adopted ground-effect principles 40 years later: porpoising, an oscillating cycle in which the car is drawn too close to the ground and the underbody airflow stalls, causing it to pop back up again.

Having missed its opportunity to build on first-mover advantage in the ground-effect field, Lotus was already fading from the lead group as the 1980s dawned. Williams, Ferrari, and a resurgent McLaren would take the lead in an era defined by technical innovation on the track and political conflict off it. Brabham too would cease to be a force, as Bernie Ecclestone grew distracted by his endless quest for loot.

Greater cornering speeds because of ground-effect aero, and the FIA's attempts to contain it through legislation, became one of two areas of conflict between the teams and the governing body in the early 1980s. The other was power and, by extension, money. Ecclestone, naturally, was at the heart of it.

BEHIND THE SCENES

TEAM BUILDING

When British driver Martin Brundle lined up on the grid for his very first Grand Prix, at Rio de Janeiro in March 1984, he was sitting in a blue, sponsor-less Tyrrell 012. Ten years earlier, the team that still assembled its cars in a woodshed had just won its third drivers' title with Jackie Stewart at the wheel.

Despite the growth and professionalism in the sport, the Surrey-based team had barely moved on. Brundle remembers how just 12 people went to Brazil for the '84 season opener. And two of that dozen included himself and his teammate Stefan Bellof. The other members of the team were owner Ken Tyrrell (who would often drive the team's transporter to European races) and his wife Nora. That left eight mechanics to look after the two race cars. "My wife Liz and Nora made the sandwiches for the team for the weekend," said Brundle. "It's moved on a bit since, hasn't it?"

The previous year, the once great outfit had won its 23rd F1 race. It continued in the sport for another 14 years but never won another Grand Prix. Tyrrell quickly fell behind the opposition, unable to keep up the cost and demands of F1.

When Williams won its second World Championship in 1981, it had 200 people working for the team. In the subsequent years, F1 squads have spiraled with many having a workforce now of over 1,000.

Head counts rose as Formula 1 became more technologically advanced. Gains were being sought in every area: aerodynamics, electronics, and suspension design, while more tools were being utilized in the search for performance. That included wind tunnel usage and the use of Computational Fluid Dynamics (CFD) where car parts are tested in simulation before being manufactured. The rate of car development became industrialized on a grander scale. Williams and McLaren were the first to create marketing departments to obtain commercial backers. But as some teams discovered, it wasn't just quantity. The quality of the staff was still critical despite the growth in numbers of personnel. And in the fast-paced, competitive world of F1, if a piece doesn't fit, it needs to be changed quickly.

"When you think you have chosen the right team, when you find you get them together and some of the chemistry doesn't work, then you need to take a step back," said former team owner Ross Brawn. "I was never a great fan of the Human Resource (HR) department until I went to Ferrari. You need an HR director and some HR people who can really connect with the troops. At Brawn GP I met with my HR director every week to get a summary of what was going on and where we had issues."

Such a department was simply superfluous for an F1 team in Ken Tyrrell's day.

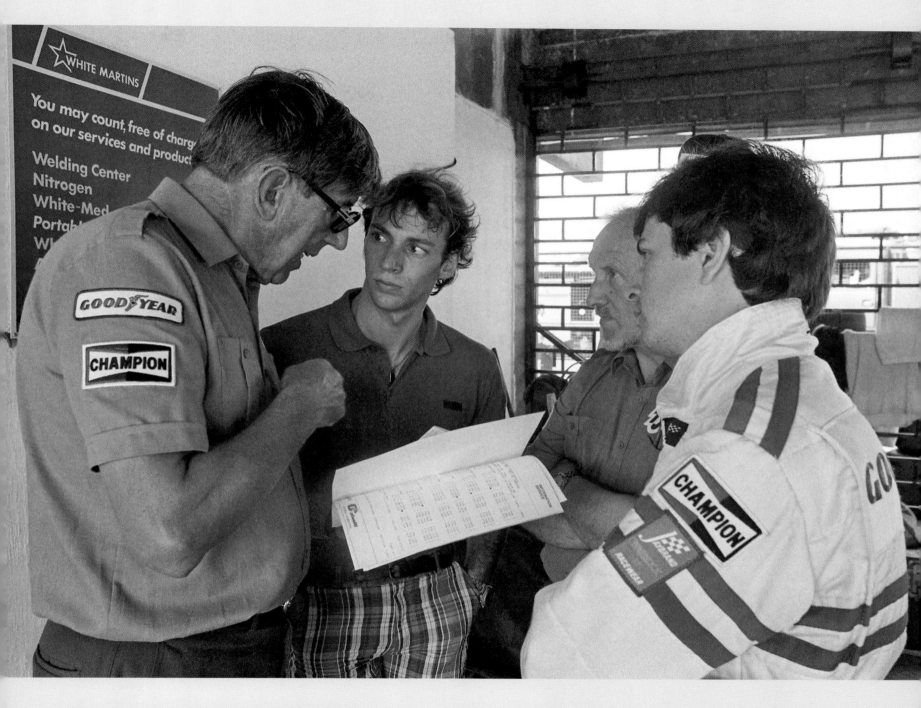

A goodly portion of the entire Tyrrell team, 1984.
Owner Ken Tyrrell (left) chats with drivers Stefan
Bellof (second from left) and Martin Brundle (right).
Today's teams can easily number upwards of 1,000.

Ground zero for what became known as the FISA-FOCA war was the arbitrary fine slapped on McLaren's John Watson by Jean-Marie Balestre, the newly installed head of the FIA's sporting committee, after a crash in the 1979 season opener. Watson wasn't even invited to plead his case. Balestre's delusions of grandeur extended to renaming his committee, the Commission Sportive Internationale (CSI), as the Fédération Mondiale du Sport Automobile—note the "Mondiale" ("world"). For this he was slapped down by the FIA's executive committee and had to settle for Fédération Internationale du Sport Automobile (FISA). Although he would become president of the FIA in 1985, at this stage Balestre was merely a vice president and well exceeding his authority. Diktats from on high were his stock-in-trade.

To the teams that made up FOCA—predominantly British-based and Cosworth-powered—Balestre and the alignments he was beginning to establish with new car-manufacturer-backed teams such as Renault and Alfa Romeo represented an existential threat. Engine power was no longer a level playing field. Manufacturers had deeper pockets—and Balestre was showing a disturbing tendency to unilaterally announce new technical regulations that seemed to favor them, such as a higher minimum weight limit (a pointless and technically regressive change—unless you were Alfa Romeo and had a

(ABOVE LEFT)
1982 Swiss GP
After world champion Alan Jones retired, Swede Keke Rosberg joined Williams. He was consistently on the podium throughout the season, and despite only winning one race at the Swiss GP, it was enough to give him the driver's title.

(ABOVE RIGHT)
1983 United States GP
With up to 750bhp available from the 1.5-liter turbocharged engines, the days of the dominant Ford DFV were coming to an end. After numerous accidents took out the leaders, McLaren's John Watson snatched a remarkable victory at Long Beach from 22nd on the grid.

1982 United States GP

At a remodeled circuit in Long Beach, Alfa Romeo driver Andre de Cesaris (No. 22) was on pole ahead of a returning Niki Lauda (No. 8) in his McLaren. Pironi and Prost hit the wall and retired as did Arnoux (No. 16). Lauda passed de Cesaris after a mistake, going on to take the checkered flag.

1982 German GP

After the tragic accident that took the life of Villeneuve in qualifying at Zolder, Ferrari brought in Patrick Tambay to fill his seat. In another collision reminiscent of Villeneuve's, Pironi crashed in qualifying at Hockenheim, having set the fastest lap. He was badly injured and never raced again. New teammate Tambay won.

1983 Belgian GP

The Belgian GP was back at Spa-Francorchamps for the first time since 1970. Prost was on pole in the Renault but lost the lead to de Cesaris at the start. The Italian had a slow pit stop, allowing Prost to finish first and Tambay's Ferrari (No. 27) second.

heavy engine). Renault's 1.5-liter turbo, once a laughing stock, was now powerful and reliable enough to open the question of whether there could be genuine parity between turbos and naturally aspirated engines–and so it proved as forced induction became expensively popular.

Both sides agreed that F1 car performance had reached dangerous levels but couldn't agree on how to keep it in check. FOCA wanted turbo engines banned; the manufacturers argued in favor of aerodynamic changes. When FISA announced a forthcoming ban on the adjustable side "skirts" vital to sealing underbody airflow, FOCA saw the direction of travel and fought back. Ecclestone and his sidekick Max Mosley sought to undermine Balestre at every turn, even petitioning the FIA to take control of F1 out of FISA's hands. Escalating pettiness between both sides led to an ugly stand-off at the Spanish Grand Prix, originally scheduled to be round seven of the 1980 season, but that was struck from the records after it was run by the national auto club without FIA sanction–and without Ferrari, Renault, and Alfa Romeo. All because of an argument over unpaid fines incurred by FOCA drivers.

Ferrari was nominally a member of FOCA, try as Balestre might to persuade Enzo Ferrari to resign from it, but in 1980 the team's 312 T5 car was miserably uncompetitive—defending world champion Jody Scheckter scored points in just one race—so Enzo exerted more influence off the track than on it, playing both sides off against one another to his advantage. Since the shape of the T5's flat-12 engine militated against effective deployment of ground-effect venturi, banning side skirts was in Ferrari's interests.

(ABOVE)
1984 Belgian GP
McLaren dominated the 1984 season with an epic battle between teammates Lauda and Prost, winning 12 out of 16 rounds. Michele Alboreto led from pole and took Ferrari's only victory at Zolder for the Belgian GP after both McLarens retired.

(LEFT)
1983 South African GP
Piquet won his second drivers' title in the final round in South Africa after season leader Prost blew an engine. It was the first championship won by a turbocharged car and the last by a Brabham.

(OPPOSITE TOP)
1983 Dutch GP
For round 12 in Holland, McLaren introduced its first turbo-engined car for Lauda with the TAG V6. Piquet was on pole but went out after a collision with Prost. Arnoux and Tambay went through for a Ferrari 1-2.

(ABOVE LEFT)
1984 Monaco GP
During a wet race in Monaco, Prost was on pole ahead of Mansell's Lotus. Multiple accidents marred the racing. Ayrton Senna in his Toleman was up to second, when Prost signaled for the race to be stopped on lap 29.

(ABOVE RIGHT)
1984 Italian GP
Lauda won his fifth race of the season at Monza, propelling him ahead of Prost for the driver's title.

By the end of the season, Ecclestone and Mosley—against a tapestry of legal injunctions flying back and forth—were beginning to draw up plans for a breakaway series, even publishing a putative calendar. Sponsors took fright; the Goodyear tire company announced its withdrawal, leaving Michelin as (potentially) sole supplier to a world championship consisting of three manufacturer teams. The 1981 season-opening Argentine Grand Prix was duly postponed. Not that FOCA could afford to run its own championship—or could it? On a trip to Austria to watch a downhill ski race, Mosley, Chapman, and McLaren's Teddy Mayer were struck by a mural on the wall of their hotel's dining room depicting the siege of Salzburg. Legend had it that the castle's defenders were out of food and had just one cow left when they hit upon the idea of painting the cow a different color each day and parading it where the attacking army could see it, giving

DEFINING EVENT

1988 ITALIAN GRAND PRIX

On the evening of September 11, 1988, Don Erio Belloi rang the bells of his parish church in the little Italian town of Maranello—a tradition he always did when Ferrari was victorious. On this occasion, the celebration was particularly poignant.

All season long Gerhard Berger and Michele Alboreto were nowhere near the McLaren-Hondas of Ayrton Senna and Alain Prost. No one was. The MP4/4 was one of the most dominant cars ever to compete in Formula 1. In qualifying for the second round of the season at Imola, the two red and white machines were 3.3 seconds quicker than Nelson Piquet's Lotus in third. Throughout the year's 16 rounds, Senna won eight, Prost seven. But the whitewash was incomplete thanks to a moment's lapse of concentration at the venerated *autodromo*.

Four weeks before the Italian Grand Prix, legendary team owner Enzo Ferrari had passed away. He died at six o'clock on the morning of Sunday, August 14, at age 90. *Il Commendatore* was interred at his family's tomb where a white marble arch simply reads: "FERRARI" and the epigram: *Ad maiora ultra vitam*— Towards greater things beyond life.

Senna led teammate Prost at Monza, until the Frenchman retired with engine failure 17 laps from the finish. The two scarlet Ferraris were elevated to second and third, but victory was still unlikely. Then, on the penultimate lap, fate intervened. Senna mistimed an overtake on a back marker approaching the Rettifilo chicane. Jean-Louis Schlesser was deputizing for Nigel Mansell in a Williams and the pair made contact. Senna was spun out of contention and the *tifosi* went wild. Berger went through to take the lead, with Alboreto close behind.

On the final lap, the historic circuit descended into euphoria as the fans of the Scuderia celebrated the Old Man's passing with this against-the-odds result. Red flags depicting the black Prancing Horse on the yellow shield were waved with gusto as the two Ferraris took the checkered flag to record a memorable 1-2 and to stop McLaren's clean sweep of the season. There was not a dry eye as the church bells chimed across the country.

A 1-2 victory by Ferrari to mark Enzo's passing.

the impression of plenty. Thus inspired, Mosley proposed that FOCA run the scheduled South African Grand Prix; the promoters agreed, Ecclestone had a stockpile of old Avon tires, and the race went ahead. Carlos Reutemann won for Williams and would likely have gone on to be world champion if it had counted for points.

When the Long Beach Grand Prix promoter said it would happily run a FOCA event and Renault informed Balestre that, owing to commercial necessity, it would have to race there, FISA had to come back to the table. The ultimate result was the Concorde Agreement, named after the Place de la Concorde in Paris, where the FIA is based, but chiefly the work of Mosley and Ferrari's sporting director assistant Marco Piccinini. A commercial contract covering an initial four-year period (though its successors still shape F1 to this day), it enshrined the rights of Ecclestone to collect revenues from race promoters on behalf of the teams.

(TOP LEFT)

1984 Portuguese GP
The championship came down to the final round in Portugal. Prost was second on the grid, but Lauda could only manage 11th. Piquet led from pole, but Prost overtook him with Mansell second. Mansell spun, allowing Lauda through to secure his third title by half a point. Left to right: Prost, Lauda, Senna.

(TOP RIGHT)

1985 Portuguese GP
With Mansell's move to Williams, Lotus needed a driver and signed young Brazilian Ayrton Senna. He proved himself in round two in Portugal, taking both pole and his first win after a wet race that he led from start to finish.

(ABOVE)

1985 Monaco GP

In Monaco Senna was on pole again for the third successive time, but his engine failed after just 13 laps. Alboreto took the lead but spun on oil from a collision between Patrese and Piquet at St. Devote. Prost's McLaren went through to take the win.

(RIGHT)

1985 European GP

At the European GP at Brands Hatch, Nigel Mansell qualified third in his Williams behind Senna and Piquet. Rosberg spun trying to overtake Senna and pitted, exiting just in front of leader Senna and slowing him down. Teammate Mansell caught up, overtook the leader, and held on to earn his first F1 win.

(OPPOSITE BOTTOM)

1985 German GP

In Germany Toleman's Teo Fabi qualified in the dry before the rain started and took a surprise pole on the new Nürburgring. After Senna and Rosberg came together and Prost spun, Alboreto took his second win of the season for Ferrari.

Though his hands had been pried away from the coffers, Balestre got his way in the form of side skirts only being permitted if fixed in position, and a mandatory 6 cm (2.3 inch) ground clearance. Since the latter could only be measured while the car was at rest in the pitlane–generally by sliding a 6 cm high wooden block under it–the teams devised ingenious ways of circumventing this. Lotus's 88, essentially one chassis inside another, was banned (much to Chapman's fury) while Brabham designer Gordon Murray adapted his BT49 car with hydropneumatic struts, which kept the car at legal

(LEFT)
1986 Brazilian GP
The 1986 season was dominated by four drivers: Nigel Mansell and Nelson Piquet for Williams, Ayrton Senna at Lotus, and Alain Prost at McLaren. Piquet won round one in his home GP in Rio, with São Paulo native Senna second—a Brazilian 1-2.

(BELOW)
1986 Belgian GP
At the Ardennes circuit of Spa-Francorchamps, Gerhard Berger put his BMW-powered Benetton on the front row next to Piquet. After a first lap pileup, Berger and Prost pitted for repairs. Piquet's turbo blew, leaving Mansell and Senna to battle it out. Nigel won his first of five races.

(OPPOSITE TOP)
1986 Detroit GP
At the bumpy Detroit street circuit, the superior chassis of the Lotus 98T put Senna on pole. On the second lap, Senna missed a gear and Mansell got ahead but overheated his brakes, allowing the Brazilian back into the lead. Driving over debris, Ayrton got a puncture but fought back from sixth to take the win.

(OPPOSITE BOTTOM)
1986 Australian GP
In Australia three drivers fought for the title. Mansell took pole, but Rosberg led most of the race before retiring with a puncture. Nigel suffered a similar fate when a tire exploded at 180 mph (290 kmh); Lotus called Piquet in and Prost (1) won the race and his second title.

height while stationary but compressed at speed, enabling the underbody venturi to generate downforce. Nelson Piquet won the title in his BT49C when Reutemann inexplicably faded in the final round of the season.

The unpoliceable ride-height rule was rescinded for 1982, but this created further problems. While the pre-1981 side skirts had been designed to "ride" the track surface, retracting into the sidepod under the force of surface undulations, the fixed skirts required very stiff suspension settings to keep the car close to the ground and retain the underbody suction effect. As a result, the cars became difficult and uncomfortable to drive while remaining too quick; a serious of horrendous accidents, one resulting in the death of Ferrari star Gilles Villeneuve, prompted a new rule mandating that the cars have entirely flat bottoms between the wheels.

Tragedy at Ferrari and poor reliability for Renault opened the door for Keke Rosberg to win the world championship for Williams, despite recording just one Grand Prix victory. It would be the last title for a normally aspirated entrant until turbos were banned in 1989. Piquet and Brabham won again in 1983 in a BT52 car Murray had effectively designed from scratch in six weeks after the late imposition of the flat-bottom rule. Murray was puzzled by Ecclestone's capitulation at the time, but in the years to come, the reasons for Bernie's keenness to avoid fresh conflict with Balestre would become clear. The BT52 was also designed with a small fuel tank to maximize the effect

McLAREN MP4/1

The amalgamation of McLaren, Ron Dennis's Project Four Racing F2 operation—and backing from Marlboro—led to the creation of the one of the most innovative cars in the sport's history: the MP4/1. Dennis had put his faith in designer John Barnard, who in turn opted to develop his 1981 creation with a revolutionary new material.

In the past, carbon composites had been used on small components in F1, such as the rear-wing supports on Graham Hill's Embassy-backed cars in 1975. But the MP4/1 was the first time the whole monocoque had been made from carbon fiber. It was a seminal moment. In time, every car on the grid would be constructed from the same lightweight, yet extremely strong, material.

After a time working in the USA, designer Barnard got in touch with the Utah-based Hercules Corporation and its "Skunk Works" research and development department. It helped assemble the MP4/1 using five major parts made from carbon composites with the front suspension bulkhead the only area using a single major aluminum component.

Although the car wasn't ready for the start of the season, when John Watson got his hands on the MP4/1 at Zolder, he ran a comfortable fourth until gearbox maladies slowed his pace. The Ulsterman memorably won the 1981 British Grand Prix, taking the lead late in the race to the delight of the partisan crowd. It was McLaren's first win for four years and vindication for Marlboro, Dennis, and Barnard's carbon fiber composite car.

Few thought that a complete carbon chassis would be safe enough. But the critics were silenced when John Watson reversed his McLaren into the Monza barriers at high speed. As Watson looped his machine out of the high-speed second Lesmo bend, the rear struck the barriers, and the car instantly broke into two. Many feared it had disintegrated, but Watson walked away from the 140 mph (225 kmh) shunt unharmed.

The torsional stiffness was double that of an aluminum chassis, and the strength displayed in the impact led to an approach to McLaren by Britain's Civil Aviation Authority. The U.S. military was also interested and started to use carbon fiber as underbody cladding in their attack helicopters. Having borrowed this technology from the aerospace industry, in due course McLaren received a commendation from NASA.

The MP4/1 wasn't the easiest car to drive. Andrea de Cesaris was dubbed "de Crasheris," but it changed perceptions. Not only was it a winning car, it had arguably used a ground-breaking material that became one of the biggest innovations in Formula 1 driver safety.

James Mann

of a tactic Murray had introduced in 1982: refueling. With a pressurized nozzle delivering around 10 gallons per second, the system enabled Brabham to run "light" and thereby achieve fast enough laps to more than compensate for time spent in the pits.

Turbo outputs crept towards the 1000bhp mark as engine manufacturers resolved the key issues of "lag" (the inertia between drivers pressing the throttle and the turbos spinning up to deliver additional power), and pre-ignition caused by high boost pressures and compression ratios. Urban myth has it that BMW engineers used to urinate on the ex-production car four-cylinder blocks to "condition" them, and that Brabham's BMW engines ran on fuel developed for Nazi rockets in World War II. Sadly, neither of these stories is true.

With greater power came additional reliance on chassis rigidity, aerodynamic performance, and tires. McLaren mastered the confluence of these demands to achieve dominance from 1984 onwards. Under new management after title sponsor Marlboro tired of the team's late-1970s slump and engineered a "merger" with the Project 4 organization co-founded by Ron Dennis, formerly Jochen Rindt's chief mechanic, McLaren

(TOP LEFT)
1987 Monaco GP
Senna took victory in Monaco in the immensely powerful Lotus 99T despite issues with its computer controlled active suspension. Mansell led from pole in his Williams FW11 but retired with turbo problems. Piquet was second and Alboreto third.

(TOP RIGHT)
1987 Japanese GP
The championship was decided with one round to go in Japan. After an accident in practice, Mansell suffered a serious back injury and was out for the final two races, handing the driver's title to Piquet. Austrian Gerhard Berger won the race from pole in his Ferrari.

(ABOVE)

1988 Brazilian GP

With a regulation change for next season banning turbo engines, many teams jumped early, including Williams, Tyrrell, and Benetton. Ferrari, Lotus, and McLaren did not change. This was the right decision with Prost (No. 11) and Senna (No. 12) winning all but one race starting in Brazil.

(RIGHT)

1988 British GP

Despite restrictions limiting turbos to 2.5 bar, McLaren proved its chassis, designed by Gordon Murray who had moved from Brabham, was the best. By round eight at Silverstone, Prost had won four races to Senna's three. The Brazilian evened it up, taking the checkered flag in heavy rain.

(OPPOSITE BOTTOM)

1987 Hungarian GP

The previous season, the Hungarian GP returned to the calendar for the first time since 1936. Piquet in his Williams Honda won. Teammate Mansell took pole and led most of the race only to retire after he lost a wheel nut. Piquet moved ahead in the driver's championship.

pioneered new approaches in technology and commerce. Dennis's key hire before the merger went through in 1980 was John Barnard, an innovative and single-minded engineer returning to the UK after a successful interlude in the U.S. racing scene.

McLaren's renaissance was built on several pillars. First, Dennis secured sufficient investment for Barnard to realize his dream of building a car in lightweight composite materials rather than aluminum. The challenge here was not only to understand and learn how to work with carbon fiber's very different characteristics, but also to build the car (the first "tubs" had to be built by U.S. aerospace manufacturer Hercules because no British company would take it on) and prove that in any on-track accident it wouldn't explode into fibrous shards. In parallel Barnard executed a quiet revolution in F1 chassis design: he demanded that every single part was built according to the design, ending a tradition of improvisation on the factory floor and no car being exactly the same.

What really unleashed the power of this new approach was the Porsche-built turbo engine Dennis commissioned with investment from Mansour Ojjeh's Techniques d'Avant Garde company. In 1983 Dennis lured double world champion Niki Lauda out of retirement, and the following year, with the TAG engines now ready and a new car designed to accommodate them, he partnered Lauda with the promising Alain Prost, recently fired (for no good reason) by Renault. Between them, Lauda and Prost dominated the 1984 and '85 seasons, winning a championship each. Although Williams put up a tough fight with increasingly powerful Honda engines, Prost picked up a bonus world title in '86 when Williams had tire problems in the final round.

While the TAG engine's fuel-efficiency proved valuable as fuel-capacity limits were brought in alongside boost restrictions to curtail car performance, by 1987 Honda held sway–to the extent that Nelson Piquet claimed the championship with Williams despite suffering (and concealing) depth-perception issues after a crash in San Marino. But with Frank Williams adjusting to life as a tetraplegic after a road accident, the team's management of its drivers and its relationship with Honda suffered. Piquet left for Lotus, taking the engine deal with him, and Dennis swooped to land a similar deal for McLaren. With a bespoke V6 turbo tailored to suit even greater boost restrictions in what would be the last year before naturally aspirated engines became mandatory again, Prost and new teammate Ayrton Senna won all but one of the races in the 1988 season. The following year, as McLaren dominated again, this extraordinarily talented pair would have a spectacular fall-out, which resulted in Prost moving to Ferrari and taking the world champion's coveted number one with him.

(ABOVE)
1988 Australian GP
With only the 11 highest scores counting towards the championship, the season ran right down to the wire in Adelaide, Australia. Senna took pole, but Prost led before being passed by Berger's Ferrari. Berger crashed, clipping Arnoux's Ligier and retiring. Prost (No. 11) won, but Senna (No. 12) was second, giving him the title.

(OPPOSITE TOP LEFT)
1989 Brazilian GP
With normally aspirated engines now mandatory, Ferrari signed Nigel Mansell to drive its 3.5-liter V12 car with a new semi-automatic gearbox. In Brazil Senna took pole but clashed with Berger at turn one. Mansell triumphed on debut for Ferrari, coming through from sixth.

(OPPOSITE TOP RIGHT)
1989 Mexican GP
Senna's blistering qualifying laps won him pole 13 out of 16 races. He won round two at Imola and then in Monaco and took pole again for the Mexican GP ahead of Prost. Tires proved critical with different choices for the two McLaren teammates. Senna won with Prost fifth.

Mercurial, intense, and single-minded, Senna was a force of nature who wanted to test himself against the best. So it was almost inevitable that he would clash with Prost, whose smooth driving style belied great speed and tactical acumen. Ostensibly the argument began with a supposed agreement at San Marino in 1989 that whichever of them got away from the starting line first would have priority at the first corner. At the start Senna got there first from pole position, but the race was then stopped for an hour after an accident. Second time around Prost got the better start, but Senna overtook him at the Tosa hairpin on the first lap. Prost felt Senna had reneged on the agreement; Senna denied it existed. By the end of the season, they were only talking to each other through intermediaries and casting doubt in public over the equality of their equipment. It was a tawdry and unedifying spectacle.

Throughout the decade, F1 had benefitted from an influx of sponsors keen to take advantage of the TV exposure Ecclestone had industriously been securing. In 1980 reigning world champion Jody Scheckter was earning $1 million a year; he built his real fortune only after retiring. By the close of the 1980s, driver salaries alone had escalated to the point where, famously, Dennis and Senna reached an impasse over Senna's 1988–1990 contract that amounted to a *gap* of $1.5 million between their desired figures–and they agreed to resolve it by flipping a coin.

(BOTTOM LEFT)
1989 Canadian GP
Prost was on pole in a wet Montreal. In a race of attrition, Senna led until two laps from the end when his Honda V10 gave out. Williams driver Thierry Boutsen (shown) won and teammate Patrese was second.

(BOTTOM RIGHT)
1989 Japanese GP
Controversy clouded the result in Suzuka after the McLaren drivers came together at the chicane and stalled their engines. Senna restarted, but despite winning the race was disqualified for cutting the corner. Benetton's Alessandro Nannini (shown) won, but Senna's loss was enough for Prost to win his third title.

THE WORLD CHAMPIONS

ALAN JONES
(1980)

Strong, brave, and fearless. Alan Jones's driving style suited the ground-effect era where brute force was an advantage, in cars that were glued to the road. The son of '50s racer Stan Jones, young Alan arrived in England in 1967 looking for a drive. Money was tight, but eventually the Australian graduated to F1 in the mid-1970s. Following Frank Williams's divorce from Walter Wolf, he called upon the no-nonsense Jones to lead his reborn F1 team.

In 1979, when the Patrick Head-designed FW07 appeared from Jarama onwards, it suddenly became the car to beat. Despite not scoring the team's maiden win at Silverstone, Jones won three on the trot in the second half of the year.

Victory at the season opener in Argentina 1980 immediately showed both his and his team's intent. He added four more wins to secure the World Championship at the penultimate round in Montréal.

Frank Williams once admitted that "Jonesy" was probably his favorite driver: "He was one of the best and most combative drivers we've ever had," said Williams. "He was also a great friend and just a great bloke."

NELSON PIQUET
(1981, 1983, 1987)

After winning British F3 in 1978, the charismatic Brazilian was appointed to Bernie Ecclestone's Brabham F1 team. The formidable duo were a force to be reckoned with in the early 1980s, and in Gordon Murray's BT49, Piquet took the '81 title at the final round in Las Vegas, after championship rival Carlos Reutemann's charge faded.

The turbocharged BMWs were unreliable the following year, but in '83 Piquet was in contention for a second crown. After trailing Renault's Alain Prost early on, a volatile new fuel extracted more boost from the engine. Dominant victories at Monza and Brands Hatch led to title number two when Prost retired from the South African finale.

Piquet accepted a big-money deal to race for Williams—alongside Nigel Mansell—for '86 and '87. The rivalry with Mansell, and in particular the disagreement over who was number one in the team, boiled over and ultimately cost Williams the title.

Piquet took fewer wins than his teammate in '87 (three compared to Mansell's six) but had suffered a concussion from an impact with the Tamburello wall at Imola. Despite that, he won his third World Championship following the Brit's practice crash in Suzuka.

KEKE ROSBERG
(1982)

Throughout his early career, Keijo "Keke" Rosberg showed blinding speed so Williams deemed him a suitable replacement for the out-going Alan Jones. With Carlos Reutemann's sudden retirement, the Flying Finn found himself de facto team leader. He took a brilliant win at the Swiss GP at Dijon-Prenois in 1982, and solid performances across the year meant he overhauled the points lead of the injured Didier Pironi to scoop the World Championship.

Two further wins stand out in his career—both on street circuits—which displayed his courage and skill. The first came in a wet/dry Monaco ('83) and the second in the searing heat of Dallas a year later.

Initially Rosberg was troubled with the arrival of Nigel Mansell at Williams, but Rosberg continued to excel, famously stubbing out a cigarette to record one of the fastest laps of all time in qualifying at Silverstone in 1985. At an average speed of over 160 mph (257 kmh), it stood as a lap record for over 17 years.

ALAIN PROST
(1985, 1986, 1989)

The diminutive, curly-haired Frenchman was known as The Professor for his intelligent and methodical approach to racing. His statistics rank him as one of the greatest drivers of all time: four world titles, 51 victories, and nearly 800 points from 199 starts. But it wasn't just race craft. Prost had blistering speed, characterized by a precise, undemonstrative driving style.

He rose through the ranks of an Elf-sponsored racing program and won promotion to F1 with McLaren after winning the 1979 European F3 Championship. Decent form led to him being recruited by Renault to spearhead its campaign. Wins followed and he nearly took the crown, just losing out in the final race of 1983. Prost returned to Ron Dennis's McLaren team and once again just missed out on the title the following year—this time by half a point to teammate Niki Lauda.

Finally, Prost became France's first Formula 1 World Champion in 1985, taking five wins en route to the crown in his fuel-efficient McLaren-Porsche. Despite not having the best package a year later—as the all-powerful Williams-Honda was the car to have—his guile and consistency enabled *Le Professeur* to take a second title at the Adelaide curtain closer. He was the underdog going into the race, but when both Williams cars hit trouble with their tires, he cruised to victory to steal the title. Out-classed by Williams in the following season, in 1988 a new partnership with Honda brought success. But Prost had a new element to content with— Brazilian sensation Ayrton Senna was now his teammate at McLaren.

The pair dominated the year, with Senna emerging on top. But their relationship deteriorated, and in 1989 the title was decided in Prost's favor after a clash at the Suzuka chicane. Unhappy with the politics, he left for Ferrari, but he was on the receiving end of Senna's forceful driving as the enmity between the pair grew.

AYRTON SENNA
(1988)

Ayrton Senna da Silva was regarded as one of the greatest talents to ever sit in a racing car, and his trademark bright yellow helmet garnered fear within his rivals.

Senna raced with a relentless commitment and faith, demanding the best equipment to match his God-given talent. But his pursuit of victory at all costs came with a ruthless edge. His driving and politicking caused controversy, particularly in his dealings with teammate Alain Prost on the track—and with the former President of the FIA, Jean-Marie Balestre, off it.

After impressing in the British junior series, Senna enjoyed his first taste of F1 machinery with Williams in 1983. He entered Grand Prix racing with Toleman the following year and nearly won in a Monaco downpour. His first win came in the rains of Estoril in 1985, driving for Lotus.

Senna's prodigious talent led to him being hired by McLaren to partner Prost for 1988. With the dominant MP4/4, the pair swept all before them. Senna won eight races to Prost's seven, and in the dropped-scoring system (only the best 11 results counted), the Brazilian won his first drivers' title—90 points to the Frenchman's 87.

THE ⑤ 1990s

You can't uninvent technology. But you *can* be in a position where you can't afford it. In the 1990s, Formula 1 increasingly became a racing category defined by the schism between its haves and have-nots. A sport that spends big must earn big, exposing F1 to a series of threats and shocks through the decade: the after-effects of financial crises in key markets; the death of one of its star drivers on live television; tighter regulation on tobacco advertising, a key income stream; and the realization among key stakeholders that, while Bernie Ecclestone had made them all richer, he had spirited a disproportionate quantity of wealth and power away into his own pockets via an impenetrable network of offshore shell companies.

Jean Alesi in the Ferrari F92A, Monaco Grand Prix 1992.

In the early years of the decade, F1 accelerated towards "peak tech" almost in spite of a global economic downturn. In 1989, having moved to Ferrari, John Barnard pioneered the semi-automatic gearbox. Initially motivated by the desire to narrow the cockpit and "tub" by removing the need for a mechanical linkage, the system–operated electro-pneumatically by paddles mounted behind the steering wheel–also meant the driver could change gear faster and without taking his hand off the wheel. Though it was initially unreliable, once the cause of the failures was traced and fixed (electrical shutdown caused by engine vibrations throwing the alternator belt off), it became a must-have. But only, of course, if you could afford to develop your own.

(LEFT)
1990 San Marino GP
With no love lost between the two McLaren drivers, Alain Prost left and signed to Ferrari for the 1990 season. The first two races epitomized the season with Ayrton Senna winning in America and Prost in Brazil. Senna took pole again in San Marino, but Patrese (pictured) in the Williams won.

(BELOW)
1990 Monaco GP
In Monaco for round four, Senna led from pole but the race was stopped after Berger collided with Prost, blocking the circuit. At the restart, Senna pulled away from the pack to win. Prost and Nigel Mansell retired as did most of the other cars; only seven finished the race.

(ABOVE)

1990 Japan GP

Controversy shrouded the penultimate round in Japan as Senna narrowly led the drivers' championship ahead of Prost. Senna was on pole on the dirty side of the track. He intentionally drove into Prost at turn one as the Ferrari driver got ahead, sealing the second title for the Brazilian.

(RIGHT)

1991 Canadian GP

In his McLaren, world champion Ayrton Senna took pole and won the first four races of the season in Phoenix, Interlagos, Imola, and Monte Carlo. In Canada Mansell passed Williams's teammate Riccardo Patrese from pole. Mansell led but missed a gearchange on the final lap, allowing Nelson Piquet's Benetton (pictured) through to win.

Ferrari, still riddled with infighting after Enzo's death in 1988, had a short-lived advantage. Barnard's somewhat eccentric working practices—he refused to move to Italy, so the cars were designed and part-built in the UK then assembled in Maranello—meant he didn't last long, and by early 1990 he was on the job market again. Meanwhile old rancor contributed to a dramatic racing season as Alain Prost's move to Ferrari relieved none of the tension that had built up between him and Ayrton Senna when they were teammates at McLaren. What had begun as a dispute over Senna violating a supposed agreement over on-track etiquette had metastasized into mutual paranoia over equality of equipment, culminating in a collision in the Japanese Grand Prix that resolved the 1989 drivers' championship in Prost's favor. Senna's protests over his disqualification from that race escalated to a confrontation with Jean-Marie Balestre, now president of the FIA, and the threat of Senna losing his license—and McLaren's entry to the 1990 championship being refused.

(ABOVE)
1991 French GP
Nigel Mansell, who had left Ferrari for Williams, was Senna's main competition in 1991, winning five races starting in France at Magny-Cours. Patrese fluffed the start from pole, then Prost led. Mansell passed Prost at the hairpin and went on to win.

(LEFT)
1991 Portuguese GP
In Portugal at Estoril, Patrese's Williams was on the front row next to Berger's McLaren. At the start Patrese (No. 6) led, but Mansell got by on lap 18 only to be disqualified when a wheel came off after a pit stop. Patrese took the top step.

(ABOVE)
1992 San Marino GP
After Ferrari fired Prost for publicly criticizing the team, he took a sabbatical in 1992. The Williams FW14B's superiority won ten out of 16 rounds. Mansell won nine and the drivers' title. Here Mansell leads the pack at the start of the San Marino GP.

Although these issues were resolved, the 1990 season ended in even more rancorous circumstances. Once again Suzuka was the venue with Balestre a prime agitator. Having secured pole position, Senna successfully lobbied to have it moved to the left-hand side of the track where the grippier racing line is, figuring that having it on the "dirty" side of the track constituted an unfair disadvantage. Balestre overruled the stewards and reversed the decision. At the first corner, Senna held the inside line even though Prost's car was ahead, and the inevitable high-speed impact took them both out of the race, settling the world championship in Senna's favor. Decades on, this incident still has the power to provoke bitter arguments within the fan community.

CONCORDE DISCORD

While the sport's governing body, the FIA, had supervised and regulated the Formula 1 World Championship since 1950, it had never owned any of the rights to the races. The organizers of individual events had always struck a deal with the entrants. And in the 1970s, Bernie Ecclestone had marshalled the teams into a union to take on those negotiations.

When Max Mosley was elected to the full FIA presidency in 1993, he felt it was his duty to acquire some rights to the championship for the governing body, especially as Ecclestone was extending further control over the sport.

"I used to tell our staff he [Bernie] was like the person in the next seat on a flight who would take over the armrest if you left it clear for a moment," said Mosley. "They had to be constantly on alert to stand their ground."

Mosley had suggested a new Concorde Agreement that was a tripartite agreement between the FIA, the teams, and Bernie. It meant the FIA had a direct contract with the person who held the deals to the races that made up the championship. A 15-year agreement was mooted from 1995 to 2010.

But some of the teams were unhappy with the new arrangement, saying the championship belonged to them. They argued that without the competitors, there was no sport. In his autobiography, Mosley gave a simple analogy to counter this argument. "If you dined in a certain restaurant each night, and for many years, that didn't in some way make you its owner or entitle you to shares in it," he wrote. "It is our [the FIA's] restaurant. Bernie was the chef, a very talented chef, who had built the restaurant up, but it was still our restaurant. But privately Bernie would say to me: 'OK, but if I left to open another restaurant down the road, then where would the FIA be?' He had a point—and quite a strong one."

The threat of a breakaway championship made Mosley more determined to ink a deal. Meanwhile, on the basis of the 15-year contract, Ecclestone was eager to float his business on the stock exchange, but his financiers wanted a longer-term investment. A ten-year extension to 2020 was mooted for $300 million.

But Bernie's flotation of FOM was halted by an on-going investigation by the European Commission's Competition Department. In parallel Ecclestone was entering into a deal with German TV magnate Leo Kirch's EM.TV company. After a long series of legal negotiations over rights and trademarks, financing, and control, in April 2001 the "Hundred Year Agreement" was signed. The FIA received $313.6 million, which it immediately put into a UK charitable foundation to promote road safety, while FOM secured the commercial rights to the sport until December 31, 2110. This deal sealed the long-term fate of Formula 1 and its association with the FIA.

(ABOVE)
1991 Australian GP
The final round of the season in Australia saw torrential rain from the start. Alesi, Mansell, Berger, and others crashed, and the race was abandoned after just 26 of 81 laps. Senna led from pole and was awarded half points for the win.

(RIGHT)
1992 Canadian GP
In Monaco after Mansell lost a wheel nut and had to pit, the McLarens fought back with a win for Senna. In Canada Senna led from pole, colliding with Mansell who retired. After Senna went out with an electrical problem, Berger went through to win.

Remarkably, at the time Senna escaped sanction for the crash, for Balestre's power was fading; none other than Max Mosley would successfully challenge Balestre as head of FISA in 1991 before unseating him as president of the FIA itself two years later. Senna's title defense in '91, on his way to his third and final world championship, was something of an outlier, the result of banking consecutive victories early on in a technically conservative car as faster opposition proved less mechanically reliable. That opposition would not include Ferrari, who imploded in '91 and would not achieve consistent success again until new management had cleaned house later in the decade.

Williams, in partnership with Renault, led the charge to F1's peak tech era. Having pioneered turbocharging in the 1970s, the French car manufacturer was the first to perfect pneumatic-valve actuation in its 3.5-liter naturally aspirated V10s of the early 1990s. Doing away with conventional springs enabled the engines to rev faster, generating more power, without experiencing valve "bounce." After a fallow period in the late 1980s, Williams had recruited well, hiring Adrian Newey, an up-and-coming designer

(TOP)

1992 Belgian GP
Mansell had won the championship at the race in Hungary, then was back on pole for round 12 in Belgium. It was wet in the Ardennes at Spa-Francorchamps but drying fast. Benetton driver Michael Schumacher made the right call for dries taking his first F1 win.

(ABOVE)
1993 South African GP

After a year out of F1, Alain Prost joined Williams for the 1993 calendar. He teamed with new British driver Damon Hill, son of world champion Graham. The Frenchman won straight out the blocks in South Africa with a clean sweep of pole and fastest lap. Senna (No. 8), Prost (No. 2), Schumacher.

(OPPOSITE BELOW LEFT)
1992 Portuguese GP

Mansell's final win of the season was in Portugal where he dominated the race from pole. After multiple incidents, including a nasty accident between Patrese and Berger, Mansell slowed to pit to take his 30th career victory. He left F1 and joined the Newman Haas CART team in America.

(OPPOSITE BELOW RIGHT)
1993 European GP

For round three, the European GP was held at the Donington Park circuit, last used in the 1930s. The race was intermittently very wet and drying, and the cars made a record 63 pit stops. Senna made the right choices to take the win a minute ahead of Hill.

with an eclectic background that included race-engineering Bobby Rahal in IndyCars as well as creating several aerodynamically daring F1 cars for March.

Competitive and uncompromising, Newey was ahead of his time, and his first Williams, the FW14 of 1991, represented a clear break from the team's previous works, with a high nose cone to help steer and optimize airflow under the car as well as over it. Drivers Nigel Mansell and Riccardo Patrese likened the experience of sitting in the cockpit to lying in a bathtub with their feet resting on the taps. It was fast, but its new semi-automatic gearbox was fragile, helping Senna to rack up four consecutive victories at the start of the season—a points gap Mansell could not close despite winning five rounds from mid-season onwards. This would be the only world championship for a car powered by a V12 engine and the last for one equipped with a manual gearbox.

In 1992 Williams added computer-controlled reactive suspension to the mix, along with front and rear wings built in such a way that they flexed very slightly when the car was traveling at high speed, reducing drag. The effects were transformative. Lotus had evaluated active suspension in the early 1980s as a means of optimizing ground-effect aerodynamics, and actually ran an active system in F1 in 1987, as had Williams. But these were deemed too heavy, expensive, and unreliable. For 1992 Williams deployed an entirely new system overseen by Paddy Lowe. Using hydropneumatic actuators at each corner, its sole purpose was to react to bumps in a way that kept the entire car at a predetermined height and attitude relative to the track surface.

Armed with the reactive-suspension FW14B in 1992, Mansell was virtually unbeatable. In the first round, he outqualified Senna by 0.741s and led from lights to flag, 34s up the road from Senna and 24s from his own teammate. Patrese's struggles with the FW14B highlighted the potential hazards of the technology—at corner entry, he found the lack of "feel" for grip through the steering wheel disconcerting and confidence-sapping. Mansell had the bravery and self-belief to just hang on. Reactive suspension, later joined by anti-lock brakes, became another expensive must-have, and the gap between those who could afford such niceties and those who couldn't grew wider still.

F1's new financial and technical reality was no respecter of tradition. Teams with remarkable histories of success fizzled out. Brabham, long since sold by Bernie Ecclestone as he concentrated on building his fortune, closed in 1992; Lotus soldiered on a little longer at the back of the grid; and, while Tyrrell was "saved" by a sale to British American Tobacco in 1997, in truth, very little of the old entity survived the new regime.

An inflection point was coming, but nobody saw it yet. The teams were busy scrambling to outdo one another and catch up with Williams, while the drivers were similarly focused on ensuring they ended up in the best cars. Having compared the handling of his Ferrari unfavorably with that of a truck, a firing offence at Maranello, Alain Prost was a spectator during Mansell's dominant 1992 season—safe in the knowledge that he had already signed a contract with Williams for '93. Senna also threw his hat in the ring,

(LEFT)
1993 Australian GP
Although Prost did not win a race after round ten, he was consistently on the podium with only one retirement in Brazil to take his fourth drivers' title. In the final two races, he was second to Senna in Japan and Australia and announced his retirement.

(BELOW)
1994 Spanish GP
Damon Hill's (No. 0) first win of the season came in Spain after a gearbox problem slowed pole-man Schumacher, who had led for much of the race. Mika Häkkinen, Rubens Barrichello, and Martin Brundle all retired.

(ABOVE)

1994 German GP

Refueling was brought into question after fire engulfed Jos Verstappen's Benetton and pit crew at the German GP. Berger took the sole win for Ferrari of the season after multiple accidents and retirements saw only eight cars complete the race.

(RIGHT)

1994 Australian GP

Controversy surrounded the launch and traction control on Schumacher's Benetton, and he was disqualified from two rounds. Nevertheless, in Adelaide all was set with just one point separating him from Hill. A collision on lap 36 of 81 saw both cars retire, and Schumacher took the title.

supposedly offering to drive for free, until he was informed that Prost had got there first—and had a no-Senna clause in his contract. Still, all this interest enabled Williams to play hardball when negotiating Mansell's contract extension. This was why, despite winning a record-breaking nine races and tying up the drivers' championship after 11 of 16 rounds, Nigel stomped into the media center on race day morning at Monza and announced his retirement at the end of the season. Armed with the even faster and more sophisticated Williams FW15C, Prost veritably cruised to his fourth world title in 1993, though he was humbled by Senna in the wet European Grand Prix at Donington.

1994 SAN MARINO GRAND PRIX

For the start of the 1994 season, there had been a series of revised technical rules to eliminate so-called "driver aids." In addition, refueling had been reintroduced to enliven the show, while another idea from the IndyCar series was adopted: a pace car would slow the field down to avoid race stoppages in the wake of an accident.

When the third round of the 1994 season rolled into Imola, the events of that weekend cast a long shadow for years to come as the impact of the twin deaths of Roland Ratzenberger and Senna resonated around the world.

A day after Rubens Barrichello had enjoyed a lucky escape when he launched his Jordan into the catch fencing on the Friday, Ratzenberger was less fortunate when he hit the wall head-on during qualifying. It was the first F1 fatality since Elio de Angelis lost his life in testing eight years previously.

Senna had been particularly shocked by Roland's accident and broke down in tears on the shoulder of F1's much-loved resident doctor, Professor Sid Watkins. Less than 24 hours later, the eminent neurosurgeon was in the middle of the emergency to save his friend's life.

Senna had furled up an Austrian flag and placed it in his Williams cockpit to wave after the race in honor of Roland. But tragically, after a short Safety Car period, he too hit the wall. The watching world suddenly heaved into a wretched shock.

On lap seven, the red-flag appeared with Senna slumped in his car, motionless. "For the third time that weekend there was a frantic effort to cut the chin-strap and get a helmet off," said Watkins. "We supported Ayrton's neck and removed the helmet. His eyes were closed and he was deeply unconscious. I got an airway into his mouth rotated it and we had effective airflow. He looked serene. I raised his eyelids and it was clear from his pupils that he had a massive brain injury. We lifted him from the cockpit and laid him on the ground. As we did he sighed and, though I am totally agnostic, I felt his soul departed at that moment."

At the next race in Monaco, Karl Wendlinger was placed into an induced coma following his heavy hit with the wall. Formula 1 was in crisis. One of the sport's calming voices was that of newly installed FIA President Max Mosley. The former racer-turned-barrister steadied the ship to calmer waters and introduced a raft of safety measures.

After initial knee-jerk alterations that included adding chicanes in place of fast corners, Mosley set about a detailed plan, including upgrades to cars, drivers' kit, and circuits. But while motor racing will always be dangerous, the safety crusade led by Mosley has certainly reduced the risk in the years since 1994.

The 1994 season was tragic as newcomer Roland Ratzenberger and three-time world champion Ayrton Senna were killed at the San Marino GP. After a chaotic re-start, Benetton's Schumacher went on to win. Senna drives his Williams FW16.

(ABOVE)

1995 Pacific GP

With two races in Japan, Hill needed to win both to keep his championship chances alive. At Aida for the Pacific GP, the Williamses were on the front row, but Schumacher's pit team was faster. Despite a gearbox problem, Schumacher won the race and his second drivers' title.

(OPPOSITE TOP LEFT)

1995 San Marino GP

Due to safety concerns, regulations changes reduced engines to three liters and added the plank under the cars to lower downforce. At Imola one year on from Senna and Ratzenberger's passing, Hill secured his first win of the season after Schumacher crashed.

(OPPOSITE TOP RIGHT)

1995 British GP

By round eight at Silverstone, Schumacher had won four races to Hill's two, and Alesi had a single win in Canada. Hill was on pole, but a collision with Schumacher at Stowe took out both cars. British driver Johnny Herbert took his first win after six years in F1.

(OPPOSITE BOTTOM)

1995 Portuguese GP

Scotsman David Coulthard got his first F1 win in Portugal after leading the race from pole alongside teammate Hill. At the start, there was a nasty accident when Ukyo Katayama's Tyrrell was launched into the air on the main straight, sending him to the hospital.

Frank Williams was a racer to the very core of his being. In 1993 McLaren's MP4/8 was technically a match for the FW15C but underpowered, since after Honda's withdrawal, McLaren had been forced into a customer deal for second-string Ford V8s. Senna's bravura performances in the MP4/8 spoke of a great driver at the height of his powers; Prost's play-it-safe crawl to the title brought silverware and validation, but it didn't make Frank's soul sing. Inevitably Senna was announced as a Williams driver for 1994, and Prost signaled his own retirement rather than renew his contract and face a potential repeat of 1988–89.

Senna was now last man standing of the late-1980s stars, following the departure of Prost, Mansell, and Nelson Piquet. But Williams wouldn't have the dominant car of 1994. That, in the early season at least, would be the Benetton B194, occupied by Michael Schumacher. The talented German had shot to fame when he made a brief appearance with the young Jordan team in Belgium in '91 before being relocated in a piece of contractual sleight-of-hand orchestrated by Ecclestone and Benetton boss Flavio Briatore. Piquet, immediately outperformed by his new teammate, decided that racing in IndyCar would be a better idea. By 1994 Schumacher was a Grand Prix winner and now Senna's chief threat.

F1 is supposed to represent the pinnacle of technology as well as being the arena of the world's best drivers. Realizing that one of these propositions had come to undercut the other, the FIA moved to outlaw the full gamut of so-called "driver aids," even those that had been tested but not raced, such as Williams's continuously variable transmission. Anti-lock brakes, traction control, launch control, four-wheel steering, and active suspension went on the fire (theoretically in some cases). As a result, cars whose aerodynamics had been honed to take advantage of the stability provided by active suspension became fundamentally less stable, though Mosley would go to his grave denying this.

(ABOVE)
1996 Australian GP
Berger and Alesi left Ferrari for Benetton. Schumacher went the other way to join Irish driver Eddie Irvine at Ferrari. At the first race of the season in Australia, Hill triumphed after overtaking Canadian Williams teammate Jacques Villeneuve.

(LEFT)
1996 Monaco GP
The surprise winner of the year was Ligier's Olivier Panis at the Monaco GP. Schumacher took pole but hit the wall at Mirabeau. One after another all but three cars retired, leaving the Frenchman to take his only F1 victory ahead of Coulthard and Herbert.

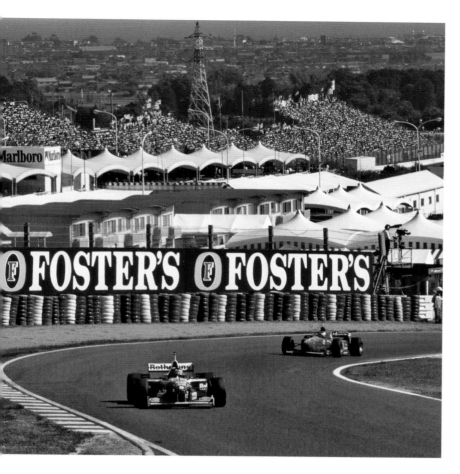

(ABOVE RIGHT)

1996 Italian GP

Ferrari had won only one race in Spain before Schumacher took the top step again in Belgium. In Monza the German was third on the grid, but after Hill spun on lap five, Schumacher won Ferrari's first home GP for seven years, ahead of Alesi and Häkkinen.

(ABOVE LEFT)

1996 Japanese GP

The drivers' title came down to the final round in Japan with Williams teammate Jacques Villeneuve as Damon Hill's only rival for the honors. The Canadian was on pole but lost a wheel. Hill went on to win the race and the drivers' title, becoming the first son of a world champion (Graham) to win a championship himself.

Williams took a big performance hit, and Senna, along with teammate Damon Hill, found the new FW16 a handful in the early races of 1994. Furthermore, Senna became convinced that Schumacher's car was illegal and pushed himself ever harder to overcome his new nemesis. The inflection point arrived in a brutal weekend at Imola. There, during Friday practice, Jordan driver Rubens Barrichello narrowly avoided being decapitated in a high-speed accident. The following day Roland Ratzenberger crashed, with fatal consequences, during qualifying when the front wing of his Simtek became detached. A palpably emotional Senna visited the scene and later stowed an Austrian flag in his cockpit, planning to wave it in Ratzenberger's honor after the race.

He never got the opportunity. On lap seven, after a brief Safety Car period, Senna led the field into the Tamburello corner–and speared straight off into the wall. A suspension component pierced his helmet. Senna was airlifted to a hospital but never regained consciousness. Extraordinarily and somewhat callously, the race was restarted and ran to its conclusion. But in the weeks to come, the very existence of F1 would be called into question, a clamor that grew yet louder when Karl Wendlinger crashed in Monaco and spent 19 days in a coma.

Safety had improved over the previous decade and a half thanks to crash testing and advanced composite construction. There was also a permanent fast-response doctor, Professor Sid Watkins, hired by Ecclestone after the avoidable death of Ronnie Peterson in 1978. But F1 had grown complacent and the San Marino Grand Prix weekend punctured its bubble of invulnerability. In response Mosley instituted a science-based safety research program and imposed short-term measures to curtail car performance.

Schumacher won back-to-back titles in 1994 and '95 against a background of questions over his and Benetton's probity. Teammate Jos Verstappen's car caught fire in the pits at the Nürburgring in '94, and Benetton was subsequently found to have tampered with its fuel rigs to speed up the flow. Refueling had been brought back as a strategy

WILLIAMS FW15C

Not only was Williams's 1993 masterpiece a sleek, beautiful car to look at, under its skin was one of the most-advanced F1 cars of all time. Patrick Head's creation featured a slew of electronic gizmos. But sadly the sophisticated technology in the FW15C was soon mothballed. For the start of the following season, driver aids were banned.

The car won ten of the 16 races in 1993, with World Champion Alain Prost taking seven victories to Damon Hill's three. Unusually, the British driver was competing with the number zero, following the absence of the reigning champion's number one entry, thanks to Nigel Mansell's switch to IndyCar.

At the heart of the '93 challenger was its active suspension, which was developed with computer software written by engineering guru Paddy Lowe. The actuators fitted to each wheel were lengthened or shortened via hydraulic pressure as they responded the loads sustained by the car. It meant that adjustments were happening in real time to ensure the chassis was constantly positioned in the most optimum level for aerodynamic efficiency. The setup meant the FW15C wasn't impacted by the usual roll, pitch, or dive of a conventionally suspended car.

Drivers also benefited from traction control, whereby power delivery was cut from Renault's RS5 67-degree 3.5-liter V10 on the detection of wheelspin. This latest iteration featured new con rods and revised inlet and combustion chambers giving the power unit an extra 30bhp, taking it to a total of 780bhp.

The gearbox was fully automatic, while power steering helped the drivers manage the extra power and downforce. The aerodynamic surfaces were the hallmark of legendary designer Adrian Newey, while the electronics extended to provide ABS braking from mid-season onwards.

Finally, there was a feature whereby the rear diffuser could be stalled to reduce the drag of the car. The software also enabled the engine to rev to an extra 300rpm thereby enabling—via a button in the cockpit—a rather useful overtaking aid. But the regulators thought the FW15C and rival cars of the time went a step too far and put more control in the drivers' hands (and feet) for 1994.

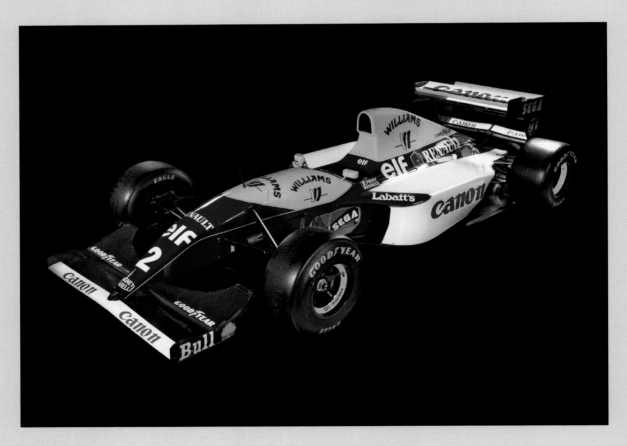

James Mann

1997 Australian GP
Williams did not renew world champion Damon Hill's contract. His replacement was German Heinz-Harald Frentzen who was quick out of the blocks, taking the fastest lap in round one in Australia. Coulthard's win was McLaren's first win in four years.

gimmick to improve the spectacle, but each team was supposed to use identical rigs with a capped fuel flow. Likewise the FIA found illegal traction control software in Benetton's laptops, accessible via a hidden menu, but were unable to prove it had been used. Schumacher's track etiquette was also questionable; he served a race ban for a flag infringement and, in the title decider, deliberately collided with Hill as the Williams went to overtake.

Subsequently Michael set his sights on a new challenge with the struggling Ferrari, importing the technical director and chief designer of Benetton–Ross Brawn and Rory Byrne–to help turn the team around. Fiat, Ferrari's parent company, had rolled the dice early in the decade, bringing in Luca di Montezemolo, team manager under Enzo Ferrari in the 1970s, as chairman in 1991. While Montezemolo's principal focus was the transformation of the road car business, whose product line had grown dated in comparison with rivals, he brought in three-time world champion Niki Lauda as a consultant on the F1 side. Lauda's solution to the team's troubles was to rehire John Barnard as technical director and submit to his demands for a UK-based design office. The quest for a high-powered team principal led Montezemolo, on Ecclestone's recommendation, to poach Jean Todt from Peugeot, where the former rally co-driver had superintended two victories at the Le Mans 24 Hours. Protected by Montezemolo from board interference and the squawkings of the Italian media, Todt set about transforming the Scuderia's outdated working practices. Having recruited Schumacher, Todt's next move was to give his new star a better car, one designed and built under one roof along with the engine, rather than assembled from schematics faxed page by page from the UK.

By 1997 the Scuderia was in a position to fight at the front again, and, as Jacques Villeneuve contrived to make heavy weather of the championship in the dominant Williams, Schumacher took the battle to the final round. There, he once again cynically tried to take his rival out, but ended up in the gravel trap—and was disqualified from the championship.

For 1998 Mosley imposed another set of rules designed to slow cars down, raising the front wing, narrowing the distance between the wheels and the centerline, and specifying grooved tires. Adrian Newey, now technical director of McLaren, was quickest to identify the profound changes to the airflow this caused in the wake of the front wheels. The team had been improving anyway after partnering with Mercedes and the result was two seasons of dominance for Mika Häkkinen, who had survived a bad accident of his own in 1995.

But the constructors' championship in 1999 would fall to Ferrari, a sign of what was to come in the following decade.

(ABOVE)
1997 Argentinian GP
In Argentina the Williams cars blocked out the front row of the grid, with Panis and Michael Schumacher behind. At turn one, Schumacher plowed into the back of Barrichello's Stewart, ending up in the gravel. Villeneuve won ahead of Irvine and Ralph Schumacher.

(ABOVE)
1997 German GP
Gerhard Berger had missed three races with a sinus problem, but was back in his Benetton for the German GP where he put the car on pole. He led the race from start to finish, save for two laps when Giancarlo Fisichella took over before getting a puncture.

(RIGHT MIDDLE)
1997 European GP
At the European GP in Jerez, the two contenders for the title lined up on the front row. Schumacher led Villeneuve into turn one, but on lap 48 of 69 the Canadian tried a pass and Schumacher turned into him, colliding and retired. The incident would earn the German disqualification and hand the championship to Villeneuve.

(RIGHT BOTTOM)
1998 Monaco GP
Coulthard won at Imola. Häkkinen won in Spain, took pole, had the fastest lap, and won in Monaco, proving that the McLaren was the fastest car on the circuit once again. Fisichella was second and Irvine third.

1998 Argentinian GP
The 1998 season was a battle between Ferrari and McLaren with Finn Mika Häkkinen winning the first two races in Australia and Brazil. In Argentina Coulthard was on pole and leading initially, then Schumacher (shown) reeled him and got by when the McLaren driver made a mistake.

(TOP)
1998 Belgian GP
At the start of a very wet Belgian GP, there was a huge accident involving 11 cars that took out seven of them. The race was stopped. At the restart, the rain continued and spare cars were used. Hill's Jordan achieved its first win, with teammate Ralf Schumacher second.

(ABOVE)
1998 Luxembourg GP
In the Luxembourg GP, with two rounds to go, Schumacher and Häkkinen were level on points. The Ferraris held the front row of the grid. Irvine initially took the lead, giving it up to Schumacher. Häkkinen got past to win and won again in Japan taking the championship.

1999 French GP
Ferrari was looking good for the 1999 season when Irvine won in Australia and Michael Schumacher won at Imola and Monaco. Häkkinen took the next two wins in Spain and Canada. Frentzen won for Jordan at Magny-Cours for the French GP.

(BELOW)

1999 British GP
Schumacher sustained a broken leg at Silverstone after hitting the barrier at the fastest part of the circuit. The injury took him out for the next six rounds. McLaren's David Coulthard won the race, with Irvine second and Ralf Schumacher third.

(LEFT)
1999 Austrian GP
With Finn Mika Salo standing in for the injured Schumacher, it was Irvine who scored his second win for Ferrari at the Austrian GP. The McLarens collided on the first lap, knocking pole sitter Häkkinen to the back of the field. He recovered to finish third with Coulthard second.

(BOTTOM)
1999 Japanese GP
It was close at the end of the season at Suzuka in Japan with either Irvine or Häkkinen potential title winners. Michael Schumacher was on pole, but the Finn beat him at turn one and then led. Irvine had started fifth after a poor qualifying and could only manage third. Häkkinen won a consecutive championship.

AYRTON SENNA
(1990, 1991)

NIGEL MANSELL
(1992)

After being disqualified from the 1989 Japanese Grand Prix—and losing the title to teammate Alain Prost—Senna executed his revenge a year later. Heading towards Suzuka's first corner, he ruthlessly took his nemesis out of the race. His foot flat to the floor. When the dust settled, Senna was champion in the most controversial of circumstances.

The Brazilian arrived at the start of 1991 in a McLaren powered by Honda's new V12. Senna won the first time out on the streets of Phoenix, before he returned to São Paulo to the scene of arguably his greatest triumph.

While leading, in the closing stages his shoulders seized in agony. With his McLaren also stuck in gear and the rain starting to fall, Senna somehow managed to reach the checkered flag. But he was overcome—mentally and physically—by the achievement of winning his home race in front of his adoring fans for the first time.

By the end of the year, Senna had clinched his third world title. Williams took a step forward in 1992, so understandably Ayrton was eager to jump ship. He signed with Williams for 1994, but sadly, the relationship with Sir Frank was cut tragically short after his fatal crash at Imola.

With his bushy moustache and broad accent, Nigel Mansell didn't look or sound like a typical Grand Prix driver. But what he lacked in panache he made up for with sublime skill and raw speed. Mansell became the most decorated driver in Williams's history, having started more races and achieved more wins (28) and poles (also 28) than any other of Sir Frank's hires.

Mansell broke his duck in the 1985 European Grand Prix at Brands Hatch and was closely matched against Brazilian teammate Nelson Piquet.

In 1986 "Red Five" scored five wins to Piquet's four. But Nigel was robbed of the world title with an infamous tire blow-out as he was lapping a backmarker along Adelaide's Dequetteville terrace. Despite the crushing blow, he came back stronger in 1987, taking a further six victories. But there was more

World Championship heartbreak when a crash at Suzuka gifted the crown to teammate Piquet. Following two disappointing seasons at Ferrari in 1989 and 1990, *Il Leone* was offered a deal to rejoin Williams—and battled hard in the title stakes—coming up second best to Senna's McLaren.

Finally, Mansell achieved his life's ambition in 1992. In the dominant active ride FW14B, Mansell started the season perfectly, winning the opening five Grands Prix of the year. But despite wrapping up the title as early as August, relations with Williams had deteriorated.

After defecting to IndyCar, Mansell returned to Sir Frank's team for a third and final time in the wake of Senna's death. He proved he was still a force when, at the grand old age of 41, he put his car on pole and won his final race for Williams in the 1994 Adelaide finale.

ALAIN PROST
(1993)

MICHAEL SCHUMACHER
(1994, 1995)

After two unsuccessful seasons at Maranello, Prost took a sabbatical in 1992 and joined Williams the following year, expecting to be teammate to Nigel Mansell. But instead he found himself alongside Damon Hill. The Professor started the year in style, winning at Kyalami in South Africa—and despite a couple of early-season hiccups—went on to take four wins on the trot mid-season. By the time of the Portuguese Grand Prix, it was clear that Prost was not enjoying the politicking in F1 anymore and announced his retirement from the sport.

His start line creep at Monaco and a run up the escape road at Hockenheim that year both received harsh in-race penalties from the stewards. It had been a fractious time fighting with the governing body, so he seemed relieved to be hanging up his helmet. In his final two races, driving the sophisticated FW15C, he finished second both times to arch-rival Senna. In the season-ending Australian Grand Prix, there were smiles between the pair when they shared a podium for the final time.

As a junior driver for the Mercedes sports car squad, Michael Schumacher was given a surprise F1 call-up after the Jordan team's incumbent driver, Betrand Gachot, had been involved in an altercation with a London taxi driver. The young German stunned everyone on his debut, qualifying a sensational seventh at Spa. Despite his race only lasting three corners because of a burnt-out clutch, Schumacher had made his mark.

By the next round at Monza, the promising racer had moved up the grid with Benetton. A year on from his debut at Spa, Michael was victorious. It was the first of 91 wins in a career in which he would rank as one of the very greatest the sport has ever seen.

Schumacher's first quest for the title came in 1994, but it wasn't without controversy. It was a season punctuated with disqualifications, race bans, and ultimately a crash with title-rival Damon Hill at the season finale that decided the championship in Schumacher's favor. He followed it up with a second trophy for Benetton the following year, which was more dominant on track and less controversial off it.

Schumacher brought to Formula 1 a new level of profession-

alism when it came to fitness. He would take a mobile gym to testing, so he could work out after a full day in the car. With barely a bead of sweat on his brow, he quickly demoralized his rivals with his relentless pursuit of physical superiority.

Schumacher was offered a Ferrari contract for 1996 and moved to Italy along with key members of his Benetton team, including designer Rory Byrne and technical director Ross Brawn. It was new Scuderia boss Jean Todt's goal to bring the drivers' championship back to Maranello for the first time since 1979.

After scoring just three wins in the first year together, Schumacher went into the 1997 Jerez showdown with a chance of the title. He lost out to Williams's Jacques Villeneuve—again in controversial circumstances—which led to the FIA excluding him from the official standings.

The following season, he stalled his Ferrari at the start of the Japanese Grand Prix to gift the title to McLaren's Mika Häkkinen. When Schumacher broke his leg on the opening lap of the 1999 British Grand Prix, it meant the Italian team's devotees had to wait another year for the return of its long-awaited drivers' crown.

DAMON HILL
(1996)

JACQUES VILLENEUVE
(1997)

MIKA HÄKKINEN
(1998, 1999)

Despite being the son of Graham Hill, young Damon's journey to Formula 1 wasn't the easiest to navigate. But filled with huge determination, he climbed to the very top of the sport to mirror his father's achievement to become World Champion.

A late-comer to racing, Damon was thrust into the Williams team to partner Alain Prost in 1993, following Mansell's departure, and his first of three consecutive Grand Prix wins started in Hungary. A year later he was partnered by Ayrton Senna and dutifully helped galvanize the team in the wake of the Brazilian's fatal accident.

A brilliant victory in the aggregate-timed 1994 Japanese Grand Prix set-up a title showdown with Michael Schumacher in Adelaide. But the Benetton man's forceful driving cruelly robbed him of the title. A poor year followed in 1995 when he continued to clash again with Schumacher and was outfoxed in both speed and strategy.

With Michael's switch to Ferrari, Hill marched confidently to the 1996 title—just keeping rookie sensation Jacques Villeneuve at bay until the final round. Hill took eight wins to Villeneuve's four, but Damon was still unceremoniously dropped by Williams at the end of the year.

After becoming IndyCar and Indy 500 champion, Jacques Villeneuve spent much of 1995 testing a Williams Formula 1 car, so he was immediately on the pace when he made his debut at the 1996 Australian Grand Prix—a race he oh-so-nearly won.

As the son of the legendary Gilles Villeneuve, young Jacques was something of a maverick, not always conforming to the expected norm. For 1997, Williams put its weight behind Jacques, at the expense of Damon Hill, and the French-Canadian duly delivered.

He scored the team's 100th win at Silverstone and set up a thrilling showdown with Michael Schumacher at the Jerez season finale. It was a great satisfaction to take the crown in only his second year. Villeneuve remained at Williams, but could only manage two podiums in 1998 for a team that had lost Renault engines and its technical ace Adrian Newey.

Villeneuve switched to the newly established BAR team and in time drifted off the pace, ultimately retiring at the end of 2006.

With a raw pace and a laconic charm, Mika Häkkinen stunned on his McLaren debut when he out-qualified established super star Ayrton Senna. The Finn had been brought into the Woking squad at Estoril following the dismissal of American driver Michael Andretti towards the end of the 1993 season.

McLaren boss Ron Dennis enjoyed a close relationship with Mika, especially after Häkkinen had a nasty accident in practice at Adelaide in 1995. The Finn required an emergency tracheotomy at the side of the track and spent time in the hospital after suffering a fractured skull.

After taking his first win for McLaren at the end of 1997, he set about a title-winning campaign the following year. With Mercedes power and a car designed by Adrian Newey, Häkkinen withheld the challenge from Schumacher and Ferrari to take eight wins in '98—and to achieve a neat total of 100 points.

A second championship followed in 1999, with his nearest challenger now Eddie Irvine, after Ferrari team leader Schumacher had broken his leg at Silverstone.

THE
⑥ 2000s

Despite the presence of major tech companies as sponsors, Formula 1's competitors barely registered a bump in the road with the bursting of the dot-com bubble in March 2000. But millennial angst was building elsewhere as old grievances over money and power gained fresh impetus.

2002 Hungarian GP
Despite Ferrari team orders giving preference to Michael Schumacher, teammate Rubens Barrichello won four races. In Hungary for round 13, it was a 1-2 finish for the Ferraris—Barrichello first and Schumacher second winning him the championship.

In the 1980s Max Mosley and Bernie Ecclestone challenged the establishment. Now they *were* the establishment. And, ironically, among the most powerful antagonists ranged against them were the very car manufacturers they had worked so hard to woo into F1. Formula 1 in the 2000s would be dominated by the fall-out of complex behind-the-scenes negotiations, at the center of which was Ecclestone's family trust company SLEC, an offshore Russian-doll structure into which Bernie had spirited F1's commercial rights.

The acrimony reflected the ballooning value of TV deals to F1's income and, through distribution of prize money, the competitors. More than ever, this was a cash-hungry business; where at the turn of the 1990s, teams might have employed between 100 and 200 staff, now these figures were reaching beyond 700. Ever more sophisticated data capture required more engineers and computational power to analyze. Many teams had more than one wind tunnel running 24/7.

Despite all this widely distributed brainpower and infrastructure, very few competitors could challenge Ferrari and Michael Schumacher consistently as Michael racked up five consecutive drivers' championships from 2000 onwards. At Benetton in the 1990s, technical director Ross Brawn had been among the first to grasp the strategic implications of refueling, often running rings around Williams even when they had a faster car. At Ferrari he and Schumacher continued this tradition, though in the early 2000s they generally had the fastest cars on the grid at their disposal too. Williams, having formed a partnership with BMW after Renault's withdrawal, seldom made the most of the increasingly powerful German V10s. In this era, Ferrari set a template for F1 strategy that stands to this day: Brawn's strategic savvy combined with a highly disciplined pit crew drilled by former Lotus mechanic Nigel Stepney, car designs optimized around small fuel tanks to "run light" (and, therefore, fast) between fuel stops, and Schumacher's ability to be quicker than anyone else on his laps into and out of the pits. Since 1994 the pitlane had been subject to an electronically governed speed limit (initially 120 kmh [75 mph] under race conditions, 100 kmh [62 mph] from 2004 onwards). Schumacher was a master of judging his entry to the pitlane perfectly so he was flying all the way up to the line marking the speed-limited zone; on the way out he had an almost supernatural feel for the grip available on the new tires.

And in the court of popular opinion, at least, Ferrari had a more than sympathetic ear from the governing body. By the end of the decade, social media enabled disgruntled fans to voice their partisan displeasure publicly and without filter. In the early 2000s, magazine and newspaper letters pages, along with web forums, provided the

(BELOW LEFT)
2000 Brazilian GP
The new millennium saw new regulations of 3-liter V10 engines for all. Ferrari was quick out of the blocks with three consecutive wins for Schumacher in Australia, Brazil, and San Marino. Schumacher leads Jarno Trulli in the Jordan at Interlagos.

(BELOW RIGHT)
2000 British GP
The British GP's move from its usual summer slot to Easter made it wet for qualifying. Ferrari's Rubens Barrichello secured pole alongside Heinz-Harald Frentzen's Jordan and led for the first 30 laps before spinning. McLaren driver David Coulthard won.

(OPPOSITE TOP)
2000 German GP
For round 11 in Germany at Hockenheim, Coulthard and Schumacher were on the front row. Barrichello was back in 18th after an oil leak forced him to drive the spare car. During a wet race, Barrichello worked his way through the field to take his first F1 win.

(OPPOSITE BOTTOM)
2000 Japanese GP
Häkkinen won in Hungary and again in Belgium, giving him four wins to Schumacher's five. The two-horse championship was close right up to the penultimate round in Japan where a win for the German driver clinched his third title.

(ABOVE LEFT)
2001 Malaysian GP
Ferrari showed its dominance again in 2001 with wins for Schumacher in rounds one and two ahead of Coulthard and teammate Barrichello. In Malaysia a tropical downpour forced many cars into the gravel traps. Schumacher held on to take his sixth consecutive win.

(ABOVE RIGHT)
2001 San Marino GP
San Marino saw the Williams team return to winning, with Michael Schumacher's little brother Ralf taking the top step. The race was a battle of attrition that saw only 12 of 20 cars finish. It was the first time two brothers had won an F1 race.

(LEFT)
2001 Austrian GP
McLaren driver David Coulthard took his second win of the season in Austria ahead of the two Ferraris despite starting down the grid in seventh place. The Scotsman eked out his fuel, allowing him to stay out longer before pitting and giving him the advantage and the victory.

main platforms for those wits who liked to quip that FIA stood for Ferrari International Assistance. As with all cognitive biases, of course, those who took this position ignored those occasions when the Scuderia didn't get a free pass from the regulator.

Although Mika Häkkinen had won the drivers' championship with McLaren in 1999—assisted by Schumacher missing several rounds with a broken leg—Ferrari won the constructors' title by four points. A controversy at the penultimate round of the season, the first to be held in Malaysia, cast a long shadow over those to come. Schumacher returned and helped teammate Eddie Irvine's fading championship hopes by holding up the McLarens while Irvine cantered to victory, but, two hours after the race, both Ferraris were disqualified after the cars were deemed illegal during the scrutineering process. The "barge boards"—vertical plates positioned on either side of the cockpit to condition the airflow around the sidepods—didn't comply with the rules. Irvine's disqualification meant Häkkinen and McLaren were world champions until the following Saturday, when the disqualification was reversed on appeal. Although Mika got the job done at the following Grand Prix, the appeal cost McLaren the constructors' championship and shook the team's faith in the sport's governance.

(ABOVE)
2002 Malaysian GP
Ferrari's dominance continued into 2002 with Michael Schumacher winning 11 out of 17 rounds and standing on the podium at every race. But it was Ralf Schumacher who snatched a win in his Williams for the Malaysian GP in Sepang with teammate Juan Pablo Montoya runner up.

(RIGHT)
2001 Hungarian GP
Michael Schumacher's win in Hungary secured his fourth drivers' title with four rounds to go. By the end of the season, he had won nine out of 17 races and was 58 points ahead of nearest rival Coulthard.

BEHIND THE SCENES

MANUFACTURER POWER

One of the great threats to Formula 1 in the early 2000s was its spiraling, exorbitant costs. Much of the spending was profligate too. For example, teams were preparing special cars just for a few laps of qualifying. Engines were fitted that could produce extra power but could last no more than 50 km (31 miles). The FIA initiated a series of measures to help bring down sky-high expenditures. But almost all them were baulked at—impossible to achieve, the teams and manufactures said.

By 2003 seven major car companies were involved in supplying engines for Formula 1: Ferrari, BMW, Mercedes, Renault, Honda, Toyota, and Ford. Between them they were spending more than €1.5 billion a year. Because costs were so steep, they started to demand more of the revenues Formula 1 accumulated. Unless there was a fairer distribution of income (Bernie Ecclestone was talking half), they would go it alone.

Together the rebel teams formed a union called FOTA (the Formula 1 Teams Association) and engaged with investment bankers, law firms, and sports management groups to formulate plans for a breakaway series: they called it the Grand Prix World Championship (GPWC).

But despite its protestations, a rival series was never a credible threat. Motor racing is not as simple as other sports that might have multiple rival governing bodies—such as boxing. "Unlike motor racing, those sports do not need massively expensive racing circuits that depend on licenses from the governing body for their everyday business," said former FIA President Max Mosley. "They can hold an event almost anywhere. In motor sport, even rallies need the local government, police, insurance companies, none of whom feel comfortable without the blessing of the established sporting authority and its safety experts."

As time wore on, the solidarity of FOTA weakened. Mosley explained simply in his autobiography that "Bernie was able to split them, firstly by paying Ferrari over the odds, then picking off the rest."

With the global economic downturn at the end of the decade, the manufacturers suddenly scarpered. Ford had already quit, then Honda withdrew, quickly followed by Toyota and BMW. Their departures could have seriously damaged F1. But Mosley had managed to push through his proposals to bring costs down: testing was banned, parc fermé was introduced on Saturday evening to stop qualifying cars, more parts were standardized, and engine usage was restricted. In due course, a budget cap was eventually set to ensure the teams had financial security. The age of manufacturer excess was over.

(ABOVE)
2002 Monaco GP
McLaren suffered reliability issues with the MP4-17 throughout the season, particularly with Räikkönen's car. Coulthard did better and won again in Monaco, taking the lead from pole sitter Montoya on lap one and holding onto the flag.

(RIGHT)
2002 Spanish GP
For round five in Spain, Schumacher achieved the Grand Slam: taking pole, fastest lap, and the win. Ferrari teammate Barrichello did not start after a gearbox failure on the grid.

McLaren and Häkkinen therefore entered the 2000s in a state of discombobulation, not helped by their new Mercedes V10's predisposition to blow up. Three consecutive DNFs (did not finish) for Schumacher mid-season helped Mika get his mojo back and take the fight to his rival. Most dramatically, at Spa, after Michael put him on the grass, Mika slingshot around a backmarker to execute one of the most spectacular overtaking moves of all time. Still, Schumacher sealed the championship at the penultimate round, and in early 2001, Häkkinen had scary incidents in Australia and Brazil, which shook his confidence and competitiveness. Michael sealed his fourth world championship with three rounds left to run as Mika announced a "sabbatical" from which he never returned. Schumacher banked his fifth, sixth, and seventh drivers' championships in quick succession, as Ferrari continued to dance beyond its competitors on the technical front, introducing a radical lightweight seamless-shift gearbox in 2002. That season's Ferrari, along with its 2004 car, were two of the most successful in F1 history. Even the great Adrian Newey was hard-pressed to follow. In his own autobiography, Newey describes the 2002 McLaren

(ABOVE)
2003 Australian GP
With the Belgian GP cancelled due to a row about tobacco advertising, there were just 16 rounds for the 2003 calendar. Ferrari's dominance was challenged at the start of the season by McLaren, with Coulthard winning in Australia and Räikkönen in Malaysia.

as "flawed, not one of my best" and his 2003 design, the MP4-18, was bold in every aspect but proved fundamentally flawed and was never raced. Newey blamed a new committee-style management structure imposed by McLaren after Jaguar made a bid to poach him.

Ferrari's victory streak had a stultifying effect on TV viewing figures. And despite the perception that the FIA had a favorable outlook when it came to Ferrari, alarms were ringing in the corridors of power. Alarmed at the increasing costs of racing, Mosley was already bringing in regulations aimed at capping the number of new engines and gearboxes teams could use, and restricting the number of days on which they could test. Controlling this would also, he believed, improve the on-track spectacle by limiting the amount of performance-improving data that could be gathered outside race weekends. The nagging voice of Ecclestone was also detected when Mosley began to tinker with the technical and sporting regulations explicitly to spice up the on-track spectacle. The qualifying system went through many iterations, partly to introduce an element of uncertainty to the results, but chiefly to service demands from broadcasters, via Ecclestone, that cars should be on track throughout the session.

All other factors being equal, the grip levels offered by a circuit would steadily increase as more rubber was laid down by the cars, so the action in qualifying tended to be concentrated at the end of the hour when the track was at its fastest. The idea of having a specific qualifying hour, rather than deciding grid positions based on fastest lap times in any practice session, dated from 1996. Between 2003 and 2005, the format went through a number of iterations based on drivers taking to the circuit one-by-one and having a single opportunity to set a time. While theoretically more exciting, it was loathed by competitors who viewed it as unfair. Attempts to debug it failed; one format in which grid spots were determined by an aggregate of two sessions—one with low fuel and one with race fuel—was so widely reviled it was dropped after six rounds. In 2006 F1 adopted the multi-element elimination format, which, by and large, prevails today.

(ABOVE)
2003 Monaco GP
Michael Schumacher got back on form,
winning the next three rounds in San
Marino, Spain, and Austria. Colombian
Montoya started from third on the grid and
won in Monaco, beating Räikkönen by just
over half a second.

Another controversial mid-decade change had the welcome, for some, effect of putting Ferrari's dominance on hiatus. Michelin's arrival in 2001 had initiated a tire war, which rapidly became acrimonious. Ferrari's tight partnership with Bridgestone meant the Japanese tires were optimized to suit the Scuderia's cars, so many rivals rushed to embrace Michelin. Tensions escalated to a point where, late in the '03 season, Bridgestone and Ferrari complained about Michelin's front tires having more rubber in contact with the track than the rules permitted. The FIA changed its measurement rubric and found the tires illegal—more fuel for "Ferrari International Assistance" theorists—and Michelin had to rush out a new, compromised construction. As the cars got ever faster through 2004, Mosley moved to constrain performance again, making aerodynamic changes to reduce downforce, mandating that engines had to last a minimum of two race weekends, and banning tire changes except in the case of punctures. The idea was that to be more durable, the tires would need to be based on harder (and therefore slower) rubber. But Bridgestone was already operating several steps harder than Michelin because it favored a stiffer sidewall construction that generated more heat at the contact patch. This, combined with Ferrari having to move away from a design concept optimized for frequent tire changes, led to the Scuderia winning just one race in 2005—the ridiculous Indianapolis Grand Prix where just six cars started.

(LEFT)

2003 Brazilian

At Interlagos Barrichello was on pole, but after a red-flag following a huge accident for Alonso's Renault on lap 54, Räikkönen was announced the winner. The result would be overturned later due a timing issue, promoting second-place Jordan driver Fisichella to the top step—his first and Jordan's final F1 win.

(BOTTOM)

2003 United States GP

Michael Schumacher extended his lead in the championship over Montoya, winning at the United States GP at Indianapolis from ninth on the grid. Montoya finished sixth after a drive-through penalty for causing a collision with Barrichello, ending his title challenge.

2004 Bahrain GP
Bahrain and China hosted the only two new races for 2004. Ferrari continued to prove its superiority over the rest of the field, winning 15 of 18 rounds. At the new Sakhir circuit, Michael Schumacher won pole, fastest lap, and the race. Barrichello was second and BAR driver Jenson Button third.

Wider change was coming. At Ferrari, Todt had an eye on a position further up the corporate food chain, Byrne was considering a well-earned retirement, and Brawn planned a sabbatical. In amongst all the succession planning, there was the question of what to do about Schumacher, who had made his debut as a fresh-faced 21-year-old but was now in his mid-30s. Increasingly, F1 was a young man's game. In 2000 Jenson Button arrived at the age of 20 with just two seasons of single-seater experience. The following season, 21-year-old Kimi Räikkönen made his debut amid concerns that he had only contested 23 car races. Also that year, 19-year-old Fernando Alonso contested his first Grand Prix with the back-of-the-grid Minardi team, but since he was managed by Benetton team principal Flavio Briatore, he was pre-destined for greater things.

2005 UNITED STATES GRAND PRIX

The atmosphere on the Indianapolis grid for the 2005 United States Grand Prix was febrile. I recall trying to listen into a huddle of TV crews and journalists who were grilling F1 supremo Bernie Ecclestone. Would 14 cars really come into the pits to retire before the start? It didn't seem possible. But my heart sank when they did.

For years Formula 1 had tried to win favor with the U.S. audience. Throughout the 1980s, the sport lurched from one city street track to another. At the turn of the century, it had found a home at Indianapolis. But there was little respect from F1 for the hallowed home of the Indy 500. An uninspired infield course was built, and the Brickyard's famous Turn 1 was driven *the other way* around. Michael Schumacher had even enquired whether the famous strip of original bricks could be smoothed down so as not to hinder his launch off the grid.

During Friday practice of the 2005 United States Grand Prix, two accidents occurred that would have a lasting impact on the relationship between F1 and the U.S. fanbase.

The Toyota TF105s of Ralf Schumacher and Ricardo Zonta both suffered left-rear tire failures. After an investigation by Michelin's engineers, they discovered another half a dozen problems amongst the other six teams running their rubber. The issues were attributed to the unusual lateral/vertical loadings caused by the high-speeds on the final banked corner on the lap. As a result, Michelin advised its teams that they do no more than ten cumulative laps for the remainder of Saturday practice.

Meanwhile, the six Bridgestone runners—Ferrari, Jordan, and Minardi—had no issues running flat-out through that corner. Because one-third of the grid was not affected, it was impossible to reach an unanimous decision to tame the cars through the banked Turn 13.

The Michelin-shod teams demanded a chicane be built, but the FIA was adamant that alterations to a circuit must comply to their own rigorous safety procedures and could not be simply changed overnight. Other suggestions included a speed limit for that corner. But would Bridgestone runners have adhere to this? Would there be an alternative racing line for the slower cars? Perhaps the Michelin teams could drive through the pits on every lap?

As the clock ticked down to the race start, the deadlock remained. The Michelin runners withdrew from the race and just six cars took the start. Michael Schumacher scored his 84th Grand Prix victory, the hollowest of his career.

Michelin refunded the Indy race-goers, but then withdrew from F1 at the end of the following year. The sport has only had a sole tire suppler since then, first Bridgestone then Pirelli took over in 2010. Indianapolis hosted its last F1 race in 2007, as a new, permanent home was built in Austin, Texas, and the popular Circuit of The Americas venue successfully fostered a new relationship with Formula 1.

2005 United States GP

For the U.S. GP, only six cars competed after all the Michelin tired cars withdrew on safety grounds due to the banked circuit at Indianapolis. The Bridgestone-shod teams—Ferrari, Minardi, and Jordan—raced in front of a disappointed crowd. Michael Schumacher won his only victory of the season.

(LEFT)
2004 Monaco GP
Renault driver Jarno Trulli was the only one to upset Michael Schumacher's rhythm of 12 consecutive wins. Trulli won in Monaco after the German collided with Montoya in the tunnel following the safety car.

(BELOW LEFT)
2004 Belgian GP
In the Ardennes forests of Belgium, Trulli narrowly beat Michael Schumacher to take pole, with Renault teammate Alonso third. During an accident-packed race, Räikkönen started tenth, steadily moved up the field, and scored McLaren's only win of the season.

By the middle of the decade, these young men had marked themselves out as the future of F1. In 2003 Alonso, age 22, became the youngest Grand Prix winner of all time, beating Bruce McLaren's record that had stood since 1959. Five years later it would be beaten again. Alonso's rise mirrored that of his Renault team as the road car manufacturer committed huge resources following its acquisition of Benetton in 2001. In this era the team operated two separate design groups, both working under technical director Mike Gascoyne, but with one working on the present car while the other developed next year's. It was Alonso and Renault who toppled Schumacher and Ferrari in 2005 and again in '06 before Alonso—sorting the deal himself, suprising his own manager—moved to McLaren. Honda also committed increasing sums to F1, acquiring the British American Racing organization (formerly Tyrrell) and establishing Button as its star. This proved less successful since Button didn't win a Grand Prix until 2006, not that this prevented him becoming an obsession among British tabloid newspapers. Räikkönen, poached by McLaren from the midfield Sauber team (in a deal so financially lucrative that Sauber was able to build a new wind tunnel), also challenged for the '05

(ABOVE)
2004 Chinese GP

At the inaugural Chinese GP in Shanghai, Michael Schumacher started from the pit lane after an engine change. He had already won his seventh drivers' title and could only manage 12th. The victory went to Barrichello, with Button and Räikkönen behind.

(RIGHT)
2005 San Marino GP

A new FIA regulation for 2005 was no tire changes except for weather. The Renaults looked fast from the start, with Fisichella winning in Australia and Alonso in Malaysia, Bahrain and Imola after Räikonen retired and an epic battle for the lead with Micheal Schumacher.

title before the car reliability let him down. Just as disaffection with McLaren set in, Räikkönen's managers received an offer from Ferrari (Montezemolo himself) to replace Schumacher in 2007. A rather surprised Michael was presented with Räikkönen's hiring as a fait accompli and given the opportunity to announce his "retirement" at the 2006 Italian Grand Prix.

Further cost-cutting measures included the replacement of 3-liter V10 engines with 2.4-liter V8s with frozen specifications and the imposition of a universal electronic Engine Control Unit to prevent teams employing traction control. By the middle of the decade, manufacturers were beginning to balk at the continued expense. Ford was first to topple, selling Jaguar Racing to the Red Bull soft drink empire in 2005. This business was regarded as such a joke that when Adrian Newey announced his intention to move there, McLaren didn't even force him to serve his contractual notice period. It would come to regret that.

Hiring Alonso would also prove to be a mis-step–or at least, hiring him at the same time as promoting its young prodigy, Lewis Hamilton, to an F1 seat. Hamilton, the first driver of color to reach the peak of motorsport, burned with an ambition to match his extraordinary talent. He would be number two to nobody, putting him in almost instant conflict with his double-world-champion teammate, who expected number-one treatment that he did not receive. Their partnership in 2007 dissolved into an ugly spat over status, leading them to sabotage each other on track and creating an opportunity for Räikkönen to win the drivers' championship at the final round as Hamilton's 21-point lead dwindled to a one-point deficit. But this was just part of the intrigue that season as it was discovered that, as part of the wider regime change at Ferrari, Nigel Stepney had been blocked from promotion to a more senior technical position–and stolen a tranche of secret technical documents that he passed to McLaren chief designer Mike Coughlan. Their intention was to jointly seek better jobs elsewhere and keep the blueprints as a reference from which to draw ideas, but the subterfuge was discovered when Coughlan's wife took them to a high street "copy shop" for duplication.

"Spy-gate," as the controversy became dubbed, concluded with McLaren being fined a record $100 million and stripped of its constructors' points. Few would argue that the sum was vindictive and reflected Mosley's long-standing enmity with team boss Ron Dennis. Over the winter, the threat of expulsion from the championship hovered over the team if a forensic examination of its 2008 design bore any trace of Ferrari "DNA."

(OPPOSITE TOP)

2005 Chinese GP

By the final round in China, Alonso, age 24, had already taken the drivers' title, the youngest ever, and he won again. Despite both Räikkönen and the Spaniard having won seven races each, the Renault driver appeared on the podium more times.

(OPPOSITE BOTTOM)

2006 Bahrain GP

For the 2006 season, the honors were split equally between Ferrari and Renault with Button's Honda the only other car to win a race in Hungary. Alonso won the first round in Bahrain after a pit stop to change tires brought him out just ahead of Michael Schumacher.

(RIGHT)

2006 San Marino GP

In San Marino Michael Schumacher took pole ahead of the Hondas of Button and Barrichello with Alonso back in fifth. On the first lap, there was a collision at the Villeneuve curve that brought out the safety car. Despite a determined chase by Alonso, Schumacher took the checkered flag.

FERRARI F2004

The domination of Formula 1 by Ferrari at the beginning of the 2000s meant that any number of its cars could have been a contender for the best machine of the decade. But it is perhaps the culmination of the years of work and the evolution of both the F1-2000 and F2002 that led to its 2004 challenger becoming the class of the field.

The car took 15 wins, 12 pole positions, 14 fastest laps, eight 1-2 finishes, and 262 points out of a possible 324. Michael Schumacher scored 13 of those wins and secured the title with four rounds to spare.

Overseen by technical director Ross Brawn, vehicle designer Rory Byrne worked seamlessly with Paolo Martinelli and Gilles Simon on the ultra-reliable 053 V10 to create one of the most impressive cars to emerge from the Prancing Horse's stable.

"The 2003 season was a close call for us," said Brawn at the end of the following year. "We had a fantastic season in 2002 and perhaps that invigorated our opposition. In 2003 we saw that we'd not progressed as much as we should have done—on the cars, on the tires, on the engine. And it takes a while to react to these things. We did sort ourselves out and I think 2004 reflects that."

Compared to its predecessors, the F2004 featured a shortened wheelbase, a lower center of gravity, and revised suspension. Aerodynamic flow was improved through a redesign of the gearbox, bodywork, radiators, and exhaust.

Ferrari also harnessed its relationship with Bridgestone to extract the maximum performance from its tires. Dutch engineer Kees van de Grint worked closely with Schumacher to seek any advantage they could. While the Michelin runners were occasionally better suited to one lap pace and became a qualifying threat, the ability to gain lap time on fresh rubber was particularly powerful for Ferrari. In an eventful French Grand Prix that year, Schumacher triumphed thanks to a brilliant four-stop strategy. The F2004 represented the Maranello's final flourish of domination before Renault finally caught and surpassed them.

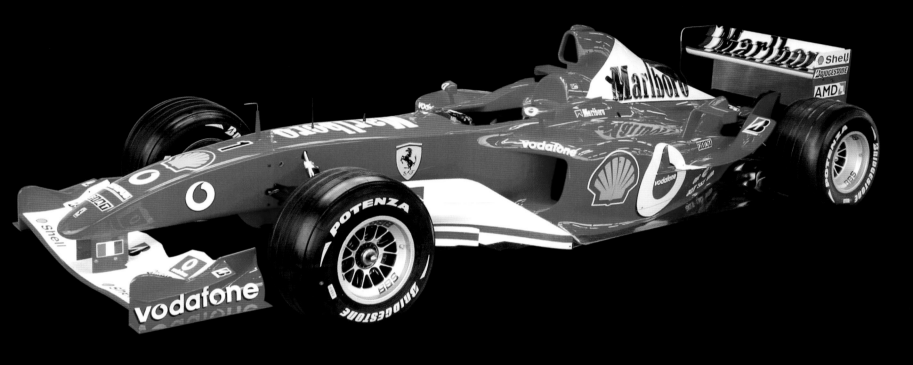

James Mann

McLaren passed the test, and Hamilton, now partnered with the more compliant Heikki Kovalainen, fought a memorable title battle through 2008 against Ferrari's Felipe Massa, prevailing in the final round by one point after making a vital overtake at the penultimate corner. But it had been a bitter campaign tinged by more controversy over officiating when Hamilton was demoted from first to third in the Belgian Grand Prix. And yet this was subsequently overshadowed by a greater scandal when it was revealed that Renault had cheated in the Singapore Grand Prix, ordering Nelson Piquet Jr. to crash deliberately, triggering a Safety Car deployment that put Alonso in a position to win the race from an unfavorable grid spot. Massa had been leading that race until the Safety Car period, when a pitlane blunder led to him leaving the "box" with his fuel hose still attached. The points swing in this race proved crucial in the title battle.

(TOP RIGHT)

2006 Hungarian GP
In Hungary Jenson Button qualified his Honda fourth but was placed 14th on the grid after a penalty for an engine change. After a wet race with numerous accidents, the Honda driver was victorious for the first time.

(TOP LEFT)

2006 Brazilian GP
Renault only won a single race in the second half of the season when Alonso put Felipe Massa into second place in Japan. That result was reversed in the final round in Brazil with Massa winning his home race. Alonso secured his second drivers' title.

(TOP)
2007 Canadian GP
In Canada Hamilton took his first pole with Alonso alongside on the front row. The race was marred by a high-speed accident for Robert Kubica's Sauber and a battle between the McLaren teammates. After the restart, Lewis Hamilton took his first first-place F1 podium.

(RIGHT)
2007 Turkish GP
The third running of the Turkish GP saw Ferrari's Massa on pole next to Hamilton. Both McLarens started poorly, and Räikkönen moved up to second holding the place to the finish making it a Ferrari 1-2.

(OPPOSITE BOTTOM)
2007 Malaysian GP
For 2007 McLaren had two new drivers— double world champion Fernando Alonso, who had left Renault, and rookie Lewis Hamilton. Räikkönen won the first race in Australia for his new team, Ferrari, and Alonso round two in Malaysia.

(OPPOSITE TOP)
2007 Brazilian GP

By the final round in Brazil, Hamilton had a four-point lead over Alonso and seven points on Räikkönen. At the start, Alonso passed Hamilton and then Räikkönen passed him before Hamilton suffered a gearbox problem, slowing him to seventh place at the flag. The championship went to the Finn by one point.

(OPPOSITE BOTTOM)
2008 Canadian GP

Hamilton won straight out of the blocks in Australia for the 2008 season. Then again at Monaco in round five with the Ferraris sharing the other four races equally. In Canada Polish driver Robert Kubica took the top step with BMW Sauber teammate Nick Heidfeld second.

In an uncompetitive year, Renault's team had been under pressure from above to achieve better results. Ditto Honda, who had tempted Ross Brawn away from his sabbatical to become team principal. Arriving at the start of that 2008 season, Brawn quickly concluded the car was a basket case and channeled all resources to the 2009 project. Here there was opportunity because Mosley was wheeling out a new technical formula to encourage overtaking, with wider front wings and narrower rear ones, combined with electrical push-to-pass systems augmenting engine power.

Honda would never see the benefit of a cash-intensive program in which the final car was the result of ideas cherry-picked from the work of three separate design teams. In December 2008, spooked by road car sales plummeting in the global financial crisis, Honda announced an immediate withdrawal from F1. Toyota, BMW, and Renault would soon follow. Brawn acquired Honda's team for a nominal £1 and, despite having to make staff cuts and run on a skeleton budget, ran Button to the world title. McLaren, who had kindly facilitated a Mercedes engine supply "for the good of the sport," could only look on aghast as the German manufacturer bought Brawn at the end of the year.

Along with Williams and Toyota, Brawn had spotted a loophole in the regulations that enabled them to run a twin-plane diffuser between the rear wheels, boosting aerodynamic downforce. It wasn't quite as advantageous as folklore made out–neither Toyota nor Williams won a race–but it was useful. When the FIA declared the devices legal, the other teams were outraged, believing it to be a politically motivated swipe by Mosley against McLaren and Ferrari for their prominent role in the Formula One Teams Association, a thorn in his side.

At the end of the year, FOTA would have its way. Mosley, embattled by tabloid revelations about his private life, the death of his son from a drug overdose, and more political ructions surrounding his attempts to expand the grid by opening a handful of entries to low-budget teams running homologated powertrains, stood down. Was this a victory of the competitors against the establishment? Only partially.

(ABOVE)
2008 Brazilian GP

Going in to the final round at São Paulo, Hamilton was seven points ahead of Massa and needed to finish fifth if the Brazilian won his home race. As the rain came down, Massa comfortably led from pole and won. Vettel held fifth ahead of Hamilton, but both passed Timo Glock's Toyota on the final lap, giving the title to the Englishman.

(ABOVE)
2008 Italian GP

Sebastian Vettel became the youngest driver to win a GP when he beat McLaren's Heikki Kovalainen at Monza by 12 seconds to take his and Toro Rosso's first F1 victory. The race started behind a safety car due to the extremely wet conditions. Vettel led from pole to finish line.

2009 Monaco GP

At the end of the 2008 season, Honda withdrew from F1 and sold the team to former technical director Ross Brawn. The team retained drivers Barrichello and Button and switched to the Mercedes powerplant. The combination proved superb, and Button won six out of the first seven races. In Monaco it was a Brawn 1-2.

2009 British GP

KERS (kinetic energy recovery systems) was introduced as an option, but only McLaren, Ferrari, Sauber, and Renault included it in their power trains. At the British GP in Silverstone, Vettel took his second win of the season for Red Bull, having been promoted from the junior team Toro Rosso.

(ABOVE)
2009 Belgian GP
In Belgium the pack was shaken as Fisichella took pole in the Force India ahead of Trulli's Toyota and Heidfeld's Sauber. After a series of collisions and pit stops, Räikkönen's Ferrari came out ahead and won with Fisichella second.

(RIGHT)
2009 Brazilian GP
Red Bull won the last three races of the 2009 season, but it wasn't enough to catch Button who took the drivers' title by nine points. Here's Australian Mark Webber winning the Brazilian GP after getting ahead of pole-sitter Barrichello; he would finish fourth in the championship.

MICHAEL SCHUMACHER
(2000, 2001, 2002, 2003, 2004)

Schumacher's status as one of the greatest drivers to have ever competed in Formula 1 was cemented by an extraordinary run of success during the first five years of the new century. Managed by the shrewd Jean Todt, with technical expertise from Ross Brawn, the German ace dominated the first half of the decade with Ferrari.

It had been 21 years since Jody Scheckter last won the drivers' title for the Scuderia, but Schumacher finally achieved that all-important quest. He took nine wins in 2000, and another nine a year later, to commence his run of five consecutive championships.

But Ferrari's single-minded pursuit of victory could be controversial at times. Michael had won four of the opening five rounds of 2002, but at the next race in Austria, the team imposed orders in favor of the points leader. On the final lap,

poor Rubens Barrichello was forced to give up victory for his teammate. The fans were unimpressed, particularly as Michael was able to wrap up the championship as early as July that year.

The supremacy continued as Schumacher was aided by a remarkable level of reliability. Although McLaren's Kimi Räikkönen ran him close in 2003, the German topped the points tally once again and in 2004 the steamroller culminated with Schumi winning 12 of the first 13 races of the year. He stayed at Maranello until the end of 2006, thereafter making a comeback with Mercedes after a few years away. Soon after retirement in 2013, Schumacher suffered a skiing accident. Since then the seven-time world champion has sadly remained out of the public eye, recovering from his life-changing injuries.

FERNANDO ALONSO
(2005, 2006)

One of the most competitive drivers to grace Formula 1, it's hardly surprising Fernando Alonso would become the youngest driver to win an F1 race (2003 Hungarian Grand Prix, age 22). Two years later he broke Emerson Fittipaldi's 33-year record to become the youngest driver to win the World Championship (Max Verstappen has since become the youngest GP winner, while Sebastian Vettel the youngest champion).

As he approaches his mid-40s, Alonso has enjoyed a remarkable longevity. The Spaniard continues to race with the same competitive spirit he first manifested 24 years earlier.

Alonso burst onto the scene with Renault to finally break years of Ferrari dominance. The youngster provided a breath of fresh air as he romped to his first of back-to-back championships for Flavio Briatore's Enstone team in 2005.

Aided by new rules that banned in-race pit stops, his Michelin-shod Renault fared better than the Ferraris on Bridgestones. The following year he won seven Grands Prix—as did Schumacher—but it was Alonso who took his second title by 13 points.

Fernando's ambition, prodigious talent, and intelligence behind the wheel led many to think he'd win multiple titles. Ultimately though, after spells with McLaren, Ferrari, Alpine, and Aston Martin (to date), he's never achieved a third crown. His last Grand Prix victory came in 2013.

KIMI RÄIKKÖNEN
(2007)

Every now and again a driver emerges with such natural talent, he can be plonked straight into a Grand Prix car and shine. Finland's Kimi Räikkönen was one of those prodigies. He'd only driven 23 car races before the Sauber team decided to give him his Formula 1 debut. At the age of 21, Kimi scored points with sixth place at his first race at Melbourne in 2001. Despite his ice cold demeanor, he was the hottest driver in the sport, with first McLaren, then Ferrari acquiring his services.

With a laid-back persona that was virtually horizontal, Räikkönen became Michael Schumacher's successor at Ferrari. He won on his Maranello debut in 2007 and remarkably put together a championship campaign in a year embroiled by the "Spygate" scandal.

In the final race of the year, three drivers had the chance to take the title for the first time since 1986. Despite Kimi being seven points behind the McLaren of Lewis Hamilton (and three behind Alonso) going into the Brazilian Grand Prix showdown, Kimi secured his sixth win against-the-odds to claim the World Championship.

Räikkönen never reached the same heights again, but continued to have a long career in the sport. In his 349 starts he managed a total of 21 victories, 18 poles, and 46 fastest laps. He was admired by fans who loved his no-nonsense, monosyllabic approach to Grand Prix racing.

LEWIS HAMILTON
(2008)

As a young boy, Lewis Hamilton famously approached McLaren boss Ron Dennis and asked for his telephone number, telling him he would one day race for his team. Dennis supported Hamilton through a meteoric junior single-seater career and incredibly gave the British driver his wish, offering him a Formula 1 seat in 2007.

Hamilton made an immediate impact, overtaking his double world champion teammate Fernando Alonso at the first corner of his debut race. It was a remarkable rookie season in which he nearly won the championship—and finished on equal points with Alonso.

It was clear Hamilton was a special talent who would go on to be statistically the greatest Grand Prix driver of all time. In his second season, he took five wins—including a brilliant home performance in the Silverstone rain—to put himself in contention for the crown.

The drivers' championship was decided in the most dramatic of climaxes. At the last corner of the final race of the year in Brazil, with the rain falling, Lewis passed Timo Glock to secure fifth place and sensationally snatch the title from race winner Felipe Massa. The Brazilian had already crossed the finish line and thought he'd done enough. "Felipe did a fantastic job, but when I passed Glock I thought I was going to explode, I think everyone was," recalled Hamilton.

JENSON BUTTON
(2009)

In 2000, Jenson Button made his F1 debut with Williams at age 20, before moving to Renault and then BAR-Honda. With a decent car underneath him, Jenson was hard to beat, but too often in his career he drove machinery that was below-par.

There was shock in the winter of 2008 when Honda suddenly decided to quit F1. It left the entire Brackley operation in limbo. Team boss Ross Brawn made a concerted bid to save the organization and founded Brawn GP. To everyone's surprise, a clever interpretation of the new regulations led to a rocketship of a car. Jenson Button led Rubens Barrichello to score a extraordinary 1-2 at the season-opening Grand Prix of 2009.

The Briton went on to win six of the first seven races of the year as Brawn GP made history, becoming the first constructor to win the title in its debut season. Although Button didn't win another race after mid-season, he did enough to take the crown at the penultimate round in Brazil. He accrued further victories with his switch to McLaren, but never again reached the dizzying highs of that extraordinary title season.

THE ⑦ 2010s

2016 Japanese GP
In Japan for race 17, Rosberg saw his final win of the season. He took the drivers' championship title by five points from Hamilton after finishing second in each of the remaining rounds.

FIA president Max Mosley's fall came about chiefly because his old ally Bernie Ecclestone decided he had become a liability. When Mosley came to power, he had claimed he would have little involvement because "F1 ran itself." By the end, all the great work he had done to champion safety–not just on track but in the road car world–had been overshadowed by the bullying tactics he and his regime employed to get their own way. This rancor had led to the vital Concorde Agreement only being re-signed year-on-year, after protracted wrangles, rather than a ten-year term from 2007, and by 2009 FOTA had made it clear to Ecclestone that the price of a peaceful settlement was Mosley's head on a silver platter. Once they got their wish, the unanimity of the members evaporated and Ecclestone successfully employed his old divide-and-rule tactics to break FOTA. When former Ferrari team principal Jean Todt was voted in as Mosley's successor, the cynics dusted down the old "Ferrari International Assistance" tropes–but what marked out Todt's regime was a light-touch approach to the competitors and the commercial rights holder.

Those cynics who believed Todt to be Mosley's continuity candidate had a swift reality check. Having inherited a number of Mosley measures in 2010, he allowed some of the most prized ones to die. In the bleak midwinter of 2008–09, seemingly in the midst of a manufacturer-team exodus, and facing the threat of FOTA organizing a breakaway championship, Mosley had announced a tender process for new teams to join the grid in 2010. They would use a cost-controlled "standard" powertrain supplied by Cosworth and Xtrac–and, provided they operated within a $52 million budget cap, they would be granted greater technical freedoms to offset the disadvantage of having

(LEFT)
2010 Chinese GP
In China for round three, Vettel's Red Bull was on pole with Mark Webber alongside. Alonso, in third, picked up a drive-through penalty for jumping the start. As rain fell, world champion Button took the lead. At the flag it was a 1-2 for the McLaren team with Hamilton second.

(BOTTOM)
2010 Bahrain GP
After finishing as runners up for the constructors' title in 2009, Red Bull was fired up for the new season. First honors, however, went to new Ferrari signing Fernando Alonso in Bahrain. Teammate Felipe Massa finished second after race leader Sebastian Vettel suffered spark plug problems.

2010 Abu Dhabi GP
Four contenders fought it out for the drivers' title in the final round in Abu Dhabi. Vettel and Hamilton on the front row, Alonso third, and Webber fifth. Button went ahead during the pit stops, but the lead reverted to Vettel, who won the race and his first world championship.

(RIGHT)
2010 British GP
At the British GP, the battle between the Red Bull teammates heated up. Vettel ran wide, trying to beat pole-man Webber into turn one, picking up a puncture in the process. Webber would go on to win his third victory of the season. Hamilton was second and Rosberg third.

less money to spend. Within weeks of the three chosen teams being announced that summer, the FIA and FOTA concluded a truce over the breakaway threat. The teams committed to a voluntary so-called "Resource Restriction Agreement," and the FIA quietly dropped the budget-cap idea as Todt slipped his feet under the executive desk. By 2016 all the new teams that joined the grid in 2010 were dead.

Kinetic Energy Recovery Systems (KERS), a Mosley initiative to lend some environmental credibility and road-car synergies while adding overtaking opportunities, were dropped by mutual consent of the entrants ahead of a better-considered reintroduction in 2011. Though laudable in concept—recycling power that would have been dissipated as heat under braking into an electrical boost—the execution had been poor since the permitted power boost didn't offset the weight penalty of carrying the devices. But Mosley's proposal to ban in-race refueling did go through, and it had fascinating ramifications.

In the refueling era, pitstop length was determined by the amount of fuel being put into the car at the cap of 12 liters per second. Generally this took eight or nine seconds, giving a degree of flexibility in terms of how long the mechanics at each corner of the car could take to remove the old wheels and tires and fit fresh ones. Now the only limit was how fast the mechanics could change the wheels—and this triggered an arms race in both equipment and the human performance field. Red Bull, drilled by perfectionist team manager Jonathan Wheatley, led the way in bringing pit stops to below the three-second-mark. It was hitting peaks elsewhere too.

In 2008, driving for Red Bull's junior team, Sebastian Vettel beat Fernando Alonso's five-year-old record to become F1's youngest-ever race winner at 21 years, two months, and 11 days. Elevation to the "main" squad followed, and by the age of 23 he was F1's youngest-ever world champion too. It had taken Adrian Newey three seasons to rid

(ABOVE LEFT)

2011 Canadian GP

In Canada Button broke Vettel's run of three consecutive wins after the race was stopped due to heavy rain. At the restart, the Brit collided with Alonso, dropping him to the back. Button worked his way through the pack to overtake Vettel and win on the final lap.

(ABOVE RIGHT)

2011 German GP

Alonso won his sole race of 2011 at Silverstone, and Hamilton took his second win in round ten at Germany's Nürburgring. Starting from the front row, Hamilton got ahead of pole sitter Webber and held on to the flag.

(ABOVE)

2011 Indian GP

Vettel secured his second world championship at the Japanese GP with four rounds to go despite finishing second. He won again in Korea and India, finishing the season over a hundred points ahead of Button. Here he is arriving in Parc Ferme in India.

(RIGHT)

2012 Chinese GP

The 2012 season was a closer run than the previous year, with 20 rounds under contention. Mercedes and Rosberg scored their first win, both as an F1 team and driver in China, despite protests about their "F duct" technology reducing drag on the rear wing.

(OPPOSITE TOP)

2011 Australian GP

The new season started as 2010 had ended, with Red Bull dominant. Sebastian Vettel took the first two races in Australia and Malaysia. At Albert Park in Melbourne, he won from pole after Hamilton damaged his undertray and was unable to keep up. Russian Renault driver Vitaly Petrov was third.

BEHIND THE SCENES

TV REVOLUTION

There was no television coverage of the first-ever World Championship Grand Prix at Silverstone in 1950. However, the BBC did broadcast a smattering of radio commentary. In the *Radio Times* listings guide published in England on May 5, 1950, it has the schedule for the BBC Light Programme. On the day of the race, it stated that the commentary on the "warming-up lap" and the start of the race would begin at 2:50 pm, before they cut away from Silverstone for The Johnny Paradise Orchestra at 3:15 pm.

That's quite a contrast to the live coverage of every race that is transmitted by 75 TV companies in 180 countries today. During live Formula 1 broadcasts, you can choose to ride on-board with all 20 drivers, listen to their team radio, monitor sector times to the thousandth of a second, know if they are on used or new tires, track their position anywhere on the circuit—and all in 4K ultra-high definition.

The entire TV operation is housed in a mini city just outside the Formula 1 paddock and travels to every race along with hundreds of miles of fiber-optic cables. In Formula 1's TV headquarters in Biggin Hill, London, a 140-strong team handles the constant video and audio streams that are beamed across the globe in the blink of an eye. But covering the sport with nearly 50 cameras positioned around every circuit—including a helicopter gyro-stabilized lens—comes at a cost. The eye-watering sums paid by the TV companies for rights forced them to push the sport behind the pay-wall, while free-to-air broadcasters were left to screen highlights.

Bernie Ecclestone built much of his wealth on selling F1 to television companies, and he saw its potential when it moved from analogue to digital transmissions. But he was never as receptive to the power of the internet—as it was initially tougher to monetize.

The change of F1 ownership in 2017 led to a revolution, particularly in the sport's social media output and the realization that the on-demand giants were the new big players. Allowing cameras into Grand Prix racing's secretive world has opened up the sport to a whole new market. The success of Netflix's *Drive to Survive* docuseries has brought new and younger fans to the sport—particularly in the U.S. And the next big thing is Hollywood. Apple TV's production of the 2025 Brad Pitt-starring *F1* movie—with an 11th team allowed to shoot during race weekends—is set to take F1 to more eyeballs than ever before. Makes you wonder what Johnny Paradise would have made of it all?

Pole sitter and eventual race winner Mario
Andretti is interviewed in the pit lane at
the Japanese Grand Prix, October 1976.

(ABOVE)
2012 Spanish GP
In Spain Williams achieved its first F1 victory in eight years when Venezuelan Pastor Maldonado took the flag in Barcelona. Jumped at the start by Alonso, the Williams driver won back the lead, passing both the Ferrari and Räikkönen's Lotus to win.

(LEFT)
2012 Belgian GP
By round 12 in Belgium, the championship was still wide open with seven drivers vying for the title. At the start there was a collision between Hamilton and Romain Grosjean, who then hit the back of Sergio Pérez's Sauber, launching into the air and landing on Alonso's Ferrari, narrowly missing the driver.

Red Bull's design department of the antiquated attitudes and design processes of the Jaguar Racing days, and he'd targeted the rules change of 2009 as an opportunity to make the best of a clean-sheet approach. Missing the double-diffuser loophole was a mis-step, but by the end of the year, Newey's RB5 was the fastest car in the grid. And, although Fernando Alonso and Jenson Button won the first two rounds of 2010 for Ferrari and McLaren, by the end of that season the same could be said for the RB6. The trend continued with the RB7, RB8, and RB9 as Vettel ran to consecutive world titles between 2010 and 2013.

(ABOVE)
2013 Australian GP
For the first race of 2013 in Australia, Vettel was on pole and led away leaving front-row teammate Webber behind with a KERS problem. The race became all about tire management. Räikkönen moved up the field staying out longer and taking the lead in the Lotus. He went on to win ahead of Alonso.

(RIGHT)
2012 Singapore GP
Vettel found his form again in Singapore having only won one race so far that season. Starting from third on the grid in the hot and humid night race, the German took the lead when Hamilton's gearbox failed. He went on to win and continued winning for the three consecutive races, giving him his third title.

Fundamental to Red Bull's success was the trendsetting concept of running an extreme "rake" angle in which the rear of the car ran higher off the ground than the front, improving the downforce-creation ability of the underfloor diffuser. The effect approximated what happens if you partially cover the end of a hosepipe with your thumb: the water accelerates as it flows through the gap. Red Bull also relocated the exhaust outlets to floor level so the hot air augmented the effect. In subsequent seasons its engine supplier, Renault, would play tricks with engine mapping to keep hot air flowing even when the driver lifted off the accelerator pedal. Vettel proved himself a

(RIGHT)
2014 Canadian GP
In Canada Red Bull driver Daniel Ricciardo broke the chain of wins for Mercedes, taking his career maiden victory from sixth on the grid. With just one lap to go, a huge accident between Massa and Pérez brought the safety car out, ending the race with the Australian in the lead.

(BELOW RIGHT)
2014 Malaysian GP
With a new engine format featuring a 1.6-liter turbo with ERS-K, the 2014 season became a rivalry between Mercedes teammates Nico Rosberg and Lewis Hamilton. Rosberg won the calendar opener in Australia, and Hamilton took pole, fastest lap, and the win in Malaysia.

(OPPOSITE TOP)
2013 Monaco GP
On the twisty tight Monaco street circuit, the Mercedes team filled the front row of the grid. In an accident-packed dramatic race, six cars were damaged, the safety car featuring heavily. At the flag, pole-sitter Nico Rosberg managed to hang on, with Vettel just three seconds behind.

(OPPOSITE BOTTOM LEFT)
2013 Hungarian GP
In Hungary midway through the season, Hamilton won his first race for Mercedes. Starting from pole he swapped the lead with Vettel and Webber. He came out in the lead after the final round of pit stops to win his fourth Hungarian GP. Vettel would win every remaining race that season.

(OPPOSITE BOTTOM RIGHT)
2013 Indian GP
Vettel won in India, giving him an unassailable lead for the championship. He also won the next three races in Abu Dhabi, U.S., and Brazil. He earned a total of 13 victories equaling that of Michael Schumacher to take his fourth and final drivers' title.

master of exploiting this effect in a way teammate Mark Webber couldn't. Having been closely matched through 2010–to the point of colliding while fighting for position in Turkey–the Red Bull drivers took different performance trajectories thereafter.

Red Bull wasn't the only team innovating. McLaren's MP4-25 featured a hidden system, known internally as "RW80" but dubbed "the f-duct" owing to its inlet vent being positioned in the "f" of the Vodafone logo on the car's nose. Ducting from this vent fed through the chassis, along the inside of the cockpit, then divided into further conduits towards the rear of the car via a fluidic switch. Another duct fed into the system via the airbox above the driver's head. In its first iteration, the system was activated by the driver covering a hole in the duct with his knee; later McLaren moved it so he used his elbow. In normal conditions, the air flowing through the system passed through a channel leading out behind the engine cover. While traveling along a straight, the driver would cover the hole in the cockpit duct, triggering the fluidic switch to divert air down a high-level duct towards the upper plane of the rear wing, where it "stalled" the airflow. This dramatically lowered the aerodynamic "drag" caused by the rear wing, yielding a higher top speed.

2014 JAPANESE GRAND PRIX

In the immediate aftermath of the 2014 Japanese Grand Prix, the sport's governing body, the FIA, set up a special accident panel to gain a better understanding of the crash that befell Marussia driver Jules Bianchi.

Under darkening Suzuka skies and heavy rain, Bianchi lost control of his car and hit a recovery vehicle that had been deployed to retrieve the Sauber of Adrian Sutil, which had spun off on the previous lap.

Bianchi suffered a diffuse axonal injury in the accident and died nine months later having never gained consciousness. Although it was determined that safety procedures were followed correctly on the day, the FIA was committed to introducing new safety measures to reduce the likelihood of a similar incident happening again.

The first of these measures was the establishment of a mechanism to reduce a driver's speed in the wake of an accident. In the past it was at the discretion of the driver how much he lifted when approaching a section of the track that was under double waved yellow flags. It was felt the wording in the International Sporting Code that a driver must "be prepared to stop" was perhaps better observed if a mandatory speed limit was introduced.

In the season following Bianchi's accident, if there was a stationary vehicle on track that required assistance from marshals, Race Control would now initiate a Virtual Safety Car (VSC). Rather than have a physical car slow everyone down, the whole track becomes neutralized (so no one can get an advantage) and drivers must reduce their speed by around 30 percent—strictly adhering to a delta time for each sector.

The second major outcome was a change to the cars themselves. Following a phase of development, a new cockpit safety device was introduced. After tests with an aeroscreen were rejected, it was decided in 2018 to fit each car with a halo. This simple, cage-like structure was placed in front and around the cockpit to help deflect objects away from a driver's head.

While there was criticism of the device at the time, particularly with a historical desire to keep F1 as an open-cockpit, open-wheel formula, those dissenters have been silenced after subsequent incidents have occurred where it was clear a driver's life has been saved thanks to the halo's introduction.

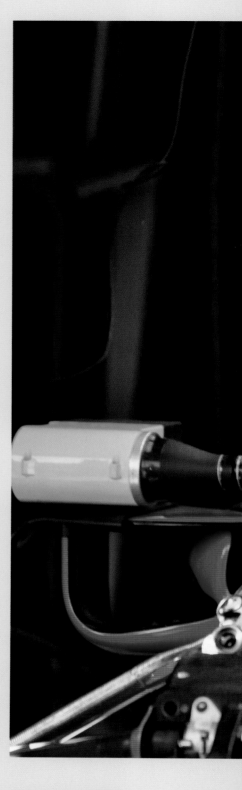

Halo device on 2018 Ferrari SF-71H.

Naturally other teams had to copy the system, but this involved a lot of reverse engineering, often with suboptimal results, because all F1 chassis were homologated after the crash-testing stage and couldn't be changed. For safety reasons, the FIA banned such devices at the end of the year, but Charlie Whiting, the FIA's race director and technical delegate, saw merit in the idea of defeating drag if it could be de-risked. The problem it solved was that the new technical formula brought in for 2009 had not only failed to improve overtaking, it had made the situation worse. As demonstrated by the Honda/Brawn car and followed by others, the wider front wing could be loaded with devices and flow conditioners to steer air around the front wheels. A ban on additional wing elements in the so-called Y250 axis—an area of 250 mm (10 inches) on either side of the centerline—merely opened up opportunities for teams to shape the inner wingtips in such a way that they set up vortices that accelerated airflow between the nose and front wheels. Throughout this decade, front wings would become so critical to overall car performance that cars couldn't follow each other close enough through corners to attack on the straights.

Whiting's solution for 2011 was the Drag Reduction System, a moveable rear-wing plane actuated by a button on the steering wheel, and electronically governed so it can only be deployed in defined areas on each track. Many fans deride it as an artificial overtaking aid, and it still has flaws—cars can end up stalemated in long trains because the car ahead also has DRS—but it remains in the rulebook to this day.

Other events in 2010 would also shape the future of F1. Team orders had been banned since 2002, when Ferrari prompted widespread fury at the Austrian Grand Prix by ordering Rubens Barrichello to cede the lead to Michael Schumacher. At Hockenheim in 2010, Felipe Massa took an early lead ahead of Ferrari teammate Alonso, only to receive the coded message "Fernando is faster than you" along with an apology from race engineer Rob Smedley. Massa duly let Alonso through. It was a clear order and, although Ferrari escaped being excluded from the results, it was fined $100,000. Nevertheless the FIA decided, after much deliberation, that the team orders ban was unpoliceable. At the end of the season, it was struck from the rules.

(BELOW)
2014 German GP
At the German GP at Hockenheim, Hamilton was relegated to the back of the grid after crashing heavily in qualifying. Rosberg took pole. He kept out of trouble from the lead as multiple collisions slowed the competition. Rosberg won his fourth race of the season.

(LEFT)
2014 United States GP
Mercedes drivers were on the podium for every race. Hamilton took the top step 11 times to Rosberg's five. At the U.S. GP in Austin, pole-sitter Rosberg narrowly avoided a collision as Hamilton overtook him on lap 24 to win the race and his second driver's title.

(ABOVE)

2015 Malaysian GP
Defending champions Lewis Hamilton and Mercedes dominated the season, winning three races with honors split ten to six for Hamilton and Rosberg. Vettel who had left Red Bull for Ferrari, won the other rounds starting in Malaysia.

(RIGHT)

2015 Monaco GP
For the first time, a virtual safety car was used during the Monaco GP after Verstappen hit the back of Grosjean's car at Sainte Devote on lap 64 of 78. Hamilton pitted, but on exit Mercedes teammate Rosberg was ahead and went on to win.

A month earlier, in mid-June, Lewis Hamilton and Button finished 1-2 for McLaren in a bizarre Canadian Grand Prix that would come to define F1 until the present day. Bridgestone had been F1's sole tire supplier since 2007 and, under Max Mosley, the FIA had made a number of tweaks to the regulations in the aim of improving the spectacle, including a return to slick tires in 2009 and a rule that all drivers had to use two different tire compounds in each race. Even so, most Grands Prix panned out with just one pit stop, frustrating the stated aim of introducing tactical variation. At Montreal that June weekend, a number of factors came together to deliver a dramatic multi-stop race: resurfaced areas of the track that yielded low grip, changeable weather conditions, and a super-soft tire compound that degraded faster than expected. Ecclestone decreed that in the future all races should be like this—and, when Pirelli won the contract to be F1's sole tire supplier from 2011 onwards, the company committed to making it happen.

(TOP LEFT)

2015 Russian GP

Rosberg was on pole for the second running of the Russian GP in Sochi around the Olympic Park street circuit. Rosberg retired with throttle problems, Grosjean crashed early on, and Räikkönen and Bottas collided. Third place went to Force India driver Sergio Pérez.

(TOP RIGHT)

2016 Spanish GP

Nico Rosberg maintained his form and the Mercedes team its dominance winning the first four rounds of the 2017 season. In Spain for race five, rookie Max Verstappen took his first win for Red Bull. He replaced Daniil Kvyat ahead of the race from Toro Rosso.

(ABOVE)
2016 European GP
There was controversy for round eight at the European GP held on the streets of Baku, Azerbaijan, because the race clashed with the final laps of the Le Mans 24 Hours. Rosberg took to the top step again, leading from pole ahead of Vettel's Ferrari by 18 seconds at the flag.

(RIGHT)
2016 German GP
Hamilton won his sixth race of the season at Hockenheim, compared to Rosberg's five, giving him a six-point lead in the drivers' title standings. Nico started on pole, but Lewis was first by turn one and held the lead ahead of Ricciardo and Verstappen's Red Bulls.

(OPPOSITE BOTTOM)
2015 United States GP
Hamilton took an unassailable lead in the drivers' championship at the U.S. GP in Austin, Texas, beating Rosberg on a damp track. The win ahead of Rosberg secured his second title with three rounds to go despite his teammate winning all the remaining races.

MERCEDES F1 W05 HYBRID

The introduction of hybrid engine regulations to Formula 1 in 2014 presented a huge challenge for the major car manufacturers. Complex packaging of an all-new battery pack and exhaust-fed motor generator led to a significant redesign at the rear of the cars. Even before the first '14 machines hit the track, it was clear Mercedes-Benz High Performance Powertrains had an edge with the new regulations. But perhaps, even team boss Toto Wolff was surprised at just how dominant the F1 W05 Hybrid would be.

One of the decisions that led Formula 1 to adopt hybrid technology was to appease the manufacturers, who were under pressure from increasingly concerned governments (and their electorates) to pioneer sustainable solutions in the face of the growing climate emergency.

The electrification of F1 had already started with the introduction of KERS (a kinetic energy recovery system) in 2009. Mercedes benefitted as it already had in-house hybrid experience through recruitment at its Brixworth engine HQ during the KERS era and separately in the production of its SLS AMG Electric Drive sports car.

Under the engine cover, the turbo compressor was separated from the turbine by a long shaft through the vee of the engine. Positioning the compressor at the front of the power unit allowed shorter plumbing routes for the water-air intercooler, as well as freeing up space to improve airflow to the rear wing.

The aerodynamic superiority of the F1 W05 was supplemented at the front by a cleverly designed suspension wishbone that enhanced the performance of the front wing. It all added up to a package that was on a different competitive level to the opposition.

Lewis Hamilton had made a smart decision to leave McLaren to join Mercedes the year before the hybrid era started. Piloting the W05, he was victorious in 11 of the season's 19 races with teammate Nico Rosberg claiming five wins. It was the first in a golden era for the Silver Arrows as they ascended to win the most successive constructors' titles (eight) in F1 history.

(ABOVE)

2017 Monaco GP
The Ferraris locked out the front row in Monaco with Räikkönen on pole. Vettel stayed out longer during the race, pitting after his teammate and taking the win on the twisty historic street circuit. This propelled him further ahead of Hamilton who could only manage seventh place.

The 2010 season ended with Alonso, Vettel, Webber, and Hamilton in contention for the title. It would rarely get as close until the end of the decade. F1 cars grew ever more ugly as new safety regulations, brought in to reduce "submarining" incidents where one car went under another on impact, meant higher, pointier noses. As with ground-effect cars three decades earlier, the FIA struggled to contain the practice of using exhaust gases and clever engine mapping to augment downforce. FOTA and the Resource Restriction Agreement disintegrated, leaving Mercedes, seemingly the only team to have observed it honestly, at a disadvantage. Their lack of competitiveness was rendered even more public by the high-profile hiring of Schumacher out of retirement for three seasons from 2010. He was a shadow of his former self.

The new Pirellis delivered on brief but proved frustratingly sensitive, a trend the Italian company could never quite dial out. Across the family of compounds, the tires delivered decent grip until the point that grip went "off the cliff" in F1 parlance, but if drivers pushed too hard too soon, that deterioration point would arrive too quickly. Many races settled into dull phases of tire management where everyone in the field was lapping more slowly than they theoretically could. In 2013 Pirelli introduced a new construction based on a steel radial "belt" rather than Kevlar, intending to give better single lap-performance but also faster thermal degradation—the aim being to boost speeds and prevent one-stop races. But a series of punctures at the British Grand Prix prompted them to revert—and the previous construction suited Red Bull's car better. Vettel won nine consecutive races over the final half of the season, matching Alberto Ascari's 60-year-old record. He had already broken many others in preceding seasons.

(RIGHT)
2017 Russian GP

The 2016 world champion Nico Rosberg announced his retirement before the new season. Finnish driver Valtteri Bottas joined the Mercedes team. He won his first race in Russia at the Sochi Autodrom for round four, overtaking both Ferraris at the start.

(BELOW RIGHT)
2017 Malaysian GP

At the Malaysian GP in Sepang, Vettel started at the back of the grid after failing to set a qualifying time due to an engine change. Hamilton was on pole, but the Red Bull cars were faster. Verstappen overtook him on lap four, holding on to win his second F1 victory.

A reset was required and it came in the form of new technical regulations for 2014. Among the existential threats facing F1 was the paucity of engine suppliers. With Honda, Toyota, and BMW gone in the aftermath of the global financial crisis, only Ferrari, Mercedes, and Renault remained. And Renault, which had sold its team to venture capitalists after the Singapore scandal broke, signaled its intention to go unless the engine rules offered some synergy with the future direction of road cars. The new package was framed around a downsized hybrid powertrain, with a turbocharged 1.6-liter V6 internal combustion engine augmented by energy recovery from the brakes and turbo, and limited to consuming just 100 kg (37 gallons) of fuel during a race. Most intriguing of all was the Motor Generator Unit–Heat (MGU-H) element, which opened the possibility of eliminating turbo "lag" by electrically spinning the turbines.

(TOP)

2017 United States GP

Lewis Hamilton took the U.S. GP and his fourth driver's title in Austin, leading nearly from pole to checkered flag with three rounds still to run. The final races were won by Verstappen, Vettel, and Bottas splitting the honors and leaving Hamilton ahead by 46 points.

(ABOVE)
2018 Chinese GP
In China Ricciardo suffered an engine failure in practice and only managed sixth in qualifying with Vettel on pole. Midway during the race, rookie teammates Brendon Hartley and Pierre Gasly collided and the safety car came out. Both Red Bulls pitted for fresh tires, allowing Ricciardo to overtake Hamilton, Vettel, and Bottas for the win.

(OPPOSITE BOTTOM LEFT)
2018 Bahrain GP
Ferrari got off to a great start winning the first two races in Australia and Bahrain. Vettel was on pole at the Sakhir circuit, where he held the lead throughout the race. Vettel was unable to change his soft tires after his teammate Räikkönen hit a mechanic in the pit lane after an unsafe release.

(OPPOSITE BOTTOM RIGHT)
2018 Austrian GP
The Mercedes were on the front row of the grid for the Austrian GP with Bottas on pole. The cars retired with hydraulic failure as did Hamilton suffering a fuel problem. Verstappen won with Räikkönen second, Vettel third, then the two Haas cars of Grosjean and Kevin Magnussen, their best finish. Here, Magnussen leads Nico Hülkenberg and Esteban Ocon.

But there were many unanticipated downsides. The new powertrains were heavier, requiring the minimum car weight to increase from 642 kg (1,415 lbs) to 690 kg (1,521 lbs), continuing an upward trend. In 2008 it had been 595 kg (1,312 lbs). It made the cars harder on tires and less eager to change direction quickly. New rules framing the shape and size of the front impact structures were poorly phrased, leading to probably the ugliest generation of F1 cars ever. Worse still, only Mercedes was properly prepared, having invested early and conquered durability problems with the MGU-H, which spins at around 125,000 rpm. Ross Brawn had given the go-ahead in 2011, but by 2014 he had been pushed out in favor of Niki Lauda and ex-racer Toto Wolff as the Mercedes board grew impatient with indifferent performance on track. It had been Lauda who snared the services of Lewis Hamilton for 2013. From 2014, with the best engine and car, Hamilton was virtually untouchable and won all but one of the drivers' championships remaining in the decade. Mercedes elevated him from a one-time champion, frustrated by McLaren's yo-yo performance, to a seven-time champion, potentially the greatest driver of all time.

In contrast, Ferrari's hybrid powertrain was flawed and Renault's just plain disastrous. Several customers, including Red Bull, could barely manage more than a few laps in 2014 pre-season testing, and the pattern of underperformance continued through the hybrid era. Predictably a scrabble ensued among the drivers for better seats. Vettel, who had a muted season in comparison to new teammate Daniel Ricciardo, moved to Ferrari in place of Alonso, who had a falling out with the second of the Scuderia's three different team principals that year. Alonso, to the surprise of many, returned to McLaren and patched up his relationship with Ron Dennis, lured by the promise of Honda's imminent return.

(LEFT)
2018 Brazilian GP
In the closing rounds of 2018, Hamilton had the drivers' title in the bag making it his fifth world championship win. At the penultimate race in Brazil, he was on pole, but Verstappen managed to get by on lap 40 yet lost it again colliding with Force India driver Esteban Ocon.

Unfortunately for Alonso, Ferrari's performance took a generally upward trajectory while the first four seasons of Honda's return were catastrophically poor. Come the end of 2018, he decided to go sportscar racing instead.

Fans–and, perhaps more significantly, Ecclestone–railed against the lack of noise generated by the new engines, as well as yet more seasons of one team winning all the time. Occasional race victories and one championship for Hamilton's teammate Nico Rosberg, along with the messily public disintegration of their long-standing friendship, didn't move the public-interest dial enough. Ecclestone pushed for–and got–an amended technical formula for 2017 with wider, more dramatic-looking cars and bigger tires. Nice in theory, but wider cars made overtaking more difficult, along with introducing another rise in weight.

(ABOVE)
2019 German GP
Verstappen won the Red Bull home GP in Austria and again in Germany after a wet start at Hockenheim. The Red Bull cars were slow off the line and easily passed. On a drying track, Hamilton lost control from the lead behind the safety car and Verstappen took advantage, going on to regain the lead and take the win.

(TOP)

2019 Belgian GP
Ferrari fought back with a run of three consecutive wins mid-season starting at Spa-Francorchamps. Charles Leclerc (No. 16) took his maiden victory ahead of Hamilton's Mercedes by less than a second.

(ABOVE)

2019 Mexican GP
In Mexico, Leclerc was promoted to pole after Verstappen was penalized for failing to slow under a yellow flag. Trying for the undercut, Leclerc pitted early, but it didn't work. Hamilton took the lead and the win. He finished the season with 413 points and his sixth driver's title.

The new generation of cars also featured the "halo" cockpit safety device, chosen from several alternative proposals in response to Jules Bianchi's tragic accident in the 2014 Japanese Grand Prix. Having pushed it through, Todt was furious when teams, drivers, and fans complained that the halo was ugly and made it difficult to identify who was in the cockpit. Those complaints faded with time and a series of incidents in which the halo demonstrably saved drivers from serious injury.

SEBASTIAN VETTEL
(2010, 2011, 2012, 2013)

Red Bull arrived in Formula 1 as a disruptive brand, with a fresh and youthful energy. At the heart of its philosophy was a program to unearth young talent. For all the burgeoning drivers that fell by the wayside, Sebastian Vettel was one who soared.

Given a seat in Red Bull's sister outfit Toro Rosso, he remarkably gave the Italian-based team its first victory in Formula 1—in the rains of Monza in 2008. The following year he was promoted to the senior Red Bull squad just as the Christian Horner–run organization was evolving into an F1 powerhouse.

Four drivers went into the 2010 season finale with a shot at the title. Vettel emerged ahead despite not topping the table at any point in the preceding eight months. He beat Alonso's record to become the youngest-ever world champion at 23 years and 134 days. The youthful German continued to sweep all before him in 2011 as the RB7 was the class of the field. He took 11 wins and secured a second title in Japan with four races to spare.

In 2012, seven different drivers won the opening seven rounds in a competitive start to the year. However, another strong campaign from the Milton Keynes outfit kept Vettel in contention until the final round. Despite spinning on the opening lap in that São Paulo showdown, he scrambled over the line in his hobbled car to deny Fernando Alonso from winning for Ferrari.

Vettel's final world championship season started in controversial fashion when he ignored a team instruction to stay behind teammate Mark Webber in the Malaysian Grand Prix. The order, known as "Multi 21" (car two must stay ahead of car one), deepened the intra-team rivalry between the pair. Vettel was unperturbed, and after the summer break went on a record-breaking nine consecutive win streak to claim title number four.

After leaving Red Bull, Sebastian attempted to emulate his hero Michael Schumacher and bring the crown back to Maranello. But he fell short. Ferrari was just not on a par with the all-dominant Mercedes in the new hybrid era.

LEWIS HAMILTON
(2014, 2015, 2017, 2018, 2019)

NICO ROSBERG
(2016)

After leaving McLaren to join Mercedes in 2013, Lewis Hamilton was in the best seat in Formula 1 when the new engine regulations came into effect at the start of 2014. The advanced 1.6-liter V6 hybrid turbocharged power unit replaced the old 2.4-liter V8s and Mercedes's engine department motored clear of the opposition.

It was the beginning of a record-breaking stranglehold on the sport for the Hamilton/Mercedes partnership, who toppled Red Bull's hegemony in the process. In time, Hamilton smashed the records set by Michael Schumacher in the previous decade—equaling his seven championships—and vaulting clear in the wins, poles, and fastest laps count. It was a measure of Lewis's unrelenting desire that after another title-winning season, he returned to the race track in subsequent years more determined to succeed than ever.

From the beginning of the hybrid era, Mercedes was immediately in the ascendency. In that first season of 19 rounds, the team amassed 18 poles and 16 victories. Hamilton's 11 wins in '14 was similarly matched by a further ten in 2015.

With his teammate Nico Rosberg finishing runner-up each time, the young German dug deep to stop Hamilton's relentless march—which he eventually succeeded in doing in 2016. Following Rosberg's shock retirement, genial Finn Valtteri Bottas partnered Hamilton at the team and, despite the odd win, wasn't able to mount a sustained challenge to Lewis's mastery.

At Monza in 2017, Hamilton took his 69th pole to eclipse Michael Schumacher's record. A year later he equaled Juan Manuel Fangio's five world titles and recorded the fastest ever pole lap in history in qualifying at Monza (clocked at average speed of 164.266 mph [264.35 kmh]).

Ferrari and Vettel failed to overhaul the might of the Silver Arrows, and in 2019 Hamilton triumphed another 11 times to add title number six to his prodigious tally.

Like father and son pairing Graham and Damon Hill, Nico Rosberg became the second driver in the 75-year history of the sport to claim a world title after his father Keke. To achieve such a feat, Nico had to overcome the greatest driver of his generation—in the same car—and he went to great lengths to achieve his ambition.

The teenage Rosberg knew Lewis Hamilton well, as the pair were teammates in karting. Despite their close relationship as youngsters, their friendship became strained in the pressure cooker environment of Formula 1. Their biggest falling out came early on in Rosberg's title-winning year. The Mercedes teammates clashed on the opening lap of the Spanish Grand Prix with both blaming the other. In a fractious season between the duo, Rosberg finally did enough to win the crown at a tense Abu Dhabi season finale.

But such was the toll it took on the Monaco-residing German, that he had no hesitation in hanging up his helmet immediately afterwards and informed Mercedes he was quitting F1 within days of his epic championship triumph.

THE
⑧ 2020s

For decades, F1 had tried unsuccessfully to crack America. Including the Indianapolis 500 as a championship-counting event during the 1950s wasn't enough of an incentive to get participants on either side of the Atlantic to make the crossing. U.S. Grands Prix held at venues such as Sebring, Riverside, Long Beach, Las Vegas, Detroit, and Phoenix were either loss-making or not profitable enough. Watkins Glen was popular and offered a sizeable prize purse, but car performance outgrew its safety features. Putative races in New York and elsewhere foundered in the wake of the 2005 Indy debacle. Against all expectations, though–almost to the surprise of all involved–in the 2020s F1's audience in America blossomed. Not only did the financially troubled U.S. Grand Prix in Austin suddenly turn a profit, it was joined by brash new events in Miami and Las Vegas, with other Stateside venues desperate to join.

2024 Bahrain GP
Verstappen got off to his winning ways in Bahrain and Saudi Arabia, but 2024 wasn't going to be as straightforward as the previous season. McLaren, Ferrari, and Mercedes became more competitive throughout the season.

211

2020 Austrian GP
A late start and limited calendar in 2020 due to Covid-19 pandemic restrictions saw the first two races in Austria in July won by Mercedes. Bottas won the first, with Leclerc's Ferrari second and McLaren's Lando Norris third. Hamilton won the Styrian GP a week later.

None of this would have happened if Bernie Ecclestone was still superintending F1's commercial rights. Besides his incredible ability to keep the teams at each other's throats so they couldn't present a united front against him, Bernie had pulled off the feat of hawking the commercial rights around various owners, adding billions of dollars to his personal wealth, while convincing all of them to leave him in charge. As the money rolled in, huge TV deals bolstered by sanctioning fees from new races (predominantly in Asia and the Middle East), you could see why. And if the Korean and Indian Grands Prix of the 2010s quickly went the way of those old U.S. Grands Prix, leaving costly white-elephant circuits behind, the supply of countries eager to spend taxpayers' money–or sovereign wealth–on the prestige of hosting F1 seemed inexhaustible.

But the 2006 transfer of the commercial rights from the creditor banks of a previous owner (a bankrupt German media conglomerate) to the venture-capitalist group CVC Capital Partners would prove to be Ecclestone's undoing. CVC paid themselves huge dividends while loading the business with debt, requiring continuous growth and cash inputs. Ecclestone wouldn't sanction any activity unless there was cash up front, so F1 didn't get involved in social media apart from heavy-handedly policing copyright on YouTube. Worse, scandal was brewing over an allegation that he bribed a senior banker to steer the sale to CVC because it would keep him in the driving seat. In 2014 he paid $80 million to settle out of court. When the U.S. giant Liberty Media acquired the commercial rights in 2017 for a reported $8 billion, it was clear its modern corporate governance wasn't going to mesh with Bernie's handshake-deal approach. He was quickly shuffled into a "chairman emeritus" non-job before Liberty's executives clamped the proverbial gold watch on his wrist and escorted him to the exit.

(RIGHT)
2020 Italian GP
At Monza in Italy there was a shock result when Alpha Tauri driver Pierre Gasly won after a chaotic race with multiple accidents, safety cars, and a penalty for Hamilton. A red flag saw the Frenchman take the top step ahead of Carlos Sainz Jr. and Lance Stroll.

(BELOW)
2020 Bahrain GP
By round 15, Hamilton led by a huge margin, having won 11 races and taking his seventh title. But it was Roman Grosjean who will be remembered for his miraculous escape from his Haas after a fiery collision with the barriers at the end of the first lap left him with burns to his hands but otherwise unhurt.

Among Liberty's first U-turns from F1's previous approach was to embrace social media and open the paddock to TV cameras belonging to companies not paying vast sums to screen the races. It is an abiding irony that the Covid-19 pandemic that swept across the globe in 2020, threatening the financial future of many sports, in many ways proved the making of F1. Lockdowns created a captive audience for TV, and one of the shows that gained huge traction was the F1 "documentary" series *Drive to Survive*, the first series of which had just dropped on Netflix when the pandemic forced the cancellation of the 2020 season-opening Australian Grand Prix. Long-term fans might cavil at the show's brazen sacrifice of factual accuracy at the altar of entertainment, but it proved such a hit that Ferrari and Mercedes, who had blocked access during the making of the first series, leapt aboard.

F1 was also one of the first global sports to achieve a restart in the pandemic year. It required Liberty Media to engage in an ambitious round of financial engineering, transferring billions of dollars in assets around its various holdings in order to free up cash to support struggling teams, and host Grands Prix without spectators. Running races without fans in the grandstands required an inversion of the usual model: rather than taking a fee from promoters who staged the events, Liberty in effect hired the circuits at its own cost. Doing so enabled the company to assemble a makeshift calendar, running several Grands Prix on back-to-back weekends at the same venues, avoiding default on their TV broadcast contracts. The nature of certain circuits, away from major population centers, made it possible for the Grand Prix circus to travel and operate in "bubbles" with very few personnel contracting Covid-19. Being among the first live sports to return, combined with what would become known as "the Netflix effect," not only supercharged audience growth in terms of raw numbers, it made the audience younger and more diverse, too.

(TOP LEFT)

2020 Sakhir GP

After Hamilton tested positive for Covid-19 in the second race in Bahrain, George Russell got his first Mercedes F1 drive. Russell got away well at the start and led before a botched pit stop spoiled his dream. Pérez came through for Racing Point to win his first victory after 190 starts.

(TOP RIGHT)

2021 Hungarian GP

A multi-car collision at the start of the Hungarian GP took out Stroll, Leclerc, Pérez, and Bottas. Lando Norris retired two laps later. At the restart, Ocon's Alpine was leading and he held on to take his first win as teammate Alonso held off a fast-charging Hamilton.

(RIGHT)
2021 Italian GP
Ricciardo won McLaren's first F1 race in nine years. With Norris second, they had a 1-2 team finish in Italy at Monza. Verstappen and Hamilton had taken each other out in a dramatic collision that saw the Red Bull launch over the Mercedes on lap 25.

(BOTTOM)
2021 Abu Dhabi GP
For the final round in Abu Dhabi, Hamilton and Verstappen were even on points. During a safety car period in the last few laps, Verstappen pitted for fresh tires. The lapped cars between him and race leader Hamilton were directed to unlap themselves. The Dutchman easily passed Hamilton to take the win and his first championship.

(OPPOSITE BOTTOM)
2021 Emilia Romagna GP
With a full calendar of 22 races in the schedule after the limitations of Covid, Hamilton won round one in Bahrain. Verstappen took the victory for the Emilia Romagna GP at Imola after a wet race. The grandstands were empty with no spectators allowed due to the continuing pandemic.

Paying teams the prize money owed from the previous season saved many entrants from bankruptcy. After the manufacturers took flight during the global financial crisis, most teams were in private ownership and, aside from the likes of Red Bull and its junior team, living a hand-to-mouth existence. Renault's 2016 reacquisition of the team it had sold to venture capitalists was very much an outlier. Haas, relatively new on the scene, was expected by founder Gene Haas to be financially self-sufficient, and it had been hobbled by a dalliance with a seemingly non-existent energy-drink sponsor who failed to pay. The Jordan team who had given Michael Schumacher his debut had passed through various ownerships before being snapped up by Canadian billionaire Lawrence Stroll as a vehicle for his son Lance's racing ambitions. Williams hadn't won a race since 2012 and in early 2020 was up for sale after a major sponsor defaulted on payments,

BEHIND THE SCENES

A NEW DEAL

The departure of Bernie Ecclestone at the beginning of 2017 marked the end of Formula 1's entrepreneurial era. The sale of the sport to U.S. company Liberty Media was completed that spring, in a deal which valued the sport at $8 billion. A pretty decent price tag when you consider Bernie didn't own the teams, drivers, or the circuits. What he did have the keys to was a vast filing cabinet of contracts.

Officially, Ecclestone was appointed chairman emeritus, but his departure from day-to-day running of Formula 1 coincided with it becoming more accessible. During Bernie's era, the joke about his company's modus operandi was: "The answer's no, what's the question?"

In Bernie's place came three wise men: chairman and chief executive Chase Carey (a former lieutenant of media mogul Rupert Murdoch); Sean Bratches, who looked after the sport's commercial interests; and Ross Brawn, who oversaw the sporting and technical side.

The new owners promised to protect races in the European heartland, expand into the U.S., and visit more "destination cities" around the world. The fan experience of attending a race improved (although the road traffic management of many venues didn't).

There were now Fan Zones behind grandstands, more music concerts performed by A-listers after the on-track action, and the adoption of extra Sprint races and Hot Laps (whereby passengers are taken around the course by F1 drivers at high speed).

For good or for worse, the sport has also opened its doors to more celebrities, and in its American races (Austin, Miami, and Las Vegas) there have been attempts at flamboyant pre-race ceremonies. The key here is "The Show," but as Formula 1 reaches 75 years of history, it must be careful its priorities as a sporting contest are not compromised. As one paddock wag said to me in Miami last year: "We now travel across the world to attend 24 rounds a year just to make a ten-part documentary series and a Hollywood movie."

Lewis Hamilton in the Fan Zone, French GP 2019.

(LEFT)
2022 Saudi Arabian GP
After the controversial finish to the season in 2021, the F1 race director was replaced and teams had to contend with many new regulations. As a consequence, Mercedes lost its competitiveness and Red Bull became dominant, winning in 17 out of 22 races. Here Verstappen wins round two in Saudi Arabia.

(BELOW)
2022 Austrian GP
In Austria Verstappen won the Sprint race and was on pole for the GP with the Ferraris second and third on the grid. Leclerc was clearly faster. He passed Verstappen using DRS (drag reduction system) twice to win despite battling problems with his car.

2022 Dutch GP
On the banked corners of Zandvoort at the Dutch GP, Mercedes had its best result of the year thus far with Russell finishing second and Hamilton fourth. Home hero Verstappen took his tenth win for Red Bull.

and McLaren had to make many staff redundant and sell off its Applied Technologies division. All these sagas would play out in dramatized form for *Drive to Survive* viewers. The shared sense of panic wrought an outbreak of unity among the stakeholders after years of Ecclestone-stoked division: as well as agreeing to freeze technical development through 2021 and defer the introduction of a new car format until '22, the teams secured highly lucrative terms in the latest version of the Concorde Agreement.

In playing the leading teams off against one another to smash FOTA and get the previous Concorde Agreement over the line, Ecclestone had baked in horrendous inequalities, which played out disadvantageously through the 2010s. The top four teams enjoyed substantial prize-fund bonuses—and got a seat at the rulemaking table—while the midfielders and tail-enders struggled to stay afloat. Despite initial resistance from Mercedes, the 2020 negotiations resulted in more equitable distribution of prize money, plus a budget cap to be phased in from 2021. Perhaps even more significantly, it locked in F1 as a ten-team format in which prospective new entrants would have to pay $200 million—distributed among the existing teams—to get through the door. At a stroke, teams in effect became franchises.

Another development in the more collegiate atmosphere of Liberty's ownership was a more scientific approach to framing the technical rules. In his memoir *Survive. Drive. Win.*, the former Honda and Brawn CEO Nick Fry had likened the meetings of senior figures in the Ecclestone era to an elementary school playground: ill-considered measures were rushed through while the participants shouted and threw bits of paper at each other. Post-Ecclestone, recognizing that previous changes had brought unforeseen consequences that detracted from rather than improved the spectacle, F1 and

2020 AUSTRALIAN GRAND PRIX

There are a swathe of lively bars and restaurants on the banks of the Yarra River near Flinders Street station in central Melbourne. On the Monday before the 2020 Australian Grand Prix was due to begin on Sunday, March 15, a public holiday meant this downtown area was packed with revelers, mingling and socializing. Yet within a week, a sense of fear and isolation had gripped the city and the wider world.

As the days counted down to the opening round of the 2020 season, events off the track took a sudden turn. The coronavirus was spreading—and fast. While the F1 teams and personnel managed to fly to Australia easily enough, within a few days of their arrival, airspace was being shut down across the globe.

The Thursday media day in Albert Park carried on as normal, but a few restrictions were put in place. Journalists had to sit two meters behind a belted barrier when talking to a driver. It was then announced that the next round, in Bahrain, would be a televised event only, i.e., no spectators or VIP guests would be present.

Then the first domino fell. A member of the McLaren team was isolated with coronavirus-like symptoms. Later that night a statement from the squad delivered a sucker punch. They had withdrawn from the race following a positive case of Covid-19.

The fans headed to the track for practice on the Friday morning, but the gates remained closed. After a long night of discussions, the decision was made to cancel the race. Everybody headed back home to isolate.

Within days the seven British-based Formula 1 teams were in contact with the government and the health authorities as they had put their collective resources together to help design and manufacture respiratory devices. But racing was put on hiatus until it was safe to resume.

"We must realize racing is entertainment. We take it seriously because we love it, but in the grand scheme of things it is by no means essential," said Mercedes boss Toto Wolff in an open letter to the fans.

Formula 1 impressively organized a way to return the on-track action in a little over four months from the Melbourne cancellation. An initial eight-race calendar was announced with a double-header taking place at the Red Bull Ring in Austria. This was in a controlled environment, in a rural location, at a venue effectively owned by an entrant in the sport.

Careful measures had been worked out whereby teams would exist in their own bubbles and regular testing took place on a daily basis. But the reason why Formula 1 could be the first major international sport to resume in a Covid era was the fact each participant sat helmeted in a car—social distancing has always been the norm in Grand Prix racing.

The empty track and pit lane at
Australia's Melbourne Grand Prix
Circuit on what should have been the
first race day of the 2020 season.

the FIA hired experienced engineers such as Pat Symonds and Nikolas Tombazis (both ex-Benetton) and engaged the teams in providing facilities for proper aerodynamic research. Tweaks to the front wings and rear brake assemblies in 2019 were the preface to an entirely new technical formula that sought to eliminate the problem of cars being unable to follow each other closely through corners. Long-term, the proposed solution was to rebalance the way the cars made downforce, shifting the focus from the front and rear wings to the underbody: a return to the ground-effect aerodynamic philosophy banned in 1983. If the wings contributed less to overall performance, ran the theory, then the cars would be less sensitive to "dirty air" from cars in front when running together. Never before had so much resource and experienced engineering rigor been deployed in crafting a new technical formula.

While these disconcertingly unfamiliar scenarios of the stakeholders working together for the common good played out away from the track, petty intrigues continued to prevail during racing weekends. The pandemic-induced racing hiatus of 2020 gave Mercedes a window of opportunity to fix a problem that was causing its engines to break, and it ran to a seventh consecutive constructors' championship, amid controversy over a dual-axis steering system that conferred a minor advantage in tire performance. Rivals, piqued that chassis-homologation rules prevented them from imitating it, lobbied for it to be banned. Lewis Hamilton took his seventh drivers' title, ably supported by Valtteri Bottas, who had been recruited to operate as a low-maintenance teammate after Hamilton's 2016 ructions with Nico Rosberg. It would be Hamilton's last world championship to date.

In Max Verstappen, Hamilton had found a ferociously competitive match. Verstappen was, relatively speaking, now an outlier in a sport increasingly dominated by older participants. When he made his debut in 2015, at age 17, he was the youngest driver in F1 history and the FIA changed the licensing rules to ensure such a thing

(BELOW)
2022 São Paulo GP
Qualifying was shaken up when Haas driver Kevin Magnussen took pole in wet conditions in São Paulo for the Sprint race. Mercedes' George Russell won his maiden GP and Hamilton was second. At season end, Verstappen and Red Bull retained their championship titles.

(ABOVE)
2023 Azerbaijan GP
2023 was a record breaking year for Red Bull winning all but one of the 22 races. In Azerbaijan Ferrari's Leclerc qualified on pole for the Sprint and Grand Prix but fell behind Red Bull's Perez in both races. He could only hold off Verstappen and Pérez until lap four when DRS was enabled allowing both cars to pass.

(RIGHT)
2023 British GP
At the British GP, Verstappen took a clean sweep of pole, fastest lap, and the victory. On the front row of the grid, Lando Norris beat the Dutchman off the line and led for the first few laps. On the open ex-airfield straights of Silverstone, Norris succumbed to the Red Bull's outright speed under DRS. The McLaren driver would finish second.

couldn't happen again. But it was other regulations that would freeze younger drivers out: reductions in testing days, brought in to cut costs, along with shorter practice sessions during Grand Prix weekends, plus the acute sensitivity of the Pirelli tires, put a premium on experience. By the late 2010s, the average age of the grid was rising, propelled by the likes of Kimi Räikkönen, Hamilton, and a returning Fernando Alonso cruising towards their 40th birthdays.

The intense rivalry between Hamilton and Verstappen was facilitated by Red Bull's resurgence–a factor of Honda finally getting on top of the hybrid engine's challenges and design guru Adrian Newey recommitting full-time to F1 after stepping back partially to work on the Valkyrie supercar. There was also a popular suspicion that amendments to the aerodynamic regulations at the start of 2021 were targeted at Mercedes to curb its dominance. It was a spectacle made for TV: Hamilton, the veteran "Mr. Clean" versus the brash young upstart whose on-track etiquette tended towards brusqueness. In parallel their team bosses, Toto Wolff and Christian Horner, battered each other with verbal handbags on camera. Wider broadcast of selected team radio interactions added

2023 Singapore GP
Carlos Sainz Jr. won the only race not to go to the dominant Red Bull team in Singapore for round 15. After Logan Sargeant's Williams dropped debris, a safety car was deployed, and both Verstappen and Pérez failed to pit to take advantage, finishing fifth and eighth, respectively.

2023 Las Vegas GP
The Las Vegas Strip hosted the penultimate round and the party town went F1 crazy. Leclerc was on pole but was forced off the circuit at turn one by Verstappen. Norris suffered a heavy accident after his car bottomed out on the bumpy track. Verstappen won the race ahead of Leclerc and Sergio Pérez.

to the intrigues as drivers and engineers used this platform to lobby publicly for rivals to be punished for minor infractions. Much of it was, and continues to be, rather childish.

Arguably this conversion of sport into soap opera reached a troubling inflection point in 2021, when radio involving race director Michael Masi was added to the mix. Masi was relatively new to the job after longtime race director and technical delegate Charlie Whiting died after suffering a deep-vein thrombosis in 2019. Whiting had earned the deepest respect of the competitors even if they didn't always agree with him. He was a poacher-turned-gamekeeper, chief mechanic to Nelson Piquet at Ecclestone's Brabham team in the early 1980s, when that outfit often punched holes in the envelope while pushing it. Whiting was also one of the few senior FIA personnel left over from the Mosley era, never pushed out by Jean Todt. Substantial shoes to fill, and Masi struggled from the get-go. Being hectored, lobbied, and often outright bullied in public by alpha-male team managers on the global broadcast placed him in an invidious position, not least in the controversial final round of the 2021 season.

RED BULL RB19

When Max Verstappen scored his record-breaking 19th win of the 2023 season at the final race in Abu Dhabi, he also achieved another incredible milestone. Throughout the year he led over 1,000 laps. To put that into context, only 19 drivers in the history of the World Championship have led that many laps in their entire *career*. When he brought his RB19 to a smoky halt following a series of celebratory donuts after the final race, he admitted he felt rather emotional. "It'll be very hard to have another season like this," said the victorious Dutchman.

As a mark of the RB19's reliability and Max's consistency behind the wheel, he also completed every single racing lap in 2023—all 1,325—which has only happened twice before in the history of the sport (Michael Schumacher in 2002 and Lewis Hamilton in 2019).

When the Formula 1 regulations prescribed "ground effect" cars that extracted more downforce from the car's floor and diffuser, one of the teething troubles for a number of teams was the propensity for the cars to bounce or "porpoise." Red Bull was the first to mitigate that issue successfully with the RB18, and its advantage carried over into the design of the RB19.

Despite propelling Max Verstappen to the title in '22, the RB18 was far from perfect. It started the season overweight, but it did become progressively slimmer as the year unfolded.

As a result, the RB19 was redesigned so the engineers could utilize weight distribution as a setup tool. It also featured an aggressive series of upgrades as the year advanced. Wider, narrower inlets for the sidepods, a new engine cover, and new floor all improved airflow for maximum aerodynamic efficiency. This was an impressive feat as new regs were introduced to reduce wind tunnel time under the FIA's Aerodynamic Testing Regulations (ATR) and Red Bull faced a further 10 percent reduction due to a cost-cap breach the previous year.

The success of the RB19 became its universal quality to be competitive on any type of layout: slow tracks, short-corners, long radius bends, or curb-hopping chicanes. When Verstappen took the lead in Miami, he wasn't headed at the front of the field for another 247 laps (in Austria) after dominating the next three races in Monaco, Barcelona, and Montréal.

The RB19 fell shy of a perfect season when it didn't win in Singapore, although 21 wins from 22 isn't too shabby.

Hamilton and Verstappen arrived in Abu Dhabi equal on points, only the second time in F1 history (the other being in 1974) that two championship protagonists have been tied going into the final round. After a season filled with ill-tempered interactions, the chief fear was that it might be decided by a Prost-Senna-style crash, deliberate or otherwise. What eventuated was more bizarre as Hamilton took the lead on lap one and stayed there for most of the race until a Safety Car deployment disrupted proceedings with five laps to run. With time running out, and under pressure from both leading teams on the radio, Masi disregarded the letter of the rules to engineer one final lap of racing rather than let it finish behind the Safety Car. As a result, Verstappen, on fresher tires, had an advantage over Hamilton and was able to pass—and secure the championship—on that final lap. In the post-truth era, the outcome of the 2021 Abu Dhabi Grand Prix generated a rift in the fan community that time has not healed.

The FIA's official report on the saga highlighted two rules governing Safety Car procedure that had not been applied correctly and attributed this to "human error." Although Masi had acted "in good faith," he was removed from his post amid a wider suite of changes brought in by incoming FIA president Mohammed Ben Sulayem, including a system of rotating race directors supported by a remote monitoring facility at the governing body's HQ. The plug was pulled on direct communications between the teams and the race director since this "distraction" at a critical moment was seen as a key factor in the poor decision-making. Certainly it was hard to argue against the impression that F1's recent focus on entertainment had gone too far.

(ABOVE)

2024 Miami GP
Lando Norris won his first GP from fourth on the grid after 110 starts in Miami, gaining an advantage over Verstappen during a safety car period. McLaren teammate Oscar Piastri took the fastest lap after upgrades for both cars.

(ABOVE RIGHT)

2024 British GP
The Mercedes team raised its game with George Russell taking the top step in Austria after Verstappen and Norris collided. Just a week later on a rain-swept Silverstone, Lewis Hamilton took his ninth British GP victory, his first since 2021.

(OPPOSITE)

2024 Australian GP
In Australia Carlos Sainz Jr. made a great recovery from missing the previous round due to appendicitis. He took the top step for his third career victory after pole-sitter Verstappen retired with brake failure. Leclerc made it a Ferrari 1-2 with the McLarens behind.

In common with his predecessors, Ben Sulayem began by explicitly saying he planned to keep a low profile in F1–before doing virtually the opposite. The early years of his tenure were marked by a series of often rather eccentric interventions on a variety of subjects, from chiding drivers for cursing in press conferences and on the team radio to opening a tender process for an 11th team to join the grid, seemingly without consulting the teams or the commercial rights holder. The pushback against this left the winning bidder Michael Andretti, son of 1979 world champion Mario Andretti, in limbo despite securing high-profile backing from General Motors and its Cadillac brand.

While the budget cap and new, performance-related restrictions on aerodynamic research set F1 on course towards closer competition, the first two seasons of the new ground-effect era appeared to demonstrate anything but that as Red Bull and Verstappen dominated. The key, perhaps, was Adrian Newey's experience. He wrote his graduate thesis on ground-effect aerodynamics and got his first job in F1 in 1979, as the previous era built to a peak. When the new formula was introduced in 2022 and most of the cars on the grid experienced various degrees of "porpoising" and bouncing, Newey's RB18 seemed relatively untroubled. Verstappen added second and third world championships to his trophy cabinet as his opposition struggled to keep up; in 2023 he broke still more performance records as Red Bull won all but one race.

That trend changed abruptly in 2024 as performance convergence belatedly set in and McLaren built its most consistent challenge for the championship in over a decade. The new ground-effect era had met the law of diminishing returns as several teams, including Red Bull, struggled to realize theoretical performance gains when adding technical upgrades to their cars. As Formula 1 entered its 75th season, many entrants were already scaling down development of their 2025 cars and shifting focus towards a new regulatory package for '26 built around active aerodynamics and engines with more focus on electrical deployment.

Red Bull's struggles demonstrated a historic truism that has prevailed since the days when teams consisted of a dozen or so people and were owned by the person whose name was above the factory door: all empires fall.

THE WORLD CHAMPIONS

**LEWIS HAMILTON
(2020)**

**MAX VERSTAPPEN
(2021, 2022, 2023, 2024)**

In a year troubled and delayed by the spread of the global Covid-19 pandemic, Hamilton's most recent world championship triumph was plagued by doubts as to when the next race would take place—or where. After congregating in Australia for the season opener, F1 took a hiatus of 217 days before resuming in Austria in July.

Every driver took precautions, knowing that contracting coronavirus would impact his ability to compete. From where he left off at the end of 2019, Hamilton continued his meteoric form and secured 11 wins—in a sleek, black Mercedes to honor the Black Lives Matter movement. He clinched his record-equaling seventh world title on a damp day in Istanbul.

Like Sebastian Vettel before him, Max was a product of the Red Bull young driver program, and his obvious talent accelerated his promotion to the higher-echelons of Formula 1. He was just 17 when he arrived at the sport's top table and immediately silenced the critics once he was behind the wheel. Strong performances for sister outfit Toro Rosso made it an easy decision for Red Bull to promote him to its top team.

What it didn't expect was a win first time out. When the two Mercedes drivers collided on the opening lap of the 2013 Spanish Grand Prix, Max was there to take the spoils, beating Alonso's record to become the youngest driver to ever win a Grand Prix (at 18 years and 228 days).

New chassis regulations were delayed a year due to Covid-19, so in 2021 there was a convergence between the teams. The closeness in speed between Red Bull and Mercedes set up a battle for the ages. Max, the young, forceful upstart, was not afraid to go toe-to-toe with the greatest star of the era. Verstappen

versus Hamilton was box-office stuff.

In addition to superb battling, the pair also had their controversial moments—colliding at Silverstone and Monza—and tripping over each other again at the penultimate round in Jeddah. That race set up an extraordinary winner-takes-all showdown in Abu Dhabi.

It was somewhat inevitable the final round would end in controversy. A late-race Safety Car didn't adhere to the correct procedures, and the one-lap shootout went the way of Verstappen—to the disbelief and anger of Mercedes.

With the onset of the new rules for 2022, Red Bull assumed its supremacy over the opposition and Max's second title was a breeze in comparison. He took 15 wins from 22. And if that looked easy, he was unstoppable a year later. Red Bull won 21 of 22 races, with the Dutchman scoring an unprecedented ten in a row in the middle of the year. In 2024 he succeeded once more to secure his fourth world title.

RACE RESULTS

Bold text denotes pole position. *Italics* denotes fastest lap.

1950

Date	Grand Prix	Winning driver	Car/engine
5/13	Britain	***Giuseppe Farina***	Alfa Romeo
5/21	Monaco	***Juan Manuel Fangio***	Alfa Romeo
5/30	Indy 500	*Johnnie Parsons*	Kurtis Kraft-Offenhauser
6/4	Switzerland	*Giuseppe Farina*	Alfa Romeo
6/18	Belgium	Juan Manuel Fangio	Alfa Romeo
7/2	France	***Juan Manuel Fangio***	Alfa Romeo
9/3	Italy	Giuseppe Farina	Alfa Romeo

Championship: 1 Giuseppe Farina (30 points), 2 Juan Manuel Fangio (27 points), 3 Luigi Fagioli (24 points)

1951

5/27	Switzerland	***Juan Manuel Fangio***	Alfa Romeo
5/30	Indy 500	*Lee Wallard*	Kurtis Kraft-Offenhauser
6/17	Belgium	Giuseppe Farina	Alfa Romeo
7/1	France	***Juan Manuel Fangio*/** Luigi Fagioli	Alfa Romeo
7/14	Britain	**José Froilán González**	Ferrari
7/29	Germany	**Alberto Ascari**	Ferrari
9/16	Italy	Alberto Ascari	Ferrari
10/28	Spain	*Juan Manuel Fangio*	Alfa Romeo

Championship: 1 Juan Manuel Fangio (31 points), 2 Alberto Ascari (25 points), 3 José Froilán González (24 points)

1952

5/18	Switzerland	*Piero Taruffi*	Ferrari
5/30	Indy 500	Troy Ruttman	Kuzma-Offenhauser
6/22	Belgium	***Alberto Ascari***	Ferrari
7/6	France	***Alberto Ascari***	Ferrari
7/19	Britain	*Alberto Ascari*	Ferrari
8/3	Germany	***Alberto Ascari***	Ferrari
8/17	Holland	***Alberto Ascari***	Ferrari
9/7	Italy	***Alberto Ascari***	Ferrari

Championship: 1 Alberto Ascari (36 points), 2 Giuseppe Farina (24 points), 3 Piero Taruffi (22 points)

1953

1/18	Argentina	***Alberto Ascari***	Ferrari
5/30	Indy 500	**Bill Vukovich**	Kurtis Kraft-Offenhauser
6/7	Holland	**Alberto Ascari**	Ferrari
6/20	Belgium	Alberto Ascari	Ferrari
7/5	France	Mike Hawthorn	Ferrari
7/18	Britain	***Alberto Ascari***	Ferrari
8/2	Germany	Giuseppe Farina	Ferrari
8/23	Switzerland	*Alberto Ascari*	Ferrari
9/13	Italy	*Juan Manuel Fangio*	Maserati

Championship: 1 Alberto Ascari (34.5 points), 2 Juan Manuel Fangio (28 points), 3 Giuseppe Farina (26 points)

1954

1/17	Argentina	Juan Manuel Fangio	Maserati
5/31	Indy 500	Bill Vukovich	Kurtis Kraft-Offenhauser
6/20	Belgium	***Juan Manuel Fangio***	Maserati
7/4	France	**Juan Manuel Fangio**	Mercedes
7/17	Britain	José Froilán González	Ferrari
8/1	Germany	**Juan Manuel Fangio**	Mercedes
8/22	Switzerland	*Juan Manuel Fangio*	Mercedes
9/5	Italy	**Juan Manuel Fangio**	Mercedes
10/24	Spain	Mike Hawthorn	Ferrari

Championship: 1 Juan Manuel Fangio (42 points), 2 José Froilán González (25 1/7 points), 3 Mike Hawthorn (24 9/14 points)

1955

1/16	Argentina	*Juan Manuel Fangio*	Mercedes
5/22	Monaco	Maurice Trintignant	Ferrari
5/30	Indy 500	Bob Sweikert	Kurtis Kraft-Offenhauser
6/5	Belgium	*Juan Manuel Fangio*	Mercedes
6/19	Holland	**Juan Manuel Fangio**	Mercedes
7/16	Britain	***Stirling Moss***	Mercedes
9/11	Italy	**Juan Manuel Fangio**	Mercedes

Championship: 1 Juan Manuel Fangio (40 points), 2 Stirling Moss (23 points), 3 Eugenio Castellotti (12 points)

1956

1/22	Argentina	Luigi Musso/*Juan Manuel Fangio*	Ferrari
5/13	Monaco	Stirling Moss	Maserati
5/30	Indy 500	**Pat Flaherty**	Watson-Offenhauser
6/3	Belgium	Peter Collins	Ferrari
7/1	France	Peter Collins	Ferrari
7/14	Britain	Juan Manuel Fangio	Ferrari
8/5	Germany	*Juan Manuel Fangio*	Ferrari
9/2	Italy	Stirling Moss	Maserati

Championship: 1 Juan Manuel Fangio (30 points), 2 Stirling Moss (27 points), 3 Peter Collins (25 points)

1957

1/13	Argentina	Juan Manuel Fangio	Maserati
5/19	Monaco	*Juan Manuel Fangio*	Maserati
5/30	Indy 500	Sam Hanks	Epperly-Offenhauser
7/7	France	**Juan Manuel Fangio**	Maserati
7/20	Britain	Tony Brooks/*Stirling Moss*	Vanwall
8/4	Germany	*Juan Manuel Fangio*	Maserati
8/18	Pescara	*Stirling Moss*	Vanwall
9/8	Italy	Stirling Moss	Vanwall

Championship: 1 Juan Manuel Fangio (40 points), 2 Stirling Moss (25 points), 3 Luigi Musso (16 points)

1958

1/19	Argentina	Stirling Moss	Cooper-Climax
5/18	Monaco	Maurice Trintignant	Cooper-Climax
5/26	Holland	*Stirling Moss*	Vanwall
5/30	Indy 500	Jimmy Bryan	Epperly-Offenhauser
6/15	Belgium	Tony Brooks	Vanwall
7/6	France	*Mike Hawthorn*	Ferrari
7/19	Britain	Peter Collins	Ferrari
8/3	Germany	Tony Brooks	Vanwall
8/24	Portugal	**Stirling Moss**	Vanwall
9/7	Italy	Tony Brooks	Vanwall
10/19	Morocco	*Stirling Moss*	Vanwall

Championship: 1 Mike Hawthorn (42 points), 2 Stirling Moss (41 points), 2 Tony Brooks (24 points)

Winning constructor: Vanwall

1959

5/10	Monaco	*Jack Brabham*	Cooper-Climax
5/30	Indy 500	Rodger Ward	Watson-Offenhauser
5/31	Holland	**Jo Bonnier**	BRM
7/5	France	**Tony Brooks**	Ferrari
7/18	Britain	**Jack Brabham**	Cooper-Climax
8/2	Germany	*Tony Brooks*	Ferrari
8/23	Portugal	*Stirling Moss*	Cooper-Climax
9/13	Italy	**Stirling Moss**	Cooper-Climax
12/12	USA	Bruce McLaren	Cooper-Climax

Championship: 1 Jack Brabham (31 points), 2 Tony Brooks (27 points), 3 Stirling Moss (25.5 points)

Winning constructor: Cooper

1960

1/7	Argentina	Bruce McLaren	Cooper-Climax
5/29	Monaco	**Stirling Moss**	Lotus-Climax
5/30	Indy 500	Jim Rathmann	Watson-Offenhauser
6/6	Holland	Jack Brabham	Cooper-Climax
6/19	Belgium	*Jack Brabham*	Cooper-Climax
7/3	France	*Jack Brabham*	Cooper-Climax
7/16	Britain	**Jack Brabham**	Cooper-Climax
8/14	Portugal	Jack Brabham	Cooper-Climax
9/4	Italy	Phil Hill	Ferrari
11/20	USA	**Stirling Moss**	Lotus-Climax

Championship: 1 Jack Brabham (43 points), 2 Bruce McLaren (34 points), 3 Stirling Moss (19 points)

Winning constructor: Cooper

1961

5/14	Monaco	*Stirling Moss*	Lotus-Climax
5/22	Holland	Wolfgang von Trips	Ferrari
6/18	Belgium	**Phil Hill**	Ferrari
7/2	France	Giancarlo Baghetti	Ferrari
7/15	Britain	Wolfgang von Trips	Ferrari
8/6	Germany	Stirling Moss	Lotus-Climax
9/10	Italy	Phil Hill	Ferrari
10/8	USA	Innes Ireland	Lotus-Climax

Championship: 1 Phil Hill (34 points), 2 Wolfgang von Trips (33 points), Stirling Moss (21 points)

Winning constructor: Ferrari

1962

5/20	Holland	Graham Hill	BRM
6/3	Monaco	Bruce McLaren	Cooper-Climax
6/17	Belgium	*Jim Clark*	Lotus-Climax
7/8	France	Dan Gurney	Porsche
7/21	Britain	**Jim Clark**	Lotus-Climax
8/5	Germany	*Graham Hill*	BRM
9/16	Italy	*Graham Hill*	BRM
10/7	USA	**Jim Clark**	Lotus-Climax
12/29	South Africa	Graham Hill	BRM

Championship: 1 Graham Hill (42 points), 2 Jim Clark (30 points), 3 Bruce McLaren (27 points)

Winning constructor: BRM

1963

5/26	Monaco	Graham Hill	BRM
6/9	Belgium	*Jim Clark*	Lotus-Climax
6/23	Holland	**Jim Clark**	Lotus-Climax
6/30	France	**Jim Clark**	Lotus-Climax
7/20	Britain	**Jim Clark**	Lotus-Climax
8/4	Germany	*John Surtees*	Ferrari
9/8	Italy	*Jim Clark*	Lotus-Climax
10/6	USA	Graham Hill	BRM
10/27	Mexico	**Jim Clark**	Lotus-Climax
12/28	South Africa	**Jim Clark**	Lotus-Climax

Championship: 1 Jim Clark (54 points), 2 Graham Hill (29 points), 3 Richie Ginther (29 points)

Winning constructor: Lotus

1964

5/10	Monaco	*Graham Hill*	BRM
5/24	Holland	*Jim Clark*	Lotus-Climax
6/14	Belgium	Jim Clark	Lotus-Climax
6/28	France	Dan Gurney	Brabham-Climax
7/11	Britain	**Jim Clark**	Lotus-Climax
8/2	Germany	**John Surtees**	Ferrari
8/23	Austria	Lorenzo Bandini	Ferrari
9/6	Italy	**John Surtees**	Ferrari
10/4	USA	Graham Hill	BRM
10/25	Mexico	Dan Gurney	Brabham-Climax

Championship: 1 John Surtees (40 points), 2 Graham Hill (39 points), 3 Jim Clark (32 points)

Winning constructor: Ferrari

1965

1/1	South Africa	*Jim Clark*	Lotus-Climax
5/30	Monaco	*Graham Hill*	BRM
6/13	Belgium	*Jim Clark*	Lotus-Climax
6/27	France	*Jim Clark*	Lotus-Climax
7/10	Britain	**Jim Clark**	Lotus-Climax
7/18	Holland	*Jim Clark*	Lotus-Climax
8/1	Germany	*Jim Clark*	Lotus-Climax
9/12	Italy	Jackie Stewart	BRM
10/3	USA	Graham Hill	BRM
10/24	Mexico	Richie Ginther	Honda

Championship: 1 Jim Clark (54 points), 2 Graham Hill (40 points), 3 Jackie Stewart (33 points)

Winning constructor: Lotus

1966

5/22	Monaco	Jackie Stewart	BRM
6/12	Belgium	**John Surtees**	Ferrari
7/3	France	Jack Brabham	Brabham-Repco
7/16	Britain	**Jack Brabham**	Brabham-Repco
7/24	Holland	**Jack Brabham**	Brabham-Repco
8/7	Germany	Jack Brabham	Brabham-Repco
9/4	Italy	*Ludovico Scarfiotti*	Ferrari
10/2	USA	Jim Clark	Lotus-BRM
10/23	Mexico	John Surtees	Cooper-Maserati

Championship: 1 Jack Brabham (42 points), 2 John Surtees (28 points), 3 Jochen Rindt (22 points)

Winning constructor: Brabham

1967

1/2	South Africa	Pedro Rodríguez	Cooper-Maserati
5/7	Monaco	Denny Hulme	Brabham-Repco
6/4	Holland	*Jim Clark*	Lotus-Ford
6/18	Belgium	*Dan Gurney*	Eagle-Weslake
7/2	France	Jack Brabham	Brabham-Repco
7/15	Britain	**Jim Clark**	Lotus-Ford
8/6	Germany	Denny Hulme	Brabham-Repco
8/27	Canada	Jack Brabham	Brabham-Repco
9/10	Italy	John Surtees	Honda
10/1	USA	Jim Clark	Lotus-Ford
10/22	Mexico	Jim Clark	Lotus-Ford

Championship: 1 Denny Hulme (51 points), 2 Jack Brabham (46 points), 3 Jim Clark (41 points)

Winning constructor: Brabham

1968

1/1	South Africa	*Jim Clark*	Lotus-Ford
5/12	Spain	Graham Hill	Lotus-Ford
5/26	Monaco	**Graham Hill**	Lotus-Ford
6/9	Belgium	Bruce McLaren	McLaren-Ford
6/23	Holland	Jackie Stewart	Matra-Ford
7/7	France	Jacky Ickx	Ferrari
7/20	Britain	*Jo Siffert*	Lotus-Ford
8/4	Germany	*Jackie Stewart*	Matra-Ford
9/8	Italy	Denny Hulme	McLaren-Ford
9/22	Canada	Denny Hulme	McLaren-Ford
10/6	USA	*Jackie Stewart*	Matra-Ford
11/3	Mexico	Graham Hill	Lotus-Ford

Championship: 1 Graham Hill (48 points), 2 Jackie Stewart (36 points), 3 Denny Hulme (33 points)

Winning constructor: Lotus

1969

3/1	South Africa	*Jackie Stewart*	Matra-Ford
5/4	Spain	Jackie Stewart	Matra-Ford
5/18	Monaco	Graham Hill	Lotus-Ford
6/21	Holland	*Jackie Stewart*	Matra-Ford
7/6	France	***Jackie Stewart***	Matra-Ford
7/19	Britain	*Jackie Stewart*	Matra-Ford
8/3	Germany	***Jacky Ickx***	Brabham-Ford
9/7	Italy	Jackie Stewart	Matra-Ford
9/20	Canada	***Jacky Ickx***	Brabham-Ford
10/5	USA	Jochen Rindt	Lotus-Ford
10/19	Mexico	Denny Hulme	McLaren-Ford

Championship: 1 Jackie Stewart (63 points), 2 Jacky Ickx (37 points), 3 Bruce McLaren (26 points)

Winning constructor: Matra

1970

3/7	South Africa	*Jack Brabham*	Brabham-Ford
4/19	Spain	Jackie Stewart	March-Ford
5/10	Monaco	*Jochen Rindt*	Lotus-Ford
6/7	Belgium	Pedro Rodríguez	BRM
6/21	Holland	**Jochen Rindt**	Lotus-Ford
7/5	France	Jochen Rindt	Lotus-Ford
7/18	Britain	**Jochen Rindt**	Lotus-Ford
8/2	Germany	Jochen Rindt	Lotus-Ford
8/16	Austria	*Jacky Ickx*	Ferrari
9/6	Italy	*Clay Regazzoni*	Ferrari
9/20	Canada	Jacky Ickx	Ferrari
10/4	USA	Emerson Fittipaldi	Lotus-Ford
10/25	Mexico	Jacky Ickx	Ferrari

Championship: 1 Jochen Rindt (45 points), 2 Jacky Ickx (40 points), 3 Clay Regazzoni (33 points)

Winning constructor: Lotus

1971

3/6	South Africa	*Mario Andretti*	Ferrari
4/18	Spain	Jackie Stewart	Tyrrell-Ford
5/23	Monaco	*Jackie Stewart*	Tyrrell-Ford
6/20	Holland	***Jacky Ickx***	Ferrari
7/4	France	*Jackie Stewart*	Tyrrell-Ford
7/17	Britain	*Jackie Stewart*	Tyrrell-Ford
8/1	Germany	**Jackie Stewart**	Tyrrell-Ford
8/15	Austria	***Jo Siffert***	BRM
9/5	Italy	Peter Gethin	BRM
9/19	Canada	**Jackie Stewart**	Tyrrell-Ford
10/3	USA	Francois Cevert	Tyrrell-Ford

Championship: 1 Jackie Stewart (62 points), 2 Ronnie Peterson (33 points), 3 Francois Cevert (26 points)

Winning constructor: Tyrrell

1972

1/23	Argentina	*Jackie Stewart*	Tyrrell-Ford
3/4	South Africa	Denny Hulme	McLaren-Ford
5/1	Spain	Emerson Fittipaldi	Lotus-Ford
5/14	Monaco	*Jean-Pierre Beltoise*	BRM
6/4	Belgium	**Emerson Fittipaldi**	Lotus-Ford
7/2	France	Jackie Stewart	Tyrrell-Ford
7/15	Britain	Emerson Fittipaldi	Lotus-Ford
7/30	Germany	Jacky Ickx	Ferrari
8/13	Austria	**Emerson Fittipaldi**	Lotus-Ford
9/10	Italy	Emerson Fittipaldi	Lotus-Ford
9/24	Canada	*Jackie Stewart*	Tyrrell-Ford
10/8	USA	***Jackie Stewart***	Tyrrell-Ford

Championship: 1 Emerson Fittipaldi (61 points), 2 Jackie Stewart (45 points), 3 Denny Hulme (39 points)

Winning constructor: Lotus

1973

1/28	Argentina	*Emerson Fittipaldi*	Lotus-Ford
2/11	Brazil	*Emerson Fittipaldi*	Lotus-Ford
3/3	South Africa	Jackie Stewart	Tyrrell-Ford
4/29	Spain	Emerson Fittipaldi	Lotus-Ford
5/20	Belgium	Jackie Stewart	Tyrrell-Ford
6/3	Monaco	**Jackie Stewart**	Tyrrell-Ford
6/17	Sweden	*Denny Hulme*	McLaren-Ford
7/1	France	Ronnie Peterson	Lotus-Ford
7/14	Britain	Peter Revson	McLaren-Ford
7/29	Holland	Jackie Stewart	Tyrrell-Ford
8/5	Germany	**Jackie Stewart**	Tyrrell-Ford
8/19	Austria	Ronnie Peterson	Lotus-Ford
9/9	Italy	**Ronnie Peterson**	Lotus-Ford
9/23	Canada	Peter Revson	McLaren-Ford
10/7	USA	**Ronnie Peterson**	Lotus-Ford

Championship: 1 Jackie Stewart (71 points), 2 Emerson Fittipaldi (55 points), 3 Ronnie Peterson (52 points)

Winning constructor: Tyrrell

1974

1/13	Argentina	Denny Hulme	McLaren-Ford
1/27	Brazil	**Emerson Fittipaldi**	McLaren-Ford
3/30	South Africa	*Carlos Reutemann*	Brabham-Ford
4/28	Spain	***Niki Lauda***	Ferrari
5/12	Belgium	Emerson Fittipaldi	McLaren-Ford
5/26	Monaco	*Ronnie Peterson*	Lotus-Ford
6/9	Sweden	Jody Scheckter	Tyrrell-Ford
6/23	Holland	**Niki Lauda**	Ferrari
7/7	France	Ronnie Peterson	Lotus-Ford
7/20	Britain	Jody Scheckter	Tyrrell-Ford
8/4	Germany	Clay Regazzoni	Ferrari
8/14	Austria	Carlos Reutemann	Brabham-Ford
9/8	Italy	Ronnie Peterson	Lotus-Ford
9/22	Canada	**Emerson Fittipaldi**	McLaren-Ford
10/6	USA	**Carlos Reutemann**	Brabham-Ford

Championship: 1 Emerson Fittipaldi (55 points), 2 Clay Regazzoni (52 points), 3 Jody Scheckter (45 points)

Winning constructor: McLaren

1975

1/12	Argentina	Emerson Fittipaldi	McLaren-Ford
1/26	Brazil	Carlos Pace	Brabham-Ford
3/1	South Africa	Jody Scheckter	Tyrrell-Ford
4/27	Spain	Jochen Mass	McLaren-Ford
5/11	Monaco	**Niki Lauda**	Ferrari
5/25	Belgium	**Niki Lauda**	Ferrari
6/8	Sweden	*Niki Lauda*	Ferrari
6/22	Holland	James Hunt	Hesketh
7/6	France	**Niki Lauda**	Ferrari
7/19	Britain	Emerson Fittipaldi	McLaren-Ford
8/3	Germany	Carlos Reutemann	Brabham-Ford
8/17	Austria	Vittorio Brambilla	March-Ford
9/7	Italy	*Clay Regazzoni*	Ferrari
10/5	USA	**Niki Lauda**	Ferrari

Championship: 1 Niki Lauda (64.5 points), 2 Emerson Fittipaldi (45 points), 3 Carlos Reutemann (37 points)

Winning constructor: Ferrari

1976

1/25	Brazil	Niki Lauda	Ferrari
3/6	South Africa	*Niki Lauda*	Ferrari
3/28	USA West	***Clay Regazzoni***	Ferrari
5/2	Spain	**James Hunt**	McLaren-Ford
5/16	Belgium	***Niki Lauda***	Ferrari
5/30	Monaco	*Niki Lauda*	Ferrari
6/13	Sweden	Jody Scheckter	Tyrrell-Ford
7/4	France	**James Hunt**	McLaren-Ford
7/18	Britain	***Niki Lauda***	Ferrari
8/1	Germany	**James Hunt**	McLaren-Ford
8/15	Austria	John Watson	Penske
8/29	Holland	James Hunt	McLaren-Ford
9/12	Italy	*Ronnie Peterson*	March-Ford
10/3	Canada	**James Hunt**	McLaren-Ford
10/10	USA	*James Hunt*	McLaren-Ford
20/24	Japan	**Mario Andretti**	Lotus-Ford

Championship: 1 James Hunt (69 points), 2 Niki Lauda (68 points), 3 Jody Scheckter (49 points)

Winning constructor: Ferrari

1977

1/9	Argentina	Jody Scheckter	Wolf-Ford
1/23	Brazil	Carlos Reutemann	Ferrari
3/5	South Africa	Niki Lauda	Ferrari
4/3	USA West	Mario Andretti	Lotus-Ford
5/8	Spain	**Mario Andretti**	Lotus-Ford
5/22	Monaco	*Jody Scheckter*	Wolf-Ford
6/5	Belgium	*Gunnar Nilsson*	Lotus-Ford
6/19	Sweden	Jacques Laffite	Ligier-Matra
7/3	France	***Mario Andretti***	Lotus-Ford
7/16	Britain	***James Hunt***	McLaren-Ford
7/31	Germany	*Niki Lauda*	Ferrari
8/14	Austrian	Alan Jones	Shadow-Ford
8/28	Holland	***Niki Lauda***	Ferrari
9/11	Italy	*Mario Andretti*	Lotus-Ford
10/2	USA	**James Hunt**	McLaren-Ford
10/9	Canada	Jody Scheckter	Wolf-Ford
10/23	Japan	James Hunt	McLaren-Ford

Championship: 1 Niki Lauda (72 points), 2 Jody Scheckter (55 points), 3 Mario Andretti (47 points)

Winning constructor: Ferrari

1978

1/15	Argentina	**Mario Andretti**	Lotus-Ford
1/29	Brazil	*Carlos Reutemann*	Ferrari
3/4	South Africa	Ronnie Peterson	Lotus-Ford
4/2	USA West	**Carlos Reutemann**	Ferrari
5/7	Monaco	Patrick Depailler	Tyrrell-Ford
5/21	Belgium	**Mario Andretti**	Lotus-Ford
6/4	Spain	***Mario Andretti***	Lotus-Ford
6/17	Sweden	*Niki Lauda*	Brabham-Alfa Romeo
7/2	France	Mario Andretti	Lotus-Ford
7/16	Britain	Carlos Reutemann	Ferrari
7/30	Germany	**Mario Andretti**	Lotus-Ford
8/13	Austria	***Ronnie Peterson***	Lotus-Ford
8/27	Holland	**Mario Andretti**	Lotus-Ford
9/10	Italy	Niki Lauda	Brabham-Alfa Romeo
10/1	USA	Carlos Reutemann	Ferrari
10/8	Canada	Gilles Villeneuve	Ferrari

Championship: 1 Mario Andretti (64 points), 2 Ronnie Peterson (51 points), 3 Carlos Reutemann (48 points)

Winning constructor: Lotus

1979

1/21	Argentina	***Jacques Laffite***	Ligier-Ford
2/4	Brazil	***Jacques Laffite***	Ligier-Ford
3/3	South Africa	*Gilles Villeneuve*	Ferrari
4/8	USA West	***Gilles Villeneuve***	Ferrari
4/29	Spain	Patrick Depailler	Ligier-Ford
5/13	Belgium	Jody Scheckter	Ferrari
5/27	Monaco	**Jody Scheckter**	Ferrari
7/1	France	**Jean-Pierre Jabouille**	Renault
7/14	Britain	*Clay Regazzoni*	Williams-Ford
7/29	Germany	Alan Jones	Williams-Ford
8/12	Austria	Alan Jones	Williams-Ford
8/26	Holland	Alan Jones	Williams-Ford
9/9	Italy	Jody Scheckter	Ferrari
9/30	Canada	Alan Jones	Williams-Ford
10/7	USA	Gilles Villeneuve	Ferrari

Championship: 1 Jody Scheckter (51 points), 2 Gilles Villeneuve (47 points), 3 Alan Jones (40 points)

Winning constructor: Ferrari

1980

1/13	Argentina	***Alan Jones***	Williams-Ford
1/27	Brazil	*René Arnoux*	Renault
3/1	South Africa	*René Arnoux*	Renault
3/30	USA West	***Nelson Piquet***	Brabham-Ford
5/4	Belgium	Didier Pironi	Ligier-Ford
5/18	Monaco	*Carlos Reutemann*	Williams-Ford
6/29	France	*Alan Jones*	Williams-Ford
7/13	Britain	Alan Jones	Williams-Ford
8/10	Germany	Jacques Laffite	Ligier-Ford
8/17	Austria	Jean-Pierre Jabouille	Renault
8/31	Holland	Nelson Piquet	Brabham-Ford
9/14	Italy	Nelson Piquet	Brabham-Ford
9/28	Canada	Alan Jones	Williams-Ford
10/5	USA	Alan Jones	Williams-Ford

Championship: 1 Alan Jones (67 points), 2 Nelson Piquet (54 points), 3 Carlos Reutemann (42 points)

Winning constructor: Williams

1981

3/15	USA West	*Alan Jones*	Williams-Ford
3/29	Brazil	Carlos Reutemann	Williams-Ford
4/12	Argentina	**Nelson Piquet**	Brabham-Ford
5/3	San Marino	Nelson Piquet	Brabham-Ford
5/17	Belgium	**Carlos Reutemann**	Williams-Ford
5/31	Monaco	Gilles Villeneuve	Ferrari
6/21	Spain	Gilles Villeneuve	Ferrari
7/5	France	*Alain Prost*	Renault
7/18	Britain	John Watson	McLaren-Ford
8/2	Germany	Nelson Piquet	Brabham-Ford
8/16	Austria	*Jacques Laffite*	Ligier-Matra
8/30	Holland	**Alain Prost**	Renault
9/13	Italy	Alain Prost	Renault
9/27	Canada	Jacques Laffite	Ligier-Matra
10/17	Caesars Palace	Alan Jones	Williams-Ford

Championship: 1 Nelson Piquet (50 points), 2 Carlos Reutemann (49 points), 3 Alan Jones (46 points)

Winning constructor: Williams

1982

1/23	South Africa	*Alain Prost*	Renault
3/21	Brazil	**Alain Prost**	Reanult
4/4	USA West	*Niki Lauda*	McLaren-Ford
4/25	San Marino	*Didier Pironi*	Ferrari
5/9	Belgium	John Watson	McLaren-Ford
5/23	Monaco	*Riccardo Patrese*	Brabham-Ford
6/6	Detroit	John Watson	McLaren-Ford
6/13	Canada	Nelson Piquet	Brabham-BMW
7/3	Holland	Didier Pironi	Ferrari
7/18	Britain	Niki Lauda	McLaren-Ford
7/25	France	**Réne Arnoux**	Renault
8/8	Germany	Patrick Tambay	Ferrari
8/15	Austria	Elio de Angelis	Lotus-Ford
8/29	Switzerland	Keke Rosberg	Williams-Ford
9/12	Italy	*René Arnoux*	Renault
9/25	Caesars Palace	*Michele Alboreto*	Tyrrell-Ford

Championship: 1 Keke Rosberg (44 points), 2 Didier Pironi (39 points), 3 John Watson (39 points)

Winning constructor: Ferrari

1983

3/13	Brazil	*Nelson Piquet*	Brabham-BMW
3/27	USA West	John Watson	McLaren-Ford
4/17	France	**Alain Prost**	Renault
5/1	San Marino	Patrick Tambay	Ferrari
5/15	Monaco	Keke Rosberg	Williams-Ford
5/22	Belgium	**Alain Prost**	Renault
6/5	Detroit	Michele Alboreto	Tyrrell-Ford
6/12	Canada	**René Arnoux**	Renault
7/16	Britain	*Alain Prost*	Renault
8/7	Germany	*René Arnoux*	Renault
8/14	Austria	*Alain Prost*	Renault
8/28	Holland	*René Arnoux*	Renault
9/11	Italy	*Nelson Piquet*	Brabham-BMW
9/25	Europe	Nelson Piquet	Brabham-BMW
10/15	South Africa	Riccardo Patrese	Brabham-BMW

Championship: 1 Nelson Piquet (59 points), 2 Alain Prost (57 points), 3 René Arnoux (49 points)

Winning constructor: Ferrari

1984

3/25	Brazil	*Alain Prost*	McLaren-TAG
4/7	South Africa	Niki Lauda	McLaren-TAG
4/29	Belgium	**Michele Alboreto**	Ferrari
5/6	San Marino	Alain Prost	McLaren-TAG
5/20	France	Niki Lauda	McLaren-TAG
6/3	Monaco	**Alain Prost**	McLaren-TAG
6/17	Canada	**Nelson Piquet**	Brabham-BMW
6/24	Detroit	**Nelson Piquet**	Brabham-BMW
7/8	Dallas	Keke Rosberg	Williams-Honda
7/22	Britain	*Niki Lauda*	McLaren-TAG
8/5	Germany	*Alain Prost*	McLaren-TAG
8/19	Austria	**Alain Prost**	McLaren-TAG
8/26	Holland	**Alain Prost**	McLaren-TAG
9/9	Italy	*Niki Lauda*	McLaren-TAG
10/7	Europe	Alain Prost	McLaren-TAG
10/21	Portugal	Alain Prost	McLaren-TAG

Championship: 1 Niki Lauda (72 points), 2 Alain Prost (71.5 points), 3 Elio de Angelis (34 points)

Winning constructor: McLaren

1985

4/7	Brazil	*Alain Prost*	McLaren-TAG
4/21	Portugal	**Ayrton Senna**	Lotus-Renault
5/5	San Marino	Elio de Angelis	Lotus-Renault
5/19	Monaco	Alain Prost	McLaren-TAG
6/16	Canada	Michele Alboreto	Ferrari
6/23	Detroit	Keke Rosberg	Williams-Honda
7/7	France	Nelson Piquet	Brabham-BMW
7/21	Britain	*Alain Prost*	McLaren-TAG
8/4	Germany	Michele Alboreto	Ferrari
8/18	Austria	***Alain Prost***	McLaren-TAG
8/25	Holland	Niki Lauda	McLaren-TAG
9/8	Italy	Alain Prost	McLaren-TAG
9/15	Belgium	Ayrton Senna	Lotus-Renault
10/6	Europe	Nigel Mansell	Williams-Honda
10/19	South Africa	**Nigel Mansell**	Williams-Honda
11/3	Australia	*Keke Rosberg*	Williams-Honda

Championship: 1 Alain Prost (73 points), 2 Michele Alboreto
(53 points), 3 Keke Rosberg (40 points)

Winning constructor: McLaren

1986

3/23	Brazil	*Nelson Piquet*	Williams-Honda
4/13	Spain	**Ayrton Senna**	Lotus-Renault
4/27	San Marino	Alain Prost	McLaren-TAG
5/11	Monaco	***Alain Prost***	McLaren-TAG
5/25	Belgium	Nigel Mansell	Williams-Honda
6/15	Canada	**Nigel Mansell**	Williams-Honda
6/22	Detroit	***Ayrton Senna***	Lotus-Renault
7/6	France	*Nigel Mansell*	Williams-Honda
7/13	Britain	*Nigel Mansell*	Williams-Honda
7/27	Germany	Nelson Piquet	Williams-Honda
8/10	Hungary	*Nelson Piquet*	Williams-Honda
8/17	Austria	Alain Prost	McLaren-TAG
9/7	Italy	Nelson Piquet	Williams-Honda
9/21	Portugal	*Nigel Mansell*	Williams-Honda
10/12	Mexico	Gerhard Berger	Benetton-BMW
10/26	Australia	Alain Prost	McLaren-TAG

Championship: 1 Alain Prost (72 points), 2 Nigel Mansell (70 points),
3 Nelson Piquet (69 points)

Winning constructor: Williams

1987

4/12	Brazil	Alain Prost	McLaren-TAG
5/3	San Marino	Nigel Mansell	Williams-Honda
5/17	Belgium	*Alain Prost*	McLaren-TAG
5/31	Monaco	*Ayrton Senna*	Lotus-Honda
6/21	Detroit	*Ayrton Senna*	Lotus-Honda
7/5	France	**Nigel Mansell**	Williams-Honda
7/12	Britain	*Nigel Mansell*	Williams-Honda
7/26	Germany	Nelson Piquet	Williams-Honda
8/9	Hungary	***Nelson Piquet***	Williams-Honda
8/16	Austria	*Nigel Mansell*	Williams-Honda
9/6	Italy	**Nelson Piquet**	Williams-Honda
9/20	Portugal	Alain Prost	McLaren-TAG
9/27	Spain	Nigel Mansell	Williams-Honda
10/18	Mexico	**Nigel Mansell**	Williams-Honda
11/1	Japan	**Gerhard Berger**	Ferrari
11/15	Australia	***Gerhard Berger***	Ferrari

Championship: 1 Nelson Piquet (73 points), 2 Nigel Mansell
(61 points), 3 Ayrton Senna (57 points)

Winning constructor: Williams

1988

4/3	Brazil	Alain Prost	McLaren-Honda
5/1	San Marino	**Ayrton Senna**	McLaren-Honda
5/15	Monaco	Alain Prost	McLaren-Honda
5/29	Mexico	*Alain Prost*	McLaren-Honda
6/12	Canada	***Ayrton Senna***	McLaren-Honda
6/19	Detroit	**Ayrton Senna**	McLaren-Honda
7/3	France	***Alain Prost***	McLaren-Honda
7/10	Britain	Ayrton Senna	McLaren-Honda
7/24	Germany	**Ayrton Senna**	McLaren-Honda
8/7	Hungary	**Ayrton Senna**	McLaren-Honda
8/28	Belgium	**Ayrton Senna**	McLaren-Honda
9/11	Italy	Gerhard Berger	Ferrari
9/25	Portugal	**Alain Prost**	McLaren-Honda
10/2	Spain	*Alain Prost*	McLaren-Honda
10/30	Japan	***Ayrton Senna***	McLaren-Honda
11/13	Australia	*Alain Prost*	McLaren-Honda

Championship: 1 Ayrton Senna (90 points), 2 Alain Prost (87 points),
3 Gerhard Berger (41 points)

Winning constructor: McLaren

1989

3/26	Brazil	Nigel Mansell	Ferrari
4/23	San Marino	**Ayrton Senna**	McLaren-Honda
5/7	Monaco	**Ayrton Senna**	McLaren-Honda
5/28	Mexico	**Ayrton Senna**	McLaren-Honda
6/4	USA	Alain Prost	McLaren-Honda
6/18	Canada	Thierry Boutsen	Williams-Renault
7/9	France	**Alain Prost**	McLaren-Honda
7/16	Britain	Alain Prost	McLaren-Honda
7/30	Germany	**Ayrton Senna**	McLaren-Honda
8/13	Hungary	*Nigel Mansell*	Ferrari
8/27	Belgium	**Ayrton Senna**	McLaren-Honda
9/10	Italy	*Alain Prost*	McLaren-Honda
9/24	Portugal	*Gerhard Berger*	Ferrari
10/1	Spain	***Ayrton Senna***	McLaren-Honda
10/22	Japan	Alessandro Nannini	Benetton-Ford
11/5	Australia	Thierry Boutsen	Williams-Renault

Championship: 1 Alain Prost (76 points), 2 Ayrton Senna (60 points), 3 Riccardo Patrese (40 points)

Winning constructor: McLaren

1990

3/11	USA	Ayrton Senna	McLaren-Honda
3/25	Brazil	Alain Prost	Ferrari
5/13	San Marino	Riccardo Patrese	Williams-Renault
5/27	Monaco	***Ayrton Senna***	McLaren-Honda
6/10	Canada	**Ayrton Senna**	McLaren-Honda
6/24	Mexico	*Alain Prost*	Ferrari
7/8	France	Alain Prost	Ferrari
7/15	Britain	Alain Prost	Ferrari
7/29	Germany	**Ayrton Senna**	McLaren-Honda
8/12	Hungary	**Thierry Boutsen**	Williams-Renault
8/26	Belgium	**Ayrton Senna**	McLaren-Honda
9/9	Italy	***Ayrton Senna***	McLaren-Honda
9/23	Portugal	**Nigel Mansell**	Ferrari
9/30	Spain	Alain Prost	Ferrari
10/21	Japan	Nelson Piquet	Benetton-Ford
11/4	Australia	Nelson Piquet	Benetton-Ford

Championship: 1 Ayrton Senna (78 points), 2 Alain Prost (71 points), 3 Nelson Piquet (43 points)

Winning constructor: McLaren

1991

3/10	USA	**Ayrton Senna**	McLaren-Honda
3/24	Brazil	**Ayrton Senna**	McLaren-Honda
4/28	San Marino	**Ayrton Senna**	McLaren-Honda
5/12	Monaco	**Ayrton Senna**	McLaren-Honda
6/2	Canada	Nelson Piquet	Benetton-Ford
6/16	Mexico	**Riccardo Patrese**	Williams-Renault
7/7	France	*Nigel Mansell*	Williams-Renault
7/14	Britain	*Nigel Mansell*	Williams-Renault
7/28	Germany	*Nigel Mansell*	Williams-Renault
8/11	Hungary	**Ayrton Senna**	McLaren-Honda
8/25	Belgium	**Ayrton Senna**	McLaren-Honda
9/8	Italy	Nigel Mansell	Williams-Renault
9/22	Portugal	**Riccardo Patrese**	Williams-Renault
9/29	Spain	Nigel Mansell	Williams-Renault
10/20	Japan	**Gerhard Berger**	McLaren-Honda
11/3	Australia	**Ayrton Senna**	McLaren-Honda

Championship: 1 Ayrton Senna (96 points), 2 Nigel Mansell (72 points), 3 Riccardo Patrese (53 points)

Winning constructor: McLaren

1992

3/1	South Africa	***Nigel Mansell***	Williams-Renault
3/22	Mexico	**Nigel Mansell**	Williams-Renault
4/5	Brazil	**Nigel Mansell**	Williams-Renault
5/3	Spain	***Nigel Mansell***	Williams-Renault
5/17	San Marino	**Nigel Mansell**	Williams-Renault
5/31	Monaco	Ayrton Senna	McLaren-Honda
6/14	Canada	*Gerhard Berger*	McLaren-Honda
7/5	France	***Nigel Mansell***	Williams-Renault
7/12	Britain	***Nigel Mansell***	Williams-Renault
7/26	Germany	**Nigel Mansell**	Williams-Renault
8/16	Hungary	Ayrton Senna	McLaren-Honda
8/30	Belgium	*Michael Schumacher*	Benetton-Ford
9/13	Italy	Ayrton Senna	McLaren-Honda
9/27	Portugal	**Nigel Mansell**	Williams-Renault
10/25	Japan	Riccardo Patrese	Williams-Renault
11/8	Australia	Gerhard Berger	McLaren-Honda

Championship: 1 Nigel Mansell (108 points), 2 Riccardo Patrese (56 points), 3 Michael Schumacher (53 points)

Winning constructor: Williams

1993

3/14	South Africa	*Alain Prost*	Williams-Renault
3/28	Brazil	Ayrton Senna	McLaren-Ford
4/11	Europe	*Ayrton Senna*	McLaren-Ford
4/25	San Marino	*Alain Prost*	Williams-Renault
5/9	Spain	**Alain Prost**	Williams-Renault
5/23	Monaco	Ayrton Senna	McLaren-Ford
6/13	Canada	**Alain Prost**	Williams-Renault
7/4	France	Alain Prost	Williams-Renault
7/11	Britain	**Alain Prost**	Williams-Renault
7/25	Germany	**Alain Prost**	Williams-Renault
8/15	Hungary	Damon Hill	Williams-Renault
8/29	Belgium	Damon Hill	Williams-Renault
9/12	Italy	*Damon Hill*	Williams-Renault
9/26	Portugal	Michael Schumacher	Benetton-Ford
10/24	Japan	Ayrton Senna	McLaren-Ford
11/7	Australia	**Ayrton Senna**	McLaren-Ford

Championship: 1 Alain Prost (99 points), 2 Ayrton Senna (73 points), 3 Damon Hill (69 points)

Winning constructor: Williams

1994

3/27	Brazil	*Michael Schumacher*	Benetton-Ford
4/17	Pacific	*Michael Schumacher*	Benetton-Ford
5/1	San Marino	Michael Schumacher	Benetton-Ford
5/15	Monaco	*Michael Schumacher*	Benetton-Ford
5/29	Spain	Damon Hill	Williams-Renault
6/12	Canada	*Michael Schumacher*	Benetton-Ford
7/3	France	Michael Schumacher	Benetton-Ford
7/10	Britain	*Damon Hill*	Williams-Renault
7/31	Germany	**Gerhard Berger**	Ferrari
8/14	Hungary	*Michael Schumacher*	Benetton-Ford
8/28	Belgium	*Damon Hill*	Williams-Renault
9/11	Italy	*Damon Hill*	Williams-Renault
9/28	Portugal	Damon Hill	Williams-Renault
10/16	Europe	*Michael Schumacher*	Benetton-Ford
11/6	Japan	*Damon Hill*	Williams-Renault
11/13	Australia	**Nigel Mansell**	Williams-Renault

Championship: 1 Michael Schumacher (92 points), 2 Damon Hill (91 points), 3 Gerhard Berger (41 points)

Winning constructor: Williams

1995

3/26	Brazil	*Michael Schumacher*	Benetton-Renault
4/9	Argentina	Damon Hill	Williams-Renault
4/30	San Marino	Damon Hill	Williams-Renault
5/14	Spain	**Michael Schumacher**	Benetton-Renault
5/28	Monaco	Michael Schumacher	Benetton-Renault
6/11	Canada	Jean Alesi	Ferrari
7/2	France	*Michael Schumacher*	Benetton-Renault
7/16	Britain	Johnny Herbert	Benetton-Renault
7/30	Germany	*Michael Schumacher*	Benetton-Renault
8/13	Hungary	*Damon Hill*	Williams-Renault
8/27	Belgium	Michael Schumacher	Benetton-Renault
9/10	Italy	Johnny Herbert	Benetton-Renault
9/24	Portugal	*David Coulthard*	Williams-Renault
10/1	Europe	*Michael Schumacher*	Benetton-Renault
10/22	Pacific	*Michael Schumacher*	Benetton-Renault
10/29	Japan	*Michael Schumacher*	Benetton-Renault
11/12	Australia	*Damon Hill*	Williams-Renault

Championship: 1 Michael Schumacher (102 points), 2 Damon Hill (69 points), 3 David Coulthard (49 points)

Winning constructor: Benetton

1996

3/10	Australia	Damon Hill	Williams-Renault
3/31	Brazil	*Damon Hill*	Williams-Renault
4/7	Argentina	**Damon Hill**	Williams-Renault
4/28	Europe	Jacques Villeneuve	Williams-Renault
5/5	San Marino	*Damon Hill*	Williams-Renault
5/19	Monaco	Olivier Panis	Ligier-Mugen-Honda
6/2	Spain	*Michael Schumacher*	Ferrari
6/16	Canada	**Damon Hill**	Williams-Renault
6/30	France	Damon Hill	Williams-Renault
7/14	Britain	*Jacques Villeneuve*	Williams-Renault
7/28	Germany	**Damon Hill**	Williams-Renault
8/11	Hungary	Jacques Villeneuve	Williams-Renault
8/25	Belgium	Michael Schumacher	Ferrari
9/8	Italy	*Michael Schumacher*	Ferrari
9/22	Portugal	*Jacques Villeneuve*	Williams-Renault
10/13	Japan	Damon Hill	Williams-Renault

Championship: 1 Damon Hill (97 points), 2 Jacques Villeneuve (78 points), 3 Michael Schumacher (59 points)

Winning constructor: Williams

1997

3/9	Australia	David Coulthard	McLaren-Mercedes
3/30	Brazil	*Jacques Villeneuve*	Williams-Renault
4/13	Argentina	*Jacques Villeneuve*	Williams-Renault
4/27	San Marino	*Heinz-Harald Frentzen*	Williams-Renault
5/11	Monaco	*Michael Schumacher*	Ferrari
5/25	Spain	*Jacques Villeneuve*	Williams-Renault
6/15	Canada	**Michael Schumacher**	Ferrari
6/29	France	***Michael Schumacher***	Ferrari
7/13	Britain	*Jacques Villeneuve*	Williams-Renault
7/27	Germany	***Gerhard Berger***	Benetton-Renault
8/10	Hungary	Jacques Villeneuve	Williams-Renault
8/24	Belgium	Michael Schumacher	Ferrari
9/7	Italy	David Coulthard	McLaren-Mercedes
9/21	Austria	***Jacques Villeneuve***	Williams-Renault
9/28	Luxembourg	Jacques Villeneuve	Williams-Renault
10/12	Japan	Michael Schumacher	Ferrari
10/26	Europe	Mika Häkkinen	McLaren-Mercedes

Championship: 1 Jacques Villeneuve (81 points), 2 Heinz-Harald Frentzen (42 points), 3 David Coulthard (36 points)

Winning constructor: Williams

1998

3/8	Australia	*Mika Häkkinen*	McLaren-Mercedes
3/29	Brazil	*Mika Häkkinen*	McLaren-Mercedes
4/12	Argentina	Michael Schumacher	Ferrari
4/26	San Marino	**David Coulthard**	McLaren-Mercedes
5/10	Spain	*Mika Häkkinen*	McLaren-Mercedes
5/24	Monaco	*Mika Häkkinen*	McLaren-Mercedes
6/7	Canada	*Michael Schumacher*	Ferrari
6/28	France	Michael Schumacher	Ferrari
7/12	Britain	*Michael Schumacher*	Ferrari
7/26	Austria	Mika Häkkinen	McLaren-Mercedes
8/2	Germany	**Mika Häkkinen**	McLaren-Mercedes
8/16	Hungary	*Michael Schumacher*	Ferrari
8/30	Belgium	Damon Hill	Jordan-Mugen-Honda
9/13	Italy	**Michael Schumacher**	Ferrari
9/27	Luxembourg	*Mika Häkkinen*	McLaren-Mercedes
11/1	Japan	Mika Häkkinen	McLaren-Mercedes

Championship: 1 Mika Häkkinen (100 points), 2 Michael Schumacher (86 points), 3 David Coulthard (56 points)

Winning constructor: McLaren

1999

3/7	Australia	Eddie Irvine	Ferrari
4/11	Brazil	*Mika Häkkinen*	McLaren-Mercedes
5/2	San Marino	*Michael Schumacher*	Ferrari
5/16	Monaco	Michael Schumacher	Ferrari
5/30	Spain	**Mika Häkkinen**	McLaren-Mercedes
6/13	Canada	Mika Häkkinen	McLaren-Mercedes
6/27	France	Heinz-Harald Frentzen	Jordan-Mugen-Honda
7/11	Britain	David Coulthard	McLaren-Mercedes
7/25	Austria	Eddie Irvine	Ferrari
8/1	Germany	Eddie Irvine	Ferrari
8/15	Hungary	**Mika Häkkinen**	McLaren-Mercedes
8/29	Belgium	David Coulthard	McLaren-Mercedes
9/12	Italy	Heinz-Harald Frentzen	Jordan-Mugen-Honda
9/26	Europe	Johnny Herbert	Stewart-Ford
10/17	Malaysia	Eddie Irvine	Ferrari
10/31	Japan	Mika Häkkinen	McLaren-Mercedes

Championship: 1 Mika Häkkinen (76 points), 2 Eddie Irvine (74 points), 3 Heinz-Harald Frentzen (54 points)

Winning constructor: Ferrari

2000

3/12	Australia	Michael Schumacher	Ferrari
3/26	Brazil	*Michael Schumacher*	Ferrari
4/9	San Marino	Michael Schumacher	Ferrari
4/23	Britain	David Coulthard	McLaren-Mercedes
5/7	Spain	*Mika Häkkinen*	McLaren-Mercedes
5/21	Europe	*Michael Schumacher*	Ferrari
6/4	Monaco	David Coulthard	McLaren-Mercedes
6/18	Canada	*Michael Schumacher*	Ferrari
7/2	France	*David Coulthard*	McLaren-Mercedes
7/16	Austria	**Mika Häkkinen**	McLaren-Mercedes
7/30	Germany	*Rubens Barrichello*	Ferrari
8/13	Hungary	*Mika Häkkinen*	McLaren-Mercedes
8/27	Belgium	**Mika Häkkinen**	McLaren-Mercedes
9/10	Italy	**Michael Schumacher**	Ferrari
9/24	USA	**Michael Schumacher**	Ferrari
10/8	Japan	**Michael Schumacher**	Ferrari
10/22	Malaysia	**Michael Schumacher**	Ferrari

Championship: 1 Michael Schumacher (108 points), 2 Mika Häkkinen (89 points), 3 David Coulthard (73 points)

Winning constructor: Ferrari

2001

3/4	Australia	*Michael Schumacher*	Ferrari
3/18	Malaysia	**Michael Schumacher**	Ferrari
4/1	Brazil	David Coulthard	McLaren-Mercedes
4/15	San Marino	*Ralf Schumacher*	Williams-BMW
4/29	Spain	**Michael Schumacher**	Ferrari
5/13	Austria	*David Coulthard*	McLaren-Mercedes
5/27	Monaco	Michael Schumacher	Ferrari
6/10	Canada	*Ralf Schumacher*	Williams-BMW
6/24	Europe	**Michael Schumacher**	Ferrari
7/1	France	Michael Schumacher	Ferrari
7/15	Britain	*Mika Häkkinen*	McLaren-Mercedes
7/29	Germany	Ralf Schumacher	Williams-BMW
8/19	Hungary	**Michael Schumacher**	Ferrari
9/2	Belgium	*Michael Schumacher*	Ferrari
9/16	Italy	**Juan Pablo Montoya**	Williams-BMW
9/30	USA	Mika Häkkinen	McLaren-Mercedes
10/14	Japan	**Michael Schumacher**	Ferrari

Championship: 1 Michael Schumacher (123 points), 2 David Coulthard (65 points), 3 Rubens Barrichello (56 points)

Winning constructor: Ferrari

2002

3/3	Australia	Michael Schumacher	Ferrari
3/17	Malaysia	Ralf Schumacher	Williams-BMW
3/31	Brazil	Michael Schumacher	Ferrari
4/13	San Marino	**Michael Schumacher**	Ferrari
4/28	Spain	*Michael Schumacher*	Ferrari
5/12	Austria	*Michael Schumacher*	Ferrari
5/26	Monaco	David Coulthard	McLaren-Mercedes
6/9	Canada	Michael Schumacher	Ferrari
6/23	Europe	Rubens Barrichello	Ferrari
7/7	Britain	Michael Schumacher	Ferrari
7/21	France	Michael Schumacher	Ferrari
7/28	Germany	*Michael Schumacher*	Ferrari
8/18	Hungary	Rubens Barrichello	Ferrari
9/1	Belgium	*Michael Schumacher*	Ferrari
9/15	Italy	*Rubens Barrichello*	Ferrari
9/29	USA	*Rubens Barrichello*	Ferrari
10/13	Japan	*Michael Schumacher*	Ferrari

Championship: 1 Michael Schumacher (144 points), 2 Rubens Barrichello (77 points), 3 Juan Pablo Montoya (50 points)

Winning constructor: Ferrari

2003

3/9	Australia	David Coulthard	McLaren-Mercedes
3/23	Malaysia	Kimi Räikkönen	McLaren-Mercedes
4/6	Brazil	Giancarlo Fisichella	Jordan-Ford
4/20	San Marino	*Michael Schumacher*	Ferrari
5/4	Spain	**Michael Schumacher**	Ferrari
5/18	Austria	*Michael Schumacher*	Ferrari
6/1	Monaco	Juan Pablo Montoya	Williams-BMW
6/15	Canada	Michael Schumacher	Ferrari
6/29	Europe	Ralf Schumacher	Williams-BMW
7/6	France	**Ralf Schumacher**	Williams-BMW
7/20	Britain	*Rubens Barrichello*	Ferrari
8/3	Germany	**Juan Pablo Montoya**	Williams-BMW
8/24	Hungary	**Fernando Alonso**	Renault
9/14	Italy	*Michael Schumacher*	Ferrari
9/28	USA	*Michael Schumacher*	Ferrari
10/12	Japan	**Rubens Barrichello**	Ferrari

Championship: 1 Michael Schumacher (93 points), 2 Kimi Räikkönen (91 points), 3 Juan Pablo Montoya (82 points)

Winning constructor: Ferrari

2004

3/7	Australia	*Michael Schumacher*	Ferrari
3/21	Malaysia	**Michael Schumacher**	Ferrari
4/4	Bahrain	*Michael Schumacher*	Ferrari
4/25	San Marino	*Michael Schumacher*	Ferrari
5/9	Spain	*Michael Schumacher*	Ferrari
5/23	Monaco	**Jarno Trulli**	Renault
5/30	Europe	*Michael Schumacher*	Ferrari
6/13	Canada	Michael Schumacher	Ferrari
6/20	USA	Michael Schumacher	Ferrari
7/4	France	*Michael Schumacher*	Ferrari
7/11	Britain	*Michael Schumacher*	Ferrari
7/25	Germany	**Michael Schumacher**	Ferrari
8/15	Hungary	*Michael Schumacher*	Ferrari
8/29	Belgium	*Kimi Räikkönen*	McLaren-Mercedes
9/12	Italy	*Rubens Barrichello*	Ferrari
9/26	China	**Rubens Barrichello**	Ferrari
10/10	Japan	**Michael Schumacher**	Ferrari
10/24	Brazil	*Juan Pablo Montoya*	Williams-BMW

Championship: 1 Michael Schumacher (148 points), 2 Rubens Barrichello (114 points), 3 Jenson Button (85 points)

Winning constructor: Ferrari

2005

3/6	Australia	**Giancarlo Fisichella**	Renault
3/20	Malaysia	**Fernando Alonso**	Renault
4/3	Bahrain	**Fernando Alonso**	Renault
4/24	San Marino	Fernando Alonso	Renault
5/8	Spain	**Kimi Räikkönen**	McLaren-Mercedes
5/22	Monaco	**Kimi Räikkönen**	McLaren-Mercedes
5/29	Europe	*Fernando Alonso*	Renault
6/12	Canada	*Kimi Räikkönen*	McLaren-Mercedes
6/19	USA	Michael Schumacher	Ferrari
7/3	France	**Fernando Alonso**	Renault
7/10	Britain	Juan Pablo Montoya	McLaren-Mercedes
7/24	Germany	Fernando Alonso	Renault
7/31	Hungary	*Kimi Räikkönen*	McLaren-Mercedes
8/21	Turkey	**Kimi Räikkönen**	McLaren-Mercedes
9/4	Italy	**Juan Pablo Montoya**	McLaren-Mercedes
9/11	Belgium	Kimi Räikkönen	McLaren-Mercedes
9/25	Brazil	Juan Pablo Montoya	McLaren-Mercedes
10/9	Japan	*Kimi Räikkönen*	McLaren-Mercedes
10/16	China	**Fernando Alonso**	Renault

Championship: 1 Fernando Alonso (133 points), 2 Kimi Räikkönen (112 points), 3 Michael Schumacher (62 points)

Winning constructor: Renault

2006

3/12	Bahrain	Fernando Alonso	Renault
3/19	Malaysia	**Giancarlo Fisichella**	Renault
4/2	Australia	Fernando Alonso	Renault
4/23	San Marino	**Michael Schumacher**	Ferrari
5/7	Europe	*Michael Schumacher*	Ferrari
5/15	Spain	**Fernando Alonso**	Renault
5/28	Monaco	**Fernando Alonso**	Renault
6/11	Britain	*Fernando Alonso*	Renault
6/25	Canada	**Fernando Alonso**	Renault
7/2	USA	*Michael Schumacher*	Ferrari
7/16	France	*Michael Schumacher*	Ferrari
7/30	Germany	*Michael Schumacher*	Ferrari
8/6	Hungary	Jenson Button	Honda
8/27	Turkey	**Felipe Massa**	Ferrari
9/10	Italy	Michael Schumacher	Ferrari
10/1	China	Michael Schumacher	Ferrari
10/8	Japan	*Fernando Alonso*	Renault
10/22	Brazil	**Felipe Massa**	Ferrari

Championship: 1 Fernando Alonso (134 points), 2 Michael Schumacher (121 points), 3 Felipe Massa (80 points)

Winning constructor: Renault

2007

3/18	Australia	*Kimi Räikkönen*	Ferrari
4/8	Malaysia	Fernando Alonso	McLaren-Mercedes
4/15	Bahrain	*Felipe Massa*	Ferrari
5/13	Spain	*Felipe Massa*	Ferrari
5/27	Monaco	*Fernando Alonso*	McLaren-Mercedes
6/10	Canada	**Lewis Hamilton**	McLaren-Mercedes
6/17	USA	**Lewis Hamilton**	McLaren-Mercedes
7/1	France	Kimi Räikkönen	Ferrari
7/8	Britain	*Kimi Räikkönen*	Ferrari
7/22	Europe	Fernando Alonso	McLaren-Mercedes
8/5	Hungary	**Lewis Hamilton**	McLaren-Mercedes
8/26	Turkey	**Felipe Massa**	Ferrari
9/9	Italy	*Fernando Alonso*	McLaren-Mercedes
9/16	Belgium	**Kimi Räikkönen**	Ferrari
9/30	Japan	*Lewis Hamilton*	McLaren-Mercedes
10/7	China	Kimi Räikkönen	Ferrari
10/21	Brazil	*Kimi Räikkönen*	Ferrari

Championship: 1 Kimi Räikkönen (110 points), 2 Lewis Hamilton (109 points), 3 Fernando Alonso (109 points)

Winning constructor: Ferrari

2008

3/16	Australia	**Lewis Hamilton**	McLaren-Mercedes
3/23	Malaysia	Kimi Räikkönen	Ferrari
4/6	Bahrain	Felipe Massa	Ferrari
4/27	Spain	*Kimi Räikkönen*	Ferrari
5/11	Turkey	**Felipe Massa**	Ferrari
5/25	Monaco	Lewis Hamilton	McLaren-Mercedes
6/8	Canada	Robert Kubica	BMW
6/22	France	Felipe Massa	Ferrari
7/6	Britain	Lewis Hamilton	McLaren-Mercedes
7/20	Germany	**Lewis Hamilton**	McLaren-Mercedes
8/3	Hungary	Heikki Kovalainen	McLaren-Mercedes
8/24	Europe	*Felipe Massa*	Ferrari
9/7	Belgium	Felipe Massa	Ferrari
9/14	Italy	**Sebastian Vettel**	Toro Rosso-Ferrari
9/28	Singapore	Fernando Alonso	Renault
10/12	Japan	Fernando Alonso	Renault
10/19	China	*Lewis Hamilton*	McLaren-Mercedes
11/2	Brazil	*Felipe Massa*	Ferrari

Championship: 1 Lewis Hamilton (98 points), 2 Felipe Massa (97 points), 3 Kimi Räikkönen (75 points)

Winning constructor: Ferrari

2009

3/29	Australia	**Jenson Button**	Brawn-Mercedes
4/5	Malaysia	***Jenson Button***	Brawn-Mercedes
4/19	China	**Sebastian Vettel**	Red Bull-Renault
4/26	Bahrain	Jenson Button	Brawn-Mercedes
5/10	Spain	**Jenson Button**	Brawn-Mercedes
5/24	Monaco	**Jenson Button**	Brawn-Mercedes
6/7	Turkey	*Jenson Button*	Brawn-Mercedes
6/21	Britain	***Sebastian Vettel***	Red Bull-Renault
7/12	Germany	**Mark Webber**	Red Bull-Renault
7/26	Hungary	Lewis Hamilton	McLaren-Mercedes
8/23	Europe	Rubens Barrichello	Brawn-Mercedes
8/30	Belgium	Kimi Räikkönen	Ferrari
9/13	Italy	Rubens Barrichello	Brawn-Mercedes
9/27	Singapore	**Lewis Hamilton**	McLaren-Mercedes
10/4	Japan	**Sebastian Vettel**	Red Bull-Renault
10/18	Brazil	Mark Webber	Red Bull-Renault
11/1	Abu Dhabi	*Sebastian Vettel*	Red Bull-Renault

Championship: 1 Jenson Button (95 points), 2 Sebastian Vettel (84 points), 3 Rubens Barrichello (84 points)

Winning constructor: Brawn

2010

3/14	Bahrain	*Fernando Alonso*	Ferrari
3/28	Australia	Jenson Button	McLaren-Mercedes
4/4	Malaysia	Sebastian Vettel	Red Bull-Renault
4/18	China	Jenson Button	McLaren-Mercedes
5/9	Spain	**Mark Webber**	Red Bull-Renault
5/16	Monaco	**Mark Webber**	Red Bull-Renault
5/30	Turkey	Lewis Hamilton	McLaren-Mercedes
6/13	Canada	**Lewis Hamilton**	McLaren-Mercedes
6/27	Europe	**Sebastian Vettel**	Red Bull-Renault
7/11	Britain	Mark Webber	Red Bull-Renault
7/25	Germany	Fernando Alonso	Ferrari
8/1	Hungary	Mark Webber	Red Bull-Renault
8/29	Belgium	*Lewis Hamilton*	McLaren-Mercedes
9/12	Italy	***Fernando Alonso***	Ferrari
9/26	Singapore	***Fernando Alonso***	Ferrari
10/10	Japan	**Sebastian Vettel**	Red Bull-Renault
10/24	Korea	*Fernando Alonso*	Ferrari
11/7	Brazil	Sebastian Vettel	Red Bull-Renault
11/14	Abu Dhabi	**Sebastian Vettel**	Red Bull-Renault

Championship: 1 Sebastian Vettel (256 points), 2 Fernando Alonso (252 points), 3 Mark Webber (242 points)

Winning constructor: Red Bull

2011

3/27	Australia	**Sebastian Vettel**	Red Bull-Renault
4/10	Malaysia	**Sebastian Vettel**	Red Bull-Renault
4/17	China	Lewis Hamilton	McLaren-Mercedes
5/8	Turkey	**Sebastian Vettel**	Red Bull-Renault
5/22	Spain	Sebastian Vettel	Red Bull-Renault
5/29	Monaco	**Sebastian Vettel**	Red Bull-Renault
6/12	Canada	Jenson Button	McLaren-Mercedes
6/26	Europe	***Sebastian Vettel***	Red Bull-Renault
7/10	Britain	*Fernando Alonso*	Ferrari
7/24	Germany	*Lewis Hamilton*	McLaren-Mercedes
7/31	Hungary	Jenson Button	McLaren-Mercedes
8/28	Belgium	**Sebastian Vettel**	Red Bull-Renault
9/11	Italy	**Sebastian Vettel**	Red Bull-Renault
9/25	Singapore	**Sebastian Vettel**	Red Bull-Renault
10/9	Japan	*Jenson Button*	McLaren-Mercedes
10/16	Korea	*Sebastian Vettel*	Red Bull-Renault
10/30	India	***Sebastian Vettel***	Red Bull-Renault
11/13	Abu Dhabi	Lewis Hamilton	McLaren-Mercedes
11/27	Brazil	*Mark Webber*	Red Bull-Renault

Championship: 1 Sebastian Vettel (392 points), 2 Jenson Button (270 points), 3 Mark Webber (258 points)

Winning constructor: Red Bull

2012

3/18	Australia	*Jenson Button*	McLaren-Mercedes
3/25	Malaysia	Fernando Alonso	Ferrari
4/15	China	**Nico Rosberg**	Mercedes
4/22	Bahrain	***Sebastian Vettel***	Red Bull-Renault
5/13	Spain	**Pastor Maldonado**	Williams-Renault
5/27	Monaco	**Mark Webber**	Red Bull-Renault
6/10	Canada	Lewis Hamilton	McLaren-Mercedes
6/24	Europe	Fernando Alonso	Ferrari
7/8	Britain	Mark Webber	Red Bull-Renault
7/22	Germany	**Fernando Alonso**	Ferrari
7/29	Hungary	**Lewis Hamilton**	McLaren-Mercedes
9/2	Belgium	**Jenson Button**	McLaren-Mercedes
9/9	Italy	**Lewis Hamilton**	McLaren-Mercedes
9/23	Singapore	Sebastian Vettel	Red Bull-Renault
10/7	Japan	***Sebastian Vettel***	Red Bull-Renault
10/14	Korea	Sebastian Vettel	Red Bull-Renault
10/28	India	**Sebastian Vettel**	Red Bull-Renault
11/4	Abu Dhabi	Kimi Räikkönen	Lotus-Renault
11/18	USA	Lewis Hamilton	McLaren-Mercedes
11/25	Brazil	Jenson Button	McLaren-Mercedes

Championship: 1 Sebastian Vettel (281 points), 2 Fernando Alonso (278 points), 3 Kimi Räikkönen (207 points)

Winning constructor: Red Bull

2013

Date	Country	Driver	Constructor
3/17	Australia	*Kimi Räikkönen*	Lotus-Renault
3/24	Malaysia	**Sebastian Vettel**	Red Bull-Renault
4/14	China	Fernando Alonso	Ferrari
4/21	Bahrain	*Sebastian Vettel*	Red Bull-Renault
5/12	Spain	Fernando Alonso	Ferrari
5/26	Monaco	**Nico Rosberg**	Mercedes
6/9	Canada	**Sebastian Vettel**	Red Bull-Renault
6/30	Britain	Nico Rosberg	Mercedes
7/7	Germany	Sebastian Vettel	Red Bull-Renault
7/28	Hungary	**Lewis Hamilton**	Mercedes
8/25	Belgium	*Sebastian Vettel*	Red Bull-Renault
9/8	Italy	**Sebastian Vettel**	Red Bull-Renault
9/22	Singapore	***Sebastian Vettel***	Red Bull-Renault
10/6	Korea	***Sebastian Vettel***	Red Bull-Renault
10/13	Japan	Sebastian Vettel	Red Bull-Renault
10/27	India	**Sebastian Vettel**	Red Bull-Renault
11/3	Abu Dhabi	Sebastian Vettel	Red Bull-Renault
11/17	USA	***Sebastian Vettel***	Red Bull-Renault
11/24	Brazil	**Sebastian Vettel**	Red Bull-Renault

Championship: 1 Sebastian Vettel (397 points), 2 Fernando Alonso (242 points), 3 Mark Webber (199 points)

Winning constructor: Red Bull

2014

Date	Country	Driver	Constructor
3/16	Australia	*Nico Rosberg*	Mercedes
3/30	Malaysia	***Lewis Hamilton***	Mercedes
4/6	Bahrain	Lewis Hamilton	Mercedes
4/20	China	**Lewis Hamilton**	Mercedes
5/11	Spain	**Lewis Hamilton**	Mercedes
5/25	Monaco	**Nico Rosberg**	Mercedes
6/8	Canada	Daniel Ricciardo	Red Bull-Renault
6/22	Austria	Nico Rosberg	Mercedes
7/6	Britain	*Lewis Hamilton*	Mercedes
7/20	Germany	**Nico Rosberg**	Mercedes
7/27	Hungary	Daniel Ricciardo	Red Bull-Renault
8/24	Belgium	Daniel Ricciardo	Red Bull-Renault
9/7	Italy	***Lewis Hamilton***	Mercedes
9/21	Singapore	***Lewis Hamilton***	Mercedes
10/5	Japan	*Lewis Hamilton*	Mercedes
10/12	Russia	**Lewis Hamilton**	Mercedes
11/2	USA	Lewis Hamilton	Mercedes
11/9	Brazil	**Nico Rosberg**	Mercedes
11/23	Abu Dhabi	Lewis Hamilton	Mercedes

Championship: 1 Lewis Hamilton (384 points), 2 Nico Rosberg (317 points), 3 Daniel Ricciardo (238 points)

Winning constructor: Mercedes

2015

Date	Country	Driver	Constructor
3/15	Australia	***Lewis Hamilton***	Mercedes
3/29	Malaysia	Sebastian Vettel	Ferrari
4/12	China	***Lewis Hamilton***	Mercedes
4/19	Bahrain	**Lewis Hamilton**	Mercedes
5/10	Spain	**Nico Rosberg**	Mercedes
5/24	Monaco	Nico Rosberg	Mercedes
6/7	Canada	**Lewis Hamilton**	Mercedes
6/21	Austria	*Nico Rosberg*	Mercedes
7/5	Britain	***Lewis Hamilton***	Mercedes
7/26	Hungary	Sebastian Vettel	Ferrari
8/23	Belgium	**Lewis Hamilton**	Mercedes
9/6	Italy	***Lewis Hamilton***	Mercedes
9/20	Singapore	**Sebastian Vettel**	Ferrari
9/27	Japan	*Lewis Hamilton*	Mercedes
10/11	Russia	Lewis Hamilton	Mercedes
10/25	USA	Lewis Hamilton	Mercedes
11/1	Mexico	***Nico Rosberg***	Mercedes
11/15	Brazil	**Nico Rosberg**	Mercedes
11/29	Abu Dhabi	**Nico Rosberg**	Mercedes

Championship: 1 Lewis Hamilton (384 points), 2 Nico Rosberg (322 points), 3 Sebastian Vettel (278 points)

Winning constructor: Mercedes

2016

Date	Country	Driver	Constructor
3/20	Australia	Nico Rosberg	Mercedes
4/3	Bahrain	*Nico Rosberg*	Mercedes
4/17	China	**Nico Rosberg**	Mercedes
5/1	Russia	***Nico Rosberg***	Mercedes
5/15	Spain	Max Verstappen	Red Bull-Renault
5/29	Monaco	*Lewis Hamilton*	Mercedes
6/12	Canada	**Lewis Hamilton**	Mercedes
6/19	Europe	***Nico Rosberg***	Mercedes
7/3	Austria	*Lewis Hamilton*	Mercedes
7/10	Britain	**Lewis Hamilton**	Mercedes
7/24	Hungary	Lewis Hamilton	Mercedes
7/31	Germany	Lewis Hamilton	Mercedes
8/24	Belgium	**Nico Rosberg**	Mercedes
9/4	Italy	Nico Rosberg	Mercedes
9/18	Singapore	Nico Rosberg	Mercedes
10/2	Malaysia	Daniel Ricciardo	Red Bull-Renault
10/9	Japan	**Nico Rosberg**	Mercedes
10/23	USA	**Lewis Hamilton**	Mercedes
10/30	Mexico	**Lewis Hamilton**	Mercedes
11/13	Brazil	**Lewis Hamilton**	Mercedes
11/27	Abu Dhabi	**Lewis Hamilton**	Mercedes

Championship: 1 Nico Rosberg (385 points), 2 Lewis Hamilton (380 points), 3 Daniel Ricciardo (256 points)

Winning constructor: Mercedes

2017

3/26	Australia	Sebastian Vettel	Ferrari
4/9	China	*Lewis Hamilton*	Mercedes
4/16	Bahrain	Sebastian Vettel	Ferrari
4/30	Russia	**Valtteri Bottas**	Mercedes
5/14	Spain	*Lewis Hamilton*	Mercedes
5/28	Monaco	Sebastian Vettel	Ferrari
6/11	Canada	*Lewis Hamilton*	Mercedes
6/25	Azerbaijan	Daniel Ricciardo	Red Bull-Renault
7/9	Austria	**Valtteri Bottas**	Mercedes
7/16	Britain	*Lewis Hamilton*	Mercedes
7/30	Hungary	**Sebastian Vettel**	Ferrari
8/27	Belgium	**Lewis Hamilton**	Mercedes
9/3	Italy	**Lewis Hamilton**	Mercedes
9/17	Singapore	*Lewis Hamilton*	Mercedes
10/1	Malaysia	Max Verstappen	Red Bull-Renault
10/8	Japan	**Lewis Hamilton**	Mercedes
10/22	USA	**Lewis Hamilton**	Mercedes
10/29	Mexico	Max Verstappen	Red Bull-Renault
11/12	Brazil	Sebastian Vettel	Ferrari
11/26	Abu Dhabi	***Valtteri Bottas***	Mercedes

Championship: 1 Lewis Hamilton (363 points), 2 Sebastian Vettel (317 points), 3 Valtteri Bottas (305 points)

Winning constructor: Mercedes

2018

3/25	Australia	Sebastian Vettel	Ferrari
4/8	Bahrain	**Sebastian Vettel**	Ferrari
4/15	China	*Daniel Ricciardo*	Red Bull-Renault
4/29	Azerbaijan	Lewis Hamilton	Mercedes
5/13	Spain	**Lewis Hamilton**	Mercedes
5/27	Monaco	**Daniel Ricciardo**	Red Bull-Renault
6/10	Canada	**Sebastian Vettel**	Ferrari
6/24	France	**Lewis Hamilton**	Mercedes
7/1	Austria	Max Verstappen	Red Bull-Renault
7/8	Britain	*Sebastian Vettel*	Ferrari
7/22	Germany	*Lewis Hamilton*	Mercedes
7/29	Hungary	**Lewis Hamilton**	Mercedes
8/26	Belgium	Sebastian Vettel	Ferrari
9/2	Italy	*Lewis Hamilton*	Mercedes
9/16	Singapore	**Lewis Hamilton**	Mercedes
9/30	Russia	Lewis Hamilton	Mercedes
10/7	Japan	**Lewis Hamilton**	Mercedes
10/21	USA	Kimi Räikkönen	Ferrari
10/28	Mexico	Max Verstappen	Red Bull-Renault
11/11	Brazil	**Lewis Hamilton**	Mercedes
11/25	Abu Dhabi	**Lewis Hamilton**	Mercedes

Championship: 1 Lewis Hamilton (408 points), 2 Sebastian Vettel (320 points), 3 Kimi Räikkönen (251 points)

Winning constructor: Mercedes

2019

3/17	Australia	*Valtteri Bottas*	Mercedes
3/31	Bahrain	Lewis Hamilton	Mercedes
4/14	China	Lewis Hamilton	Mercedes
4/28	Azerbaijan	**Valtteri Bottas**	Mercedes
5/12	Spain	*Lewis Hamilton*	Mercedes
5/26	Monaco	**Lewis Hamilton**	Mercedes
6/9	Canada	Lewis Hamilton	Mercedes
6/23	France	**Lewis Hamilton**	Mercedes
6/30	Austria	*Max Verstappen*	Red Bull-Honda
7/14	Britain	*Lewis Hamilton*	Mercedes
7/28	Germany	Max Verstappen	Red Bull-Honda
8/4	Hungary	Lewis Hamilton	Mercedes
9/1	Belgium	**Charles Leclerc**	Ferrari
9/8	Italy	**Charles Leclerc**	Ferrari
9/22	Singapore	Sebastian Vettel	Ferrari
9/29	Russia	*Lewis Hamilton*	Mercedes
10/13	Japan	Valtteri Bottas	Mercedes
10/27	Mexico	Lewis Hamilton	Mercedes
11/3	USA	**Valtteri Bottas**	Mercedes
11/17	Brazil	**Max Verstappen**	Red Bull-Honda
12/1	Abu Dhabi	***Lewis Hamilton***	Mercedes

Championship: 1 Lewis Hamilton (413 points), 2 Valtteri Bottas (326 points), 3 Max Verstappen (278 points)

Winning constructor: Mercedes

2020

7/5	Austria	**Valtteri Bottas**	Mercedes
7/12	Styria	**Lewis Hamilton**	Mercedes
7/19	Hungary	***Lewis Hamilton***	Mercedes
8/2	Britain	**Lewis Hamilton**	Mercedes
8/9	70th Anniversary	Max Verstappen	Red Bull-Honda
8/16	Spain	**Lewis Hamilton**	Mercedes
8/30	Belgium	**Lewis Hamilton**	Mercedes
9/6	Italy	Pierre Gasly	AlphaTauri-Honda
9/13	Tuscany	***Lewis Hamilton***	Mercedes
9/27	Russia	*Valtteri Bottas*	Mercedes
10/11	Eifel	Lewis Hamilton	Mercedes
10/25	Portugal	***Lewis Hamilton***	Mercedes
11/1	Emilia Romagna	*Lewis Hamilton*	Mercedes
11/15	Turkey	Lewis Hamilton	Mercedes
11/29	Bahrain	**Lewis Hamilton**	Mercedes
12/6	Sakhir	Sergio Pérez	Racing Point-Mercedes
12/13	Abu Dhabi	**Max Verstappen**	Red Bull-Honda

Championship: 1 Lewis Hamilton (347 points), 2 Valtteri Bottas (223 points), 3 Max Verstappen (214 points)

Winning constructor: Mercedes

2021

Date	Grand Prix	Winner	Constructor
3/28	Bahrain	Lewis Hamilton	Mercedes
4/18	Emilia Romagna	Max Verstappen	Red Bull-Honda
5/2	Portugal	Lewis Hamilton	Mercedes
5/9	Spain	**Lewis Hamilton**	Mercedes
5/23	Monaco	Max Verstappen	Red Bull-Honda
6/6	Azerbaijan	Sergio Pérez	Red Bull-Honda
6/20	France	*Max Verstappen*	Red Bull-Honda
6/27	Styria	**Max Verstappen**	Red Bull-Honda
7/4	Austria	*Max Verstappen*	Red Bull-Honda
7/18	Britain	Lewis Hamilton	Mercedes
8/1	Hungary	Esteban Ocon	Alpine
8/29	Belgian	**Max Verstappen**	Red Bull-Honda
9/5	Holland	**Max Verstappen**	Red Bull-Honda
9/12	Italy	*Daniel Ricciardo*	McLaren-Mercedes
9/26	Russia	Lewis Hamilton	Mercedes
10/10	Turkey	*Valtteri Bottas*	Mercedes
10/24	USA	**Max Verstappen**	Red Bull-Honda
11/7	Mexico City	Max Verstappen	Red Bull-Honda
11/14	São Paulo	Lewis Hamilton	Mercedes
11/21	Qatar	**Lewis Hamilton**	Mercedes
12/5	Saudi Arabia	*Lewis Hamilton*	Mercedes
12/12	Abu Dhabi	*Max Verstappen*	Red Bull-Honda

Championship: 1 Max Verstappen (395.5 points), 2 Lewis Hamilton (387.5 points), 3 Valtteri Bottas (226 points)

Winning constructor: Mercedes

2022

Date	Grand Prix	Winner	Constructor
3/20	Bahrain	*Charles Leclerc*	Ferrari
3/27	Saudi Arabia	Max Verstappen	Red Bull
4/10	Australia	*Charles Leclerc*	Ferrari
4/24	Emilia Romagna	*Max Verstappen*	Red Bull
5/8	Miami	*Max Verstappen*	Red Bull
5/22	Spain	Max Verstappen	Red Bull
5/29	Monaco	Sergio Pérez	Red Bull
6/12	Azerbaijan	Max Verstappen	Red Bull
6/19	Canada	**Max Verstappen**	Red Bull
7/3	Britain	**Carlos Sainz**	Ferrari
7/10	Austria	Charles Leclerc	Ferrari
7/24	France	Max Verstappen	Red Bull
7/31	Hungary	Max Verstappen	Red Bull
8/28	Belgium	*Max Verstappen*	Red Bull
9/4	Holland	*Max Verstappen*	Red Bull
9/11	Italy	Max Verstappen	Red Bull
10/2	Singapore	Sergio Pérez	Red Bull
10/9	Japan	**Max Verstappen**	Red Bull
10/23	USA	Max Verstappen	Red Bull
10/30	Mexico City	**Max Verstappen**	Red Bull
11/13	São Paulo	George Russell	Mercedes
11/20	Abu Dhabi	**Max Verstappen**	Red Bull

Championship: 1 Max Verstappen (454 points), 2 Charles Leclerc (308 points), 3 Sergio Pérez (305 points)

Winning constructor: Red Bull

2023

3/5	Bahrain	**Max Verstappen**	Red Bull-Honda
3/19	Saudi Arabia	**Sergio Pérez**	Red Bull-Honda
4/2	Australia	**Max Verstappen**	Red Bull-Honda
4/30	Azerbaijan	Sergio Pérez	Red Bull-Honda
5/7	Miami	*Max Verstappen*	Red Bull-Honda
5/28	Monaco	**Max Verstappen**	Red Bull-Honda
6/4	Spain	*Max Verstappen*	Red Bull-Honda
6/18	Canada	**Max Verstappen**	Red Bull-Honda
7/2	Austria	*Max Verstappen*	Red Bull-Honda
7/9	Britain	*Max Verstappen*	Red Bull-Honda
7/23	Hungary	*Max Verstappen*	Red Bull-Honda
7/30	Belgium	Max Verstappen	Red Bull-Honda
8/27	Holland	**Max Verstappen**	Red Bull-Honda
9/3	Italy	Max Verstappen	Red Bull-Honda
9/17	Singapore	**Carlos Sainz**	Ferrari
9/24	Japan	*Max Verstappen*	Red Bull-Honda
10/8	Qatar	*Max Verstappen*	Red Bull-Honda
10/22	USA	Max Verstappen	Red Bull-Honda
10/29	Mexico City	Max Verstappen	Red Bull-Honda
11/5	São Paulo	**Max Verstappen**	Red Bull-Honda
11/18	Las Vegas	Max Verstappen	Red Bull-Honda
11/26	Abu Dhabi	*Max Verstappen*	Red Bull-Honda

Championship: 1 Max Verstappen (575 points), 2 Sergio Pérez (285 points), 3 Lewis Hamilton (234 points)

Winning constructor: Red Bull

2024

3/2	Bahrain	*Max Verstappen*	Red Bull-Honda
3/9	Saudi Arabia	**Max Verstappen**	Red Bull-Honda
3/24	Australia	Carlos Sainz	Ferrari
4/7	Japan	*Max Verstappen*	Red Bull-Honda
4/21	China	**Max Verstappen**	Red Bull-Honda
5/5	Miami	Lando Norris	McLaren
5/19	Emilia Romagna	**Max Verstappen**	Red Bull-Honda
5/26	Monaco	**Charles Leclerc**	Ferrari
6/9	Canada	Max Verstappen	Red Bull-Honda
6/23	Spain	Max Verstappen	Red Bull-Honda
6/30	Austria	George Russell	Mercedes
7/7	Britain	Lewis Hamilton	Mercedes
7/21	Hungary	Oscar Piastri	McLaren-Mercedes
7/28	Belgium	Lewis Hamilton	Mercedes
8/25	Holland	*Lando Norris*	McLaren-Mercedes
9/1	Italy	Charles Leclerc	Ferrari
9/15	Azerbaijan	Oscar Piastri	McLaren-Mercedes
9/22	Singapore	**Lando Norris**	McLaren-Mercedes
10/20	USA	Charles Leclerc	Ferrari
10/27	Mexico City	**Carlos Sainz**	Ferrari
11/3	São Paulo	Max Verstappen	Red Bull-Honda
11/23	Las Vegas	**George Russell**	Mercedes
12/1	Qatar	Max Verstappen	Red Bull-Honda
12/8	Abu Dhabi	**Lando Norris**	McLaren-Mercedes

Championship: 1 Max Verstappen (437 points), 2 Lando Norris (374 points), 3 Charles Leclerc (356 points)

Winning constructor: McLaren

nouvelle huile SHELL Super
SHELL
SHELL
ANTAR ANTAR ANTAR
ALLINQUANT
SHELL

About the Authors

Stuart Codling is a respected motorsport journalist and broadcaster who covered sports car racing in the United States before joining *F1 Racing*, the world's biggest-selling Formula 1 magazine, in 2001. He has appeared as an F1 expert on TV and radio, hosted for Renault F1, and contributes to *F1 Racing, Autosport, Autocar*, and the *Red Bulletin*. Codling is the author of several Motorbooks titles, including *Formula 1 Drive to Survive The Unofficial Companion, Real Racers: Formula 1 Racing in the 1950s and 1960s, Art of the Formula 1 Race Car, Art of the Classic Sports Car*, and *The Life Monaco*. Stuart lives in Farnham, Surrey, England.

For over 20 years, **James Roberts** has worked as a journalist and feature-writer in Formula 1. He started his career at the specialist weekly *Motoring News*, then joined the world's best-selling Grand Prix magazine, *F1 Racing*, in 2007. After serving 13 years as Associate Editor, Roberts was appointed Editorial Director of *The Official Formula 1 Magazine*. After a brief period working on the official FIFA Qatar World Cup final program, Roberts is today a freelance F1 reporter who continues to travel to Grands Prix, contributing to various motor racing publications. He lives with his wife and three children on England's south coast.

James Mann is a leading professional car and motorcycle photographer with more than 30 years of experience shooting for publications, the motor industry, and businesses around the world. His work has appeared within and on the covers of more than 70 books, including Motorbooks titles *Art of the Formula 1 Race Car, The Art of the Classic Sports Car, Art of Ducati,* and *Art of the Le Mans Race Car.* James has provided stunning visuals for numerous magazines, including *Classic and Sports Car, CAR, Forza, The Sunday Times,* and *Automobile* magazine. He was chosen to photograph the British Auto Legends stamps for the Royal Mail and was recently awarded a Fellowship of the Royal Photographic Society. His website is jamesmann.com. James resides in Dorset, UK.

Acknowledgments

Working on this book has involved more than one reunion as I've had the pleasure of not only collaborating with James Mann again, but also helping to welcome my former colleague James Roberts to the world of book authorship. My thanks to Zack Miller and Brooke Pelletier at Motorbooks for their boundless energy and patience (the latter sorely tested as usual). And of course none of it would have been possible without the love and support of my wife, Julie.

Index